Metamorphoses of the Vampire in Literature and Film

Studies in German Literature, Linguistics, and Culture

Metamorphoses of the Vampire in Literature and Film

Cultural Transformations in Europe, 1732–1933

Erik Butler

CAMDEN HOUSE

Rochester, New York

First published 2010
by Camden House

Camden House is an imprint of Boydell & Brewer Inc.
668 Mt. Hope Avenue, Rochester, NY 14620, USA
www.camden-house.com
and of Boydell & Brewer Limited
PO Box 9, Woodbridge, Suffolk IP12 3DF, UK
www.boydellandbrewer.com

ISBN-13: 978-1-57113-432-5
ISBN-10: 1-57113-432-8

Library of Congress Cataloging-in-Publication Data

Butler, Erik, 1971–
    Metamorphoses of the vampire in literature and film: cultural transformations
in Europe, 1732–1933 / Erik Butler.
        p. cm. — (Studies in German literature, linguistics, and culture)
    Includes bibliographical references and index.
    ISBN-13: 978-1-57113-432-5 (hardcover: alk. paper)
    ISBN-10: 1-57113-432-8 (hardcover: alk. paper)
    1. Vampires in literature. 2. Vampires — History. 3. Horror tales, European —
History and criticism. 4. European fiction — History and criticism. 5. Vampire
films — History and criticism. 6. Social change in literature. 7. Literature and
society — Europe — History. I. Title. II. Series.
    PN56.V3B87 2010
    809'.93375—dc22

                                                                        2009042766

A catalogue record for this title is available from the British Library.

This publication is printed on acid-free paper.

Contents

Preface

THIS BOOK HAS BEEN WRITTEN in an attempt to fill gaps in scholarship, bridge academic disciplines, and present a coherent, historically informed theory of the vampire. For the most part, studies on vampirism focus on a single period, a single tradition, or productions in a single medium. There are many excellent studies examining Victorian vampires, the undead in cinema, contemporary vampire fictions, and the vampire in folklore. However, the purpose here is different. By means of site-specific, comparative analysis, the work at hand seeks to account for the logic underlying the vampire's many and conflicting forms. Besides source material in English, *Metamorphoses of the Vampire* makes extensive use of primary and secondary literature in French and German, which English-language critics tend to ignore. Much of what is discussed in the pages to follow has far-ranging implications for the study of vampires in general, yet it has never been presented to students and scholars in Australia, England, and North America. Above all, *Metamorphoses of the Vampire* proposes to explain why representations of vampirism begin in the eighteenth century, flourish in the nineteenth, and eclipse most other forms of monstrosity in the twentieth. Although the book's aims are synthetic and theoretical, the discussion is historically grounded in the analysis of particular works.

This study tries to be objective and neutral — to explore the categories established by the works themselves and, having determined their internal dynamics, to relate them to other texts and historical points of reference. The formal analysis of literature and film has provided the point of departure for each of the sections (although, for reasons of legibility and economy of space, these schematizations are not presented in the book). The resulting interpretations necessarily involve a more speculative mode of engagement with the material. Words such as "objective" and "neutral" are, of course, red flags to the critical reader. However, a fact (e.g., a name, a date, or a specific phrasing as it appears in a text) is not the same as a truth. The negative — that is, the analytical — capacity of criticism can only be brought to bear on a field of positive information, and the meaning of raw data is never self-evident, anyway.

Metamorphoses of the Vampire does not profess allegiance to any particular school of critical thought (psychoanalysis, postcolonial studies, feminism, deconstruction, and so on). Nor will the reader encounter much specialized vocabulary and jargon in this study, even though it draws on a wide range of theoretical texts. The point of theory in the natural sciences is to provide a coherent explanation of a phenomenon, whether complex or apparently simple. That is also the aim of the humanistic project at hand. A pragmatic concern underlies this book. If a given theory fails to open a field of questions that can be related to other items of discussion, it is, at best, irrelevant. There is no such thing as Theory, per se — only textual praxis.

In the spirit of candor and collaboration, then, a few remarks are in order before the vampire hunt begins.

(1) Although I propose a working definition of the word "vampire," much of the topic's interest derives precisely from the problems of identification and naming that arise whenever and wherever the monster is at work. The difficulty of seeing who or what vampires "really are" is a constitutive feature of the phenomenon. In a sense, the vampire is just an extraordinarily potent metaphor. While attempting to present as clear a picture as possible, any study of vampirism must accept that it will occasionally be bested by its evasive quarry.

(2) The point of this study is to anatomize a wide range of vampiric specimens and expose, in as nuanced and detailed a manner as possible, how each creature displays features that are historically and culturally specific; these characteristics commentate the world and social relations that have given shape to them. The autopsies of the undead (the expression derives from the works examined in chapters 1 and 5), while capable of standing on their own, are also understood as complementary parts in a unified field of inquiry. The introduction addresses the challenges of reconciling the specific and the general qualities exhibited by vampires; it also explains how isolated data and more universal claims can be brought into agreement.

(3) The study explores, first and foremost, cultural productions from Western Europe. Here, *Metamorphoses of the Vampire* readily acknowledges its debt to psychoanalysis: in large part, the study reads works as imaginary projections made by parties in England, France, and Germany; these fictions about others, elsewhere, point back to the real time and place they were authored. Questions of authenticity and the origin of the vampire myth lie largely outside the scope of inquiry. Chapter 1, which analyzes paradigmatic first cases and establishes a framework of interpretation for what follows, is no exception. Even here, the focus falls more on perceptions and self-referential discourse than on what, in the parlance of nineteenth-century historiography, "really happened."

(4) *Metamorphoses of the Vampire*, while acknowledging the importance of issues raised by cultural studies, seeks to preserve the critical perspective that distinguishes more traditional forms of scholarship. That is to say, the book does not shy away from the occasional value judgment concerning the aesthetic merits of works under examination.

This stance vis-à-vis texts is important to maintain because it permits the discussion of the modes in which cultural artifacts engage their audience. Some books and films present a more self-reflective structure, which in turn demands a greater level of attention and intellectual involvement from the reader/viewer. Mass entertainment, on the other hand, tends to appeal to intuition, emotion, and self-evidence. Because works belonging to "high" and "low" spheres of culture demand different hermeneutics, it is important, for heuristic and methodological reasons, occasionally to draw a dividing line.

(5) Finally, since this study focuses on Western European culture from about 1732 until 1933, the exploration of vampirism by female authors is not treated in much detail. For the period in question, practically all the writers and filmmakers in question are men. The works examined raise gender issues of great interest — vampires are notorious for troubling the waters of sexual identity — and these matters will receive due attention. However, it is not my intention to subvert the carefully crafted arguments of fiction, nor do I mean to claim the vampire for a political project of my own, and it is left to others to "reclaim" the vilified vampire for postmodern celebrations of difference.

As a rule, *Metamorphoses of the Vampire* quotes primary works both in the original and in translation; commentary from secondary sources is provided in English. Whenever no other credit is given, translations are mine.

Acknowledgments

THIS STUDY HAS BENEFITED, directly or indirectly, from the contributions of many others. My sincere thanks to the anonymous readers at Camden House and my editor, Jim Walker, for their help in shaping the book, as well as Matt Witkovsky at the Art Institute of Chicago for assistance in securing the rights to the cover image. The following is a list, more or less in order of appearance in my life, of people from whose intellectual generosity I have profited in one way or another: Chris Kelty, Dan Selden, Susan Stephens, Duncan Chesney, Moira Fradinger, Nicola Masciandaro, Edwin Duval, Michael Holquist, Françoise Jaouën, David Quint, Nike Agman, Marion Faber, Steve Hannaford, Hansjakob Werlen, Alan Berkowitz, Edmund Campos, James Melton, Niall Slater, Garth Tissol, Silke Delamare, James Steffen, Elizabeth Goodstein, Sander Gilman, Deepika Bahri, Jörg Kreienbrock, Anna Jakowska, and Dan Ashcroft. Thanks to Gopal Balakrishnan for drawing my attention to the work of Dolf Oehler, as well as Russell Berman, Bill Donahue, and Julian Preece for giving me the opportunity to present some of my research at conferences. The editors of the *Iowa Journal of Cultural Studies, German Quarterly,* and *New German Critique* also receive my gratitude for providing a printed forum for ideas that have found their way into the study. My parents and sister deserve recognition, as does Kimberly Jannarone; for the last decade, she has been the best companion anyone could desire. Although they are unlikely to appreciate it, my thanks, also, to the four-legged friends who have shared my life over the years.

Introduction: Cultural Teratology

M ETAMORPHOSES OF THE VAMPIRE — a title stolen from a poem by
Charles Baudelaire — examines a figure of humble origin that
achieved sudden prominence in the period preceding the Age of Revolution, had a flourishing career during this tumultuous epoch, and finally
achieved seemingly universal notoriety before it was over: the vampire.
Despite the celebrity this monster has enjoyed, however, it possesses no
distinct profile over time. For example, the aristocratic dress and debonair
ways commonly associated with the vampire today are but two of many
possible attributes, and they are relatively recent developments. Representations of vampires in literature, film, and the visual arts are many and
contradictory. Sometimes these creatures are suave and urbane. Sometimes they are rustic and crude. There are male vampires and female vampires. Not all vampires inhabit Gothic castles, and they do not uniformly
display the powers of sexual seduction that many enthusiasts consider
their distinguishing feature.

Yet all vampires share one trait: the power to move between and
undo borders otherwise holding identities in place. At this monster's
core lies an affinity for rupture, change, and mutation. Because of
its inimical relationship to stability, tradition, and order, the vampire
embodies the transformative march of history. For this reason, the vampire has not ceased to generate new representations of itself in modern
societies' transition from what Marshall McLuhan called the Gutenberg
Galaxy to the star-studded world of the silver screen. Indeed, global
culture's recent move into deepest cyberspace has only energized the
vampire further. *Metamorphoses of the Vampire* examines both iconic and
less-well-known representations of the monster in order to determine
the dynamic underlying its illusory ubiquity and timelessness. If the
vampire is easily recognizable today, the world over, it was not always
so. The vampire is a modern myth and, as such, subject to critique that
reveals its contingent conditions of existence.[1]

Metamorphoses of the Vampire seeks to demystify the social and historical forces that give form to an enduring object of fascination. At
the same time, the study is not intended simply to dispel illusions, nor
does it presume to reveal an unambiguous reality behind appearances.
Metamorphoses of the Vampire explains the generative processes that have
led to the abundance of texts featuring vampires. Above all, these works
have been composed in cultures and lands other than the monster's

native territory (which, as we will see, is a highly contested space). The reason for the popularity of the vampire in the West is that the figure permits the representation of foreignness within a recognizable framework — that is, the creature marks sites in a seemingly unified field and reveals points of trouble and discontinuity that are glossed over by received ideas and the routines of everyday life. At the same time, as a putative outsider, the vampire never wholly subverts the borders it transgresses and in fact reinforces them.

The name "vampire" designates, above all, a process of invasion. Thus, in Friedrich Wilhelm Murnau's *Nosferatu* (1922), the vampire appears on screen in combination with hordes of creeping rats that bring the plague to Europe. The vampire's takeover can also be alluring. Lord Ruthven, the vampire antihero of the influential work by John Polidori (1819), is a beguiling lady-killer who insinuates himself into victims' lives through the powers of persuasion and seduction. Sheridan Le Fanu's Carmilla, in the story of the same name (1872), appears a "very charming girl,"[2] even though she transforms into a feline bloodsucker at night. More recently, Anne Rice has written about rock-star vampires, whose commercial success beguiles adolescent hearts. Vampires rarely attack by force, but instead prefer stealth. The creature is polymorphously perverse and endlessly resourceful in its adaptability to new situations. For this reason, the vampire fulfills Freud's definition of the uncanny (*das Unheimliche*): the vampire combines the known and the unknown, the home and the world outside, and the familiar and the strange, but it inclines toward the latter pole, drawing all those who encounter it toward dark realms.[3] In all vampire fictions, the supernatural antagonist is, at one point or another, all but impossible to recognize because it has corrupted a well-fortified space and now seems to operate "from the inside out." Exemplarily, Bram Stoker's Count Dracula, who hails from Eastern Europe, unfolds his powers to greatest effect when he circulates incognito on English soil, making his victims there deviate from their established ways as they unwittingly become more and more like him.

The vampire can render spellbound an individual, a household, a nation, a hemisphere, and even the whole planet. In James Joyce's *Ulysses,* Stephen Dedalus, when confronted with the memory of his dead mother, becomes a "pale vampire . . . mouth to her moomb. Oomb, allwombing tomb."[4] This transformation reproduces the psychology described by the German poet and dramatist Friedrich Hebbel (1813–63) when he wrote: "Jeder Tote ist ein Vampir, die ungeliebten ausgenommen" (All dead are vampires, except the unloved ones).[5] Television's teenage Buffy the Vampire Slayer must protect her high school and small California town from the legions of undead that issue from the portal to the netherworld in the local cemetery. Here, the scale of vampiric invasion extends from the personal to the communal. In a further step, Dracula snarls to the Englishmen who hunt him, "you . . . shall yet be mine — my creatures, to do my bidding."[6] Julio Cortázar pits the French serial-film and comic-book hero Fantômas against multinational vampires.[7] The vampire threatens a series of homologous social units: the individual, the community member, the state, and, finally, the general "family of man."

The ranks of the undead include an astonishing number of apparently blue-blooded parties: *Lord* Ruthven, *Sir* Frances Varney, *Countess* Karnstein, *Count* Dracula, etc. E. T. A. Hoffmann's vampire in the *Serapion Brethren* is a baroness, and Anne Rice even traces a bloodline back to ancient Egypt in order to provide her vampires with an aristocratic origin. Vampires are supposed to have a pedigree that legitimates their barbarism and invests it with sophistication and terrible refinement. The vampire seems to defy time: it will still be around after its enemies have fallen. An interminable existence stretching indefinitely in both directions — into past and future alike — has elevated the creature above the mortal sphere, in mockery of the cycles of generation and decay through which human societies perpetuate themselves. Hence, in many vampire fictions, those who die from the monster's attack rise again as an undead. This new "life" — which is not one at all — deprives victims of their former personhood and transforms them into ghastly representatives of a loathsome family, race, or kind that should, it seems, have died out eons ago.

Because they have bought into the fiction of vampiric antiquity, many popular and scholarly discussions of the vampire fall victim to a lure posed by vampire stories, and they accept the monster as a near-eternal being whose existence reaches back to the ancient world. In the nineteenth century, Sir Richard Burton (1821–90), the English adventurer famed for his travels in the "Orient," presented his translation of the Sanskrit *Baital-Pachisi* to his readers as *Vikram and the Vampire;* by equating a legendary figure from ancient India with a monster that his modern, Western audience would recognize from boulevard theaters and chapbooks, Burton conferred a false air of venerability upon the vampire.[8] Montague Summers, in one of the first English-language studies of the vampire (1928), wrote that it is "world-wide and of dateless antiquity."[9] Following the same intuition, Ernest Jones in his psychoanalytic study of the nightmare (1931) pointed toward "the Assyrian and Babylonian Lilats, the Eastern Palukah, the Finnish Lord of the Underworld, the Bohemian Mora, [and] the German Alp"[10] in an effort to demonstrate the vampire's universality. More recently, Christopher Frayling has claimed "the vampire is as old as the world" and that "traces of vampirism are to be found in most cultures."[11] Felix J. Oinas precedes his discussion of Eastern European vampires by affirming that "belief in vampires exists all over the world, in India, China, Malaysia, Indonesia, and elsewhere."[12] One could add to the list innumerable writers and scholars also advancing this claim.[13]

To counter such generalized understandings of our monster, we should heed the cautionary words of one of the earliest writers on the topic of vampirism, the Benedictine monk Dom Augustin Calmet (1672–1757). At the middle of the eighteenth century, Calmet insisted on the novelty of the vampire:

> Chaque siècle, chaque nation, chaque pays a . . . ses maladies, ses modes, ses penchants, qui les caractérisent . . . ; souvent ce qui a paru admirable en un temps, devient pitoyable et ridicule dans un autre. . . .
> Dans ce siècle, une nouvelle scène s'offre à nos yeux . . . : on voit, dit-on, des hommes morts . . . revenir, parler, infester les villages, . . . sucer le sang de leurs proches, les rendre malades, et enfin leur causer la mort.

> [Each century, each people, each country has . . . its own maladies, its own fashions, [and] its own inclinations, which characterize them . . . ; often, what seemed admirable at one time becomes piteous and ridiculous at another. . . .
> In this century, a new scene has presented itself to our eyes . . . : people see, they say, dead men . . . come back, speak, plague villages, . . . suck the blood of their intimates, make them sick, and, finally, cause their death.][14]

Wishing to discredit the belief in vampires that was attested in contemporary reports from Eastern Europe (to be discussed in chapter 1) — and also to guard against allegations that he believed these creatures really existed[15] — Calmet pointed out that the vampire was "une nouvelle scène" (a modern fancy). In his discussion of vampirism, Calmet granted that there were some parallels in earlier ages — notably, maleficent corpses and witches who drank blood. However, he stressed that "en nulle histoire, on ne lit rien . . . d'aussi marqué que ce qu'on nous raconte des vampires" (in no historical account does one read anything . . . so well defined as what we hear about vampires).[16] This statement may seem to contradict what has just been said about the vampire's protean characteristics, but the problem vanishes when placed in historical perspective: Calmet was writing about reports of fantastic events in his own day, which occurred in a specific setting. In other words, the monk was saying that although the vampire may share some traits with other supernatural entities, these instances of partial overlap hardly amount to a shared identity; instead, it is necessary to examine the vampire phenomenon in its proper context. Calmet's caveat has been forgotten by many subsequent vampirologists.

In the words of Markman Ellis, "The vampire has a perverse modernity: a terror of recent invention manifested as a monster from time out of mind, from deep history."[17] The first written records that speak of a creature by the name of "vampire" are less than three hundred years old, and the first literary and artistic depictions of the monster are younger still. This is not to deny that the vampire in its first recorded form — a dead member of an illiterate, rural community (more on this point in a moment) — does not resemble other supernatural beings and therefore offer a rich field of study for folklorists.[18] For example, medieval Germany knew of the *Nachzehrer* — a restless corpse that stayed in the grave and consumed its own clothing and body, especially in times of plague; this creature, without a doubt, is a close relation of the first vampires.[19] However, such popular beliefs remained local and regional; they did not lead to a dynamic myth that could thrive both internationally and interculturally. Modern historical circumstances were required to foster such a development. Looking for the creature before the 1700s, vampirologists are doomed to shoot in the dark at an entity that never materializes long enough to stay in their sights.

A recurrent problem to be addressed throughout this study, then, will be the matter of distinguishing "real" vampires from their more distant relations. The lines are often blurry, for the number of vampires has only increased since the eighteenth century, as have the forms and attributes displayed by creatures that go by this name. The widespread inclination among vampirologists to see these monsters everywhere reveals the enormous strength of the myth. The vampire has mutated and adapted to any number of new environments. Vampires' powers of transformation make them seem timeless and ubiquitous when in fact they are not. Hence, scholarship has been led astray and "vampirized" for good reason. The monster embodies rupture and change, and even its familiar guises (capes, fangs, excellent breeding, tendency to sleep in coffins, etc.) conceal something unknown. The vampire marks the point where symbolic orders intersect and diverge, and its essence therefore proves extraordinarily difficult to define. A look beneath surface appearances — which are the means the vampire uses to carry out its predations — is required.

"Vampire" is a metaphor run amuck. Metaphors, though a familiar figure of language, always signify in excess of what they mean.[20] As Paul Ricoeur puts it, metaphors "consist of the attribution, to the subjects of discourse, of predicates that are incompatible [*incompossibles*] with them."[21] Metaphor — and indeed all figural language[22] — serves to convey meaning; however, it does so by leaping and bounding across otherwise separate spheres of signification, short-circuiting the fields of difference that hold in place the two items being equated. Where vampires are concerned and the comparisons run wild, tidy categories and classifications stand in disarray.[23] Whenever mention is made of vampires, traffic in deception is already taking place on a linguistic level, which amplifies accompanying themes of subterfuge and ruse in the fiction. To obtain the proper perspective on our monster, then, it is necessary to exercise the faculty that Ricoeur associates with the interpretive methods of Marx, Nietzsche, and Freud. These inaugurators of the "school of suspicion"[24] theorized not only the gap between signs and referents, but also the capacity of the former to mislead, mystify, and, indeed, point away from what they are supposed to mean.

The shape-shifting potential displayed by our monster is why the vampire has become a beloved trope of literary criticism. To take but one example, Gilles Deleuze and Félix Guattari have compared Franz Kafka to the most famous vampire of them all, Bram Stoker's Dracula. Analyzing Kafka's nocturnal writing habits, his odd diet, and the paradoxically intimate distance he kept from his family and fiancée, they observe:

> There is something of Dracula in Kafka. . . . He spends the night awake and, by day, is locked in his coffin-desk. . . . When he imagines a kiss, it is that of Gregor who grabs onto the naked neck of his sister, or that of K with Fräulein Bürstner, a kiss like that of "some thirsty animal lapping greedily at a spring of long-sought fresh water." To Felice, Kafka describes himself without shame or joke as extraordinarily thin, needing blood. . . . Kafka-Dracula . . . fears only two things: the cross of the family and the garlic of marriage.[25]

Kafka's private writings, most of his literary *oeuvre,* and the myriad letters through which he beckoned to his beloved while rarely letting her close to his person[26] all represent the shadow side of his hyperrationalized, daytime work as an insurance company bureaucrat. The impersonal language of business suffuses his fiction and correspondence,[27] yet Kafka twists this featureless idiom to personal ends, recuperating a sinister surplus value from the confusion he engineers. Deleuze and Guattari claim that Kafka's literary vampirism comes out in recurrent images of zoomorphic humans ("The Metamorphosis"), shadowy figures with dark connections to power (*The Trial*), lands with uncertain borders that are overseen by invisible rulers (*The Castle*), devilish contraptions that enforce laws comprehensible only at the moment of death ("In the Penal Colony"), and existences suspended eternally in an icy winter night ("A Country Doctor"). Yet nowhere does Kafka ever employ the term "vampire."

D. H. Lawrence's analysis of Edgar Allan Poe also hinges on the concept of vampirism.[28] The author of "Ligeia" and "Berenice," like Kafka, never mentions vampires by name. He, too, however, seems to encourage his readers to see the creatures between the lines of his poetry and tales.[29] Mario Praz, in his influential study of literary darkness, *The Romantic Agony,* finds vampires everywhere in nineteenth-century literature.[30] He traces them back in particular to the works of the notorious Donatien Alphonse François, Marquis de Sade. At the center of Sade's sprawling oeuvre stand two sisters, the pure Justine and the debauched Juliette. Juliette has ambition, depravity, and cynicism matching the greatest male libertines. Praz sees the beautiful but cold-blooded Juliette as the fore-runner of Prosper Mérimée's Vénus d'Ille, Théophile Gautier's Clari-monde, and Algernon Charles Swinburne's Mary Stuart — women who are either literally undead or seem only to have ice in their veins. He notes that Walter Pater even compared Leonardo da Vinci's *Gioconda* — the most famous work of Renaissance art — to the monster. "Like the vam-pire," the Victorian critic and essayist wrote ominously, "she has been dead many times, and learned the secrets of the grave."[31]

Especially over the last century or so, the term "vampire" has gained enormous currency in discussions of individual psychology, interpersonal relations, financial exchanges, and racial and political discourse. Now, at the beginning of the twenty-first century, the self-help sections of bookstores overflow with titles such as *Energy Vampires: A Practical Guide for Psychic Self-Protection, Unholy Hungers: Encountering the Psychic Vampire in Our-selves and Others*, and *Spiritual Vampires: The Use and Misuse of Spiritual Power.*[32] A recent study of literary and cinematic vampires by Nina Auer-bach analyzing the relationship between fictions of predation and the real-life cultural dynamics of 1980s Reaganomics has a title that cleverly fuses the discourses of women's studies, self-help, and late-capitalist narcissism: *Our Vampires, Ourselves.*[33] With equal penetration, feminist historian of sci-ence and cultural critic Donna Haraway has discussed twentieth-century practices of bioengineered racism in terms of "vampire culture."[34]

"Metaphorical" vampires have proliferated in modern culture just as much as the "actual" vampires that everyone knows from books, movies, and television. Whether in intellectual or in popular discourse, vampir-ism has suffused modern consciousness thoroughly. Although it remains exceedingly difficult to pin down the vampire's true nature — to drive a stake through its heart, as it were, and fix its essence once and for all — the purpose of this study is to track and corner the monster, if only to expose its many disguises.

Metamorphoses of the Vampire seeks to unearth the political dimen-sions of vampire stories and to illuminate the historical and social forces that shape them. That is, the approach taken here, while employing a number of interpretive tools that lead away from in situ analysis, endeav-ors to avoid speculation and remain grounded in positive detail as much as possible. The book explores both the center and the periphery of vam-pirism: the "full-blooded" undead as well as their relations of uncertain pedigree. In recognition of the slipperiness of it subject, it makes no claim to be comprehensive. The diffusion of the vampire myth does not follow a set pattern, and the creature's mutations are too numerous and quick to inventory exhaustively. The topic of vampirism bleeds over into questions concerning other types of invader, from microorganisms to extraterrestri-als; the Gothic imagination; the unnatural nature of technological repro-duction; and on and on. Whenever appropriate, the topics that overlap with the study's focus will be addressed; indeed, these seeming digressions will prove to be an intrinsic part of a subject matter that defies categorization, embodies contradiction, and constantly changes form. Different types of cultural artifact fall under the analytical lens: among other forms of evidence, poetry, narrative prose, journalism, political pamphlets, autobiographical writing, and film will be examined. The interpretive methods employed are also varied; the hybrid subject demands a hybrid approach.

A guiding critical principle of *Metamorphoses of the Vampire* comes from the concept of morphology elaborated by Carlo Ginzburg in *Clues, Myths, and the Historical Method*. Whereas the strictly historical approach stresses direct lines of filiation and development between events, morphology places the emphasis on formal and typological resemblances where no direct connections can be demonstrated conclusively. History is "concrete and narrative," and morphology is "abstract and diagrammatical."[35] The two optics complement each other inasmuch as they offer two angles of approach to the same phenomenon. Thus, the chapters of *Metamorphoses of the Vampire* together provide a synthetic view — a kind of mosaic — within which each element of the big picture is examined both in work-specific and in historical terms. The bifocal approach is necessary because the vampire's metamorphoses do not follow an organic model. Instead, to the extent that continuity between different instances of vampirism is apparent, it is better to speak of a process of combination and accretion, whereby the monster's old attributes can subsist alongside new ones or simply disappear, depending on the precise circumstances.

The cultural form whose shifting lineaments are tracked in *Metamorphoses of the Vampire* yields a nagging and constant exception to general rules of representation, hence the inflection of "morphology" into "teratology." The Greek root of the first half of the word, *teras,* means both "monster" and "wonder." Teratology, the science of phenomena that contravene the rules of regularity and stability, examines discontinuities between appearances and the reality to which they should, in principle, correspond. To this end, the study employs theories of philosophical, psychoanalytic, and anthropological provenance in order to explore the interrelationship between the categories of sameness and difference that the vampire throws into crisis.

In *Histoire de la folie à l'âge classique* (Madness and Civilization, 1961), Michel Foucault argued that every society, in each historical epoch, has something against which it defines itself negatively.[36] Foucault's concern was to show how the "insane" has provided a necessary point of reference for the "sane" — a terminus a quo from which logical thought and rationality obtain clarity and definition. *Metamorphoses of the Vampire* continues in Foucault's spirit inasmuch as his work offers a model for how to think about monsters, whose opposite is humanity. Mankind needs monsters in order to set apart a safe place for itself by rejecting its more unflattering and troubling sides to a non-human realm. However, *Metamorphoses of the Vampire* avoids drawing the same conclusions as Foucault. In *The Order of Things* (1966), the follow-up to his work on madness, Foucault predicted that Man would one day cease to be a rallying point for scientific and lay discourse and vanish "like a face drawn in sand at the edge of the sea."[37] Although a contested category and an unstable referent, "Man" will never go away so long as aberrations from the norm elicit "his" fascinated and horrified attention.[38] Monstrosity is the guarantor of the human.

The stakes of this study, then, are as follows. By creating non-human — indeed, inhuman — others, humans have long sought a way to reassure themselves that their own identity can be preserved. The vampire differs from "other others" through the transformative powers that it both embodies and wields, which undermine vast swathes of humanity whose characteristics vampire stories change into signs of something unnatural and threatening. *Metamorphoses of the Vampire* seeks to show both how the vampire displays these projections outwardly and, at the same time, points back to what, in a Marxian idiom, one may call the false consciousness of (supposed) victims. Instead of giving us a stable enemy, the vampire belongs to multiple worlds, including our own. It therefore reflects an anxiety that we, perhaps, do not know at all who "we" are.

Literature, film, and other cultural productions provide sources for the patterns defining sameness and difference that underlie human self-understanding. Jacques Lacan situates the beleaguered human subject in shifting sign systems that continually recast its identity. In what he calls "a new putting in question [*une remise en question*] of anthropology"[39] (that is, both an interrogation of received ideas about what the human *is*, and the insistence that one should not discard such a valuable scientific category merely because of disputes concerning its definition), Lacan presents a theory of how the signs that regulate human affairs and serve as a matrix for the operations of the individual psyche, while motivated by an intention, also exist autonomously and independently of their emitter and addressee. Insofar as the human subject must avail itself of preexisting patterns and codes in order to give form to ideas, the signifying material it uses in some measure conditions its very thought and intention. Lacan stresses the ways that foreign signifying material invisibly commands even seemingly straightforward forms of symbolism. The hidden point of otherness toward which Lacan repeatedly gestures is precisely where monsters dwell, for it is here — in imaginary pairings and acts of separation evocative of physical love and the traumas of birth and death — that the human subject finds the secret of its being.

Finally, the approach taken in *Metamorphoses of the Vampire* owes a debt to René Girard. Girard has argued that monstrosity has a deep structure — a timeless and fundamental basis. "We must think of the monstrous as beginning with the lack of differentiation [*l'indifférencia-tion*]," he writes.[40] Each and every monster presents an instance where the chain of being breaks down. Because an insult to balance and order constitutes its defining quality, the monster poses a menace that has a plurality of aspects and effects. Even though the monster is, technically, a single entity, it embodies actual multiplicity and, even more importantly, represents the threat of further chaos emerging. The latent threat of a spreading "lack of differentiation" in the world accounts for the terror it provokes. The monster, "an unstable hallucination,"[41] engenders unease and panic in those who confront it because it defies attempts to identify it. Merely by "being there," it sends out signals that the cosmos has ceased obeying recognizable laws.

Metamorphoses of the Vampire proposes to bring Girard's structuralist viewpoint into line with a historical perspective. When Girard explains how monsters transgress the categories that make the world intelligible, he remarks that "they always consist of a combination of elements borrowed from various existing forms."[42] If monsters are themselves imaginary, while their constituent parts are not, it should be possible to see how these fantastic creatures refract specific physical, social, and historical realities. No monster is an eternal being.[43]

The *Oxford English Dictionary* contains the entry "vampirarchy." This word dates to 1823 and means "a set of ruling persons resembling vampires." As we will see, the term depends on a set of significations that accrued to the root word "vampire" from about 1730 on. Though "vampirarchy" has fallen out of use — indeed, it appears never to have been widely employed — the term possesses a kind of semantic self-evidence that few would deny. This is the case because, as Chris Baldick has observed, "that venerable cliché of political discourse, the 'body politic'"[44] has long given rise to metaphors of monstrosity. To illustrate his point, Baldick quotes Sir Thomas Browne's *Religio Medici* (1643): "the multitude, that numerous piece of monstrosity, which taken asunder seeme men, and the reasonable creatures of God; but confused together, make but one great beast & a monstrosity more prodigious than Hydra."[45] When civic unrest seizes the populace, its members lose their particularizing, human traits (at any rate, in the eyes of an aristocratic observer). Transformed into "rabble," they embody a terrible, prodigious force, like an unnatural "great beast."

Thomas Hobbes, who sought to temper this same mass and forge it into a more harmonious entity, called his work on the commonwealth *Leviathan* (1651): even a well-functioning society is conceived as a kind of monster. In the twentieth century (after his ruinous engagement with National Socialism, the great horror of false unity), Carl Schmitt mobilized another metaphor of monstrosity to describe Hobbes's political theory; this image, which Hobbes himself employed, originates in the Roman playwright Plautus's dictum *homo homini lupus*. "For Hobbes," Schmitt writes, "the state of nature is a domain of werewolves, in which man is nothing but a wolf to other men."[46] More recently, Antonio Negri and Michael Hardt have attempted to resurrect the Jewish Golem to provide a model for empowered masses in the age of globalization.[47] The vampire fits into this still-developing political economy of monstrosity.

Like all monsters, the vampire embodies contradiction, represents the prospect of spreading chaos, and commands supernatural powers. However, it does so in its own particular way. The vampire has mutated many times in the course of the last three centuries, but certain attributes recur often enough to assure the continuity and consistency of its paradoxical being over time.

First, the vampire is neither wholly dead nor entirely alive. By right, it belongs to death, yet it does not respect the boundaries that should keep it dead — that is, inactive and away from the living. Instead, the vampire passes from one realm to another, transgressing the laws of God and Man, religion and science, and suspending the borders structuring the universe. These "metaphysical transgressions" are reflections of earthly affairs in disarray.

Second, the vampire goes about its work by expropriating and redistributing energy. This feature explains why the greater part of vampire fiction portrays the monster as a bloodsucker. To the extent that blood flows along the closed pathways of the body, it represents strength and life. When violence interrupts its course, blood changes aspect and becomes a sign of weakness and death. If vampires commonly feast on blood, they can just as easily leech out other forms of energy — a feature of their being that explains, among other characteristics, their recurrent association with money, for wealth proverbially assures health. A mystical substance conceals rather more material concerns.

Third, when vampires draw life from their victims, they infuse them with death and make the living resemble them. The monster's mode of attack relies on a process of denaturing assimilation to an "order" which, because of its logical — and ontological — impossibility, generates multiple and conflicting representations. Therefore, when not outright seducers, vampires are, at the very least, false friends.

Fourth and finally, the vampire defies the boundaries of space and time, and it seeks to spread terror actively. Thus, the existence of a single vampire poses the threat that more vampires will soon arrive. This is why "vampire" is a political category: the word signifies ambition of immense, but indeterminate, proportions that stands to remake the world in ways that victims cannot even imagine — hence, too, the infernal (or, at any rate, sacrilegious) qualities commonly displayed by this creature.

In anticipation of potential objections to the methods employed here, one particular point of likely contention should be addressed. Are vampires — readers familiar with popular novels and films will ask — not fundamentally sexual creatures? The answer is no. *Metamorphoses of the Vampire* does not affect prudery, and on occasion, it even draws back the curtains of metaphor to reveal the lurid secrets hidden by euphemism and literary artifice. However, the study examines the sexual aspects of vampirism — when they exist — among effects as much as causes. Even the erotically charged Victorian vampire's notorious appetite for virgin blood and predilection for gender-bending are symptoms of historical, sociological, and political conditions — facts that make certain kinds of wishes the source of scandal and intrigue, while leaving others in the proverbial closet. Vampire stories offer a playground for perversion — the deviation from genital sexuality — not an archive of repression.[48]

Just as *Metamorphoses of the Vampire* analyzes "the sexual life of the undead" both in morphological and in historical terms, it also views the other aspects of vampirism through a double lens: on the one hand, on the level of representation (genre, rhetoric, and the conventions of fiction in general), and, on the other, as part of a chronological order ("History," writ large). This is why the study insists on the modernity of the monster. Stories of the restless dead are indeed a universal phenomenon, found the world over and at all periods of time. Likewise, a connection between spirits and blood occurs across the globe and is shared by the most varied cultures.[49] What, after all, is more universal than anxiety about death and the mystery of regeneration, be it biological or spiritual? However, it does not follow that the vampire — before the twentieth century, at least — was ever a cultural figure to be found the world over.

As noted, many scholars, observing general apprehension about the dead, have inferred that the vampire is the emanation of some deep-seated truth common to all mankind — an archetype. Alternately, critics of a more postmodern mindset have argued for the "undead" as a ubiquitous presence-in-absence analogous to the "unconscious." Thereby, they seek to name, however imprecisely, the fluidity of ontology.[50] While often stimulating, such broad understandings of vampirism and the undead are too loose to be of much use here. The major works discussed in *Metamorphoses of the Vampire* all employ the word "vampire," with one exception that proves the rule (Daniel Paul Schreber's *Memoirs of My Nervous Illness,* discussed in chapter 5). This lexical point of orientation connects with a vast array of related words and things, and the signifier often winds up attaching to a core meaning by rather circuitous means. But by focusing consistently on the darkest patches in fields of gray, *Metamorphoses of the Vampire* achieves a degree of precision that studies following every trace of the undead lack, because it establishes the structural identity beneath the vampire's many manifestations.

Metamorphoses of the Vampire consists of six chapters arranged in chronological succession that explore exemplary incarnations of the vampire. In each case, the form assumed by the monster darkly mirrors a changing world and the modern subject's anxieties about shifting identities within the universe in flux.

Chapter 1 discusses the vampire craze that gripped Europe in the 1730s from two complementary points of view. The first epidemics of vampirism afflicted rural, illiterate communities in lands that had been subjected alternately to Austrian and Turkish rule. Reports of this phenomenon, when transmitted to learned societies, universities, and metropolitan journals, gave rise to a comparably feverish rash of scientific and religious debate. In both Eastern and Western sectors of Central Europe, vampiromania symptomized cultural conflict. Serbian rustics whose identity was imperiled by the machinations of two competing empires achieved a certain amount of symbolic mastery over their troubles by contriving a cause for them within their community. The vampire mediated between inside and outside, past and present, and served as an object onto which more general anxiety could be displaced. Analogously, but for a very different type of society, vampirism allowed learned Western Europeans to confront the interpenetration of foreign and domestic affairs and the competing claims of old and new philosophies. When the vampire emerged on the stage of history, it brought fears of beleaguered cultural identity and tradition into focus for East and West alike.

Chapter 2 examines the satirical strain of discourse that began at the same time as earnest vampirology, and it addresses the affinities between Enlightenment vampires and their Romantic kindred. *Philosophes* and those in the nineteenth century who continued their project of demystification employed the figure of the vampire to attack superstition, clerical dogma, and exploitative economic systems. This rhetorical use of the vampire also occurred in Romantic works that employed the vampire as a means of indicting sanctimony, hypocrisy, and oversimplified claims of reason. The Romantic vampire intensified the negative aspect of its Enlightenment precursor and, in the process, renewed its power as a metaphor for social criticism after Napoleon and the Revolutions of 1830 and 1848.

Until John Polidori's "The Vampyre," the monster had no specific external character traits; that is to say, no personality fleshes out the figures of Enlightenment satire. Chapter 3 takes as its point of departure Lord Ruthven, the first iconic representation of the vampire; despite his title, Ruthven displays the opportunistic qualities of the ascendant middle classes in the early nineteenth century. The chapter continues by examining the stage adaptations of Polidori's work that filled boulevard theaters in England, France, and Germany in the 1820s. The outstanding features shared by the many versions of Ruthven are his obscure pedigree and status as an impostor. Bloodsucking and "undeadness" receive relatively little attention in these works. Instead, the vampire's predations record the upward mobility of a new group that threatened the old order in which the clearly demarcated difference between gentry and peasantry, master and servant, had defined the social body. Lord Ruthven incorporates the energy of the locomotive, the factory system, and whirling city life; his destruction at the end of the melodramas satisfies the desire for a return to the idealized order of the past. The first few decades of the nineteenth century represent a turning point in the vampire's career because, in contrast to eighteenth-century works, the vampire is now used to tell stories of politically conservative wish fulfillment.

Necessarily — because the work comes as close as possible to providing a canonical version of the vampire — Bram Stoker's *Dracula* (1897) demands detailed scrutiny. Although the Transylvanian Count offers the most famous example of the undead, his presence in the novel that bears his name is strangely attenuated. Chapter 4 argues that Dracula's substance derives from his manipulation of the markets, exchange systems, and communications networks already in place in England, the country he invades. Though marked as an outsider, this vampire is really an insider par excellence. Stoker's novel, in the form of the vampire who has come to London, confronts English society with its own capacity for evil by casting back a reverse image of its own imperialist ambitions. Significantly, Dracula's nearly anonymous exploitation of the structures that command modern life — not his seductive, aristocratic profile — underwrites his power and enduring relevance. This faceless component of the vampire's being assured the Count's resurrection in the myriad guises he has subsequently assumed in the cultural productions of twentieth-century Europe and America.

Vampire stories of the nineteenth century often share the theme of madness. When confronted with the possible presence of otherworldly forces, almost all the protagonists of these tales question their sanity. Chapter 5 examines *Memoirs of My Nervous Illness* (1903) by Daniel Paul Schreber, a Dresden jurist who spent a decade in psychiatric institutions. The state of madness that Schreber describes offers a striking parallel to vampire fictions: the suspension of borders separating the living and the dead, parasitic exchanges of life force, and conjurations of beings intent on eroding the integrity of the social body through attacks on the private individual. Schreber's *Memoirs* provide an interface between the cultural imaginary from which fictions about the undead drew their power and the material conditions of everyday life at the turn of the century. Only the form of Schreber's delusions is fantastic; their social substance is real. Read as a historical allegory, *Memoirs* offer a strikingly lucid account of the anxieties and cultural pathologies entailed by modernization.

Chapter 6 discusses Friedrich Wilhelm Murnau's *Nosferatu* — whose titular monster, legendarily incarnated by actor Max Schreck, has become a vampire icon for the twentieth century[51] — against the backdrop of contemporary films that also explore the relationship between the cinematic image, automatism, and the undead. Like Dracula, Count Orlok and his peers represent the modern in atavistic guise. They unite in their scattered, spectral forms the cultural anxieties engendered by the economic, political, and technological changes that shaped life in the cataclysmic period the First World War inaugurated. In a broader historical view, these vampires give shape to fears concerning the emergence of the so-called "life sciences." Despite their religious visual language and archaizing trappings, the Weimar films examined in this chapter reveal grave misgivings about uniquely modern obsessions with race and the evolutionary struggle for survival.

Finally, the conclusion explains why, after two hundred years of association with Europe (and German/Austrian Central Europe, in particular), the vampire has become a naturalized American. If this monster owes its long life to modernizing forces, it is only fitting that it has moved to Southern California, the axis of the global culture industry.[52]

* * *

Before turning to the "real" vampires that plagued Serbian rustics in the 1700s, a few more words on the cultural terrain where vampires have thrived will set up the larger framework for the chapters to follow. These remarks are intended to establish the premium placed on change in modern life and modern symbolic productions in general. The vampire is a negatively coded representative of the dynamism that has increasingly characterized Western societies since the eighteenth century. The most famous work by Franz Kafka — Deleuze and Guattari's pseudo-vampire — points the way to the shadows where many of the monsters soon to be examined first gathered.

When he awakens from "unsettling dreams," Gregor Samsa finds himself transformed "zu einem ungeheueren Ungeziefer" (into a monstrous vermin).[53] Nowhere does Kafka indicate precisely what Gregor now looks like. The text contains only a partial description of the form the traveling salesman has assumed:

> Er lag auf seinem panzerartig harten Rücken und sah, wenn er den Kopf ein wenig hob, seinen gewölbten, braunen, von bogenförmigen Versteifungen geteilten Bauch, auf dessen Höhe sich die Bettdecke . . . kaum noch erhalten konnte. Seine vielen, im Vergleich zu seinem sonstigen Umfang kläglich dünnen Beine flimmerten ihm hilflos vor den Augen.

> [He was lying on his back as hard as armor plate, and when he lifted his head a little he saw his vaulted brown belly, sectioned by arch-shaped ribs, to whose dome the cover . . . could barely cling. His many legs, pitifully thin compared with the size of the rest of him, were waving helplessly before him.][54]

Putting a transformation at the beginning — or indeed *before* the beginning — of a narrative goes against the classical practice of the storyteller's art. Ovid, who provided a model and a lexicon for representing drastic changes of state and self to the entire European literary tradition until the end of the Renaissance, placed metamorphoses at the end of his tales. For him, as for his Greek forebears in Alexandrian Egypt, the metamorphosis represents the point of narrative culmination, which wraps up the uncertainties of the text and gives an explanation in the framework of a mythic "then" to a state of affairs "now" (for example, in his accounts of the creation of heavenly bodies, the origin of religious practices, and the beginning of the natural world).[55]

The reversal of chronology and the upsetting of narrative structure that distinguish Kafka's style are to a large extent symptomatic of cultural shifts that began in the eighteenth century. Kafka's displacement of metamorphosis to a position eccentric to the narrative proper corresponds to a shift in the symbolic value of transformation that gains in currency precisely when the first great novels are written. The transformative logic exemplified by the works of Kafka and earlier stylistic experimenters such as Laurence Sterne and his German admirer, Jean Paul Richter, represents a countercurrent to the classically inflected grand narratives of Balzac, Dickens, Mann, and other celebrated literary figures who let their themes develop internally — that is, in the course of the story's unfolding.

The distress that Kafka and his forebears bring to narrative structure corresponds, in works that are not so adventurous formally, to the relatively new literary theme of the dislocated private party, alone against the world. The figure of the solitary adventurer goes back to antiquity (e.g., Homer's *Odyssey*), but with the Renaissance, the anomalous individual started to receive more literary space in which to display the idiosyncrasies that constitute character: a distinguishing feature of modern narrative is that the representation of subjective experience counterbalances, at least hypothetically, the objective reality the protagonist shares with others.[56] Ian Watt has argued that the stories of Don Quixote, Don Juan, Faust, and Robinson Crusoe are exemplary of the phenomenon.[57] These figures do not share a common origin, yet they display a common, fundamental trait: each man is out for himself. Quixote is anachronistically obsessed with living according to the chivalric code, Don Juan is a pleasure-seeker who eschews lasting attachments, Faust impiously craves knowledge and power, and Crusoe is a castaway, left to create a social order of his own devising. Each of these characters represents radical subjectivity in possession of the power to make and unmake the world.

Sociologically, the literary exaltation of individualism requires the weakening of an older cultural order that, while constricting ambitious souls, also assured peace to more modest ones. As we will see, vampires thrive where the heroes of modern individualism experience their greatest triumphs: the realms of imagination, erotic exploit, knowledge-seeking, and foreign adventure. *Metamorphoses of the Vampire* shows how the vampire lacks definite contours of individuality and corrodes the identities of all those with whom it comes into contact. The same circumstances that enabled what Stephen Greenblatt, in another context, aptly calls "self-fashioning"[58] menace the greater part of undistinguished humanity with dissolution into faceless anonymity. A sort of "man in the crowd" (Poe) transfigured into the supernatural, the vampire has enjoyed a storied career as the diabolical spirit of an age characterized by mass movements, mass politics, and mass slaughter.[59] This monster, its iconic representations with cape-and-fangs notwithstanding, embodies the depersonalizing forces of modernity. Every representation of the vampire can be seen to contrast sharply with another depiction somewhere else, yet an underlying sameness arising from cultural contradictions — from which no society is free — generates these images in the first place. In this regard, the vampire displays, in exaggerated and monstrous form, the traits of its human counterparts, who, as recent generations of philosophers (particularly in France[60]) have stressed, are far from integral, unified subjects. As we will see, over time more and more agency is ascribed to the vampire, which always endeavors to "fashion" itself to suit its environment.[61]

No one knows exactly from what dreams Gregor Samsa awakens — and that is part of Kafka's game. However, the nightmare is not merely personal: it is cultural, as well. Kafka's vision of indeterminate horror has an iconic representation in Goya's famous picture in the *Caprichos* (1799): "El sueño de la razón produce monstruos" (The sleep [alternately, "dream"] of reason produces monsters). The image shows a man collapsed at a desk littered with pens and papers. He is surrounded by a swarm of flying creatures combining the features of owls, bats, and moths, which gaze out into the night with the fixed stare of enflamed human passions. Are these beings vampires? They could be.

The darkness and the nocturnal monsters looking wide-eyed into the void in turn represent the obscurity of the sleeper's cerebration. The title, inscribed in the image itself, provides an interpretive challenge because it suggests two opposite and mutually incompatible meanings. On the one hand, it can be taken to mean that Reason secretly dreams of its other, Madness; formulated in Lacanian terms: the unacknowledged desire of Order is Chaos. On the other hand, the title seems to assert that when Reason rests, Chaos results; therefore, Reason must be eternally vigilant in order to hold irrationality and concomitant terrors at bay. The aporia to which Goya gives such striking visual expression excludes a middle ground. Despite the modest title of the collection of images to which this picture belongs (*Caprichos* translates as "caprices" or "whims"), Goya provides an emblem of modernity in his art.

"The Sleep of Reason," which also reads as "The Nightmare of Reason," is the product of the social, political, and economic upheavals in what Eric Hobsbawm has called the "Age of Revolution."[62] Hobsbawm's term refers to the period of 1789–1848, which witnessed political revolution first in France and then throughout the European continent, as well as the consolidation of long-term processes conventionally known as the "Industrial Revolution." French revolutionaries justified the overturning of the established order with an appeal to secular rationalism; English industrialists legitimated their enterprise with the common-sense pragmatism of businessmen. In terms of broader social changes, the "Age of Revolution" continues until the present day, for the twin revolutions inaugurated a destabilizing appetite for novelty: new goods, new services, new markets, new social mobility, new rights, and new competition for power.

Revolutionary ways of thinking, whether embraced or rejected by later generations, represent hallmarks of modernity throughout the nineteenth, twentieth, and, now, twenty-first centuries. As we will see after a discussion of premodern, Serbian vampires, the twin revolutions of the eighteenth century, which restructured the modes of production and political organization of Europe, provided the motor for the vampire's many transformations. The forward-looking orientation of modernization, as if through an unconscious act of repression, generated a cultural dream world of sinister forces supposedly returning from a darker age to denature the present.[63]

The vampire is the most persistent creature haunting the dreams and nightmares of reason, whether in the illuminist eighteenth century, the dynamist nineteenth century, or the catastrophic early twentieth century. Patterns that lend the vampire definition emerge against a background of rupture and change. They include recurrent slippages of linguistic reference, transgressions of spatial and temporal boundaries, movements between different stations of class and culture, the confusion of biological and artificial forms of reproduction, the destabilization of communications media, the upsetting of religious codes, and the inversion of norms of sex and gender. This unstable core and affinity for throwing established systems into crisis sets the vampire apart from the monks lurking in labyrinthine monasteries, witches in league with the Devil, and Oriental voluptuaries who are roughly coeval with our monster as other specimens of "Gothic"[64] villainy. The terror that the vampire wields lies in the fact that it moves and changes as fast as modern life. It is impossible to know in which form the vampire will strike next.

Notes

1 On the modernity of a supposedly ancient category of culture and thought ("myth"), see the classic collection of essays by Roland Barthes, *Mythologies*, trans.

Annette Lavers (New York: Hill & Wang, 1972). See also Philippe Muray, *Le XIXe siècle à travers les âges* (Paris: Gallimard, 1999) for a brilliant — if controversial — dissection of political and religious mystifications that took form in the 1800s and continue today.

[2] Sheridan Le Fanu, *The Best Horror Stories* (London: Sphere Books, 1970), 99.

[3] Sigmund Freud, "The 'Uncanny,'" *Sigmund Freud: Collected Papers* (Vol. 4), trans. Joan Riviere (New York: Basic Books, 1959), 368–407.

[4] James Joyce, *Ulysses* (New York: Vintage, 1986), 40.

[5] Cited in Ernest Jones, *On the Nightmare* (New York: Grove, 1959), 101.

[6] Bram Stoker, *Dracula*, ed. Glennis Byron (Ontario: Broadview, 1998), 347.

[7] Julio Cortázar, *Vampiros multinacionales* (Mexico City: Excélsior, 1975); see the conclusion of the present study for a discussion.

[8] Richard F. Burton, *Vikram and the Vampire, or, Tales of Hindu Devilry*, ed. Isabel Burton (London: Tylston and Edwards, 1893). The *baital* (which Burton translates as "vampire") poses riddles to King Vikram and dispenses enigmatic wisdom. However, the oracular power that the baital possesses is not a capability shared by the creatures Europeans call vampires until later. Burton adds to the European vampire myth, but he does not find a genuine antecedent/analog to it. Just as Burton's Orientalism runs together varied cultures in Africa, the Near East, and India, his terminology for the supernatural elides important differences between monsters. For an overview of Burton's reckless life and ideas, see Mary S. Lovell, *A Rage to Live: A Biography of Richard and Isabel Burton* (New York: W. W. Norton, 1998).

[9] Montague Summers, *The Vampire* (London: Senate, 1995), ix. Originally published as *The Vampire, His Kith and Kin* (London: Kegan Paul, Trench, Trubner & Co., 1928).

[10] Jones, *Nightmare*, 116.

[11] Christopher Frayling, *Vampyres* (London: Faber and Faber, 1991), 4.

[12] Felix J. Oinas, *Essays on Russian Folklore and Mythology* (Columbus: Slavica, 1985), 111.

[13] Thus, the introduction to a recent collection of essays begins with a puzzling assertion: "An ambiguously coded figure, a source of both erotic anxiety and corrupt desire, the literary vampire is one of the most powerful archetypes bequeathed to us from the imagination of the nineteenth century" (Joan Gordon and Veronica Hollinger, eds., *Blood Read: The Vampire as Metaphor in Contemporary Culture* [Philadelphia: U of Pennsylvania P, 1997], 1). How can an archetype be only a little over a hundred years old?

[14] Dom Augustin Calmet, *Dissertation sur les vampires* (Grenoble: Jérôme Millon, 1998), 29–30.

[15] Three French editions appeared (1746, 1749, and 1751); the quotation is taken from the third, revised printing, which strikes a more skeptical tone. The work appeared in German translation in 1752, followed by an English version in 1759.

[16] Calmet, 31.

[17] Markman Ellis, *The History of Gothic Fiction* (Edinburgh: Edinburgh UP, 2000), 161.

[18] Useful studies of popular beliefs about vampires include Jan L. Perkowski, *Vampires of the Slavs* (Cambridge: Slavica, 1976); Alan Dundes, ed., *The Vampire: A Casebook* (Madison: U of Wisconsin P, 1998); and Peter Mario Kreuter, *Der Vampirglaube in Südosteuropa: Studien zur Genese, Bedeutung und Funktion* (Berlin: Weidler, 2001).

[19] This connection was observed — and subject to criticism — in the first scholarly discussion of vampires, which was delivered as a lecture in 1725 and appeared in print in 1728 and, with additions, in 1734. See Michael Ranfft, *Traktat von dem Kauen und Schmatzen der Toten in Gräbern*, ed. Nicolaus Equiamicus (Diedorf: Ubooks, 2006); unfortunately, the editor has changed the text *ad libitum* for purposes of "readability." On the subject of *Nachzehrer*, see Thomas Schürmann. *Nachzehrerglauben in Mitteleuropa* (Marburg: N. G. Elwert, 1990).

[20] This, in essence, is the driving concern of Jacques Derrida's "deconstruction," which finds its clearest articulation in "White Mythology: Metaphor in the Text of Philosophy," *Margins of Philosophy*, trans. Alan Bass (Chicago: U of Chicago P, 1985), 207–72.

[21] Paul Ricoeur, *Du texte à l'action* (Paris: Seuil, 1986), 19.

[22] See the writings of Paul de Man, e.g., "Semiology and Rhetoric," *Allegories of Reading: Figural Language in Rousseau, Nietzsche, Rilke, and Proust* (New Haven: Yale UP, 1982), 3–19.

[23] Michel Serres, *The Parasite*, trans. Lawrence R. Schehr (Minneapolis: U of Minnesota P, 2007), explores the relationship between chaos and order in science, social organization, and literature; "noise" is necessary, according to Serres, for structures to stand and systems to function. Vampires are nothing if not parasites: while seeming extrinsic to their hosts, they in fact entertain a complementary relationship with them; they are interference that, by revealing points of weakness, helps the system to regenerate itself.

[24] Paul Ricoeur, *Freud and Philosophy: An Essay on Interpretation*, trans. Denis Savage (New Haven: Yale UP, 1970), 32–36.

[25] Gilles Deleuze and Félix Guattari, *Kafka: Toward a Minor Literature*, trans. Dana Polan (Minneapolis: U of Minnesota P, 1986), 29–30; I have modified the translation, which is inaccurate (cf. the French edition [Paris: Éditions de Minuit, 1975], 53–54).

[26] See Elias Canetti, *Kafka's Other Trial: The Letters to Felice*, trans. Christopher Middleton (New York: Schocken, 1974); and Bernhard Siegert, *Relays: Literature as an Epoch of the Postal System*, trans. Kevin Repp (Stanford: Stanford UP, 1999), 207–18.

[27] See the documents and commentary in Franz Kafka, *The Office Writings*, ed. Stanley Corngold, Jack Greenberg, and Benno Wagner (Princeton: Princeton UP, 2008).

[28] David Herbert Lawrence, *Studies in Classic American Literature* (New York: Penguin, 1971), 70–88; see also James B. Twitchell, *The Living Dead: A Study of the Vampire in Romantic Literature* (Durham: Duke UP, 1981), 192–205.

[29] Vampires or not, Poe's cast of unsettling figures has a bearing on the issues of identity and bondage intimately tied to our monster. See J. Gerald Kennedy and Liliane Weissberg, eds., *Romancing the Shadow: Poe and Race* (Oxford: Oxford UP, 2001); contributor Joan Dayan argues that "By invoking the twofold condition of the undead, Poe tackled the problematic status of human materials" (109).

[30] Mario Praz, *The Romantic Agony*, trans. Angus Davidson (Oxford: Oxford UP, 1933), passim. More recently, Camille Paglia, in *Sexual Personae: Art and Decadence from Nefertiti to Emily Dickinson* (New York: Vintage, 1991), has continued the search in the same, somewhat indiscriminate spirit.

[31] Praz, 253; Walter Pater, *The Renaissance* (New York: The Modern Library, 1950), 103.

[32] For those seeking instruction along these lines, the publishing details are: Dorothy Harbour, *Energy Vampires: A Practical Guide for Psychic Self-Protection* (Rochester: Destiny Books, 2002); Barbara E. Hort, *Unholy Hungers: Encountering the Psychic Vampire in Ourselves and Others* (Boston: Shambhala, 1996); Marty Raphael, *Spiritual Vampires: The Use and Misuse of Spiritual Power* (Santa Fe: Message, 1996).

[33] Nina Auerbach, *Our Vampires, Ourselves* (Chicago: U of Chicago P, 1995).

[34] See Donna J. Haraway, *How Like a Leaf: An Interview with Thyrza Nichols Goodeve* (New York: Routledge, 2000), 149–54; here, Haraway summarizes arguments made in fuller detail in her book *Modest Witness@Second Millennium. FemaleMan Meets OncoMouse: Feminism and Technoscience* (New York: Routledge, 1997).

[35] Carlo Ginzburg, *Clues, Myths, and the Historical Method*, trans. John and Anne C. Tedeschi (Baltimore: Johns Hopkins UP, 1989), ix. Studies by Ginzburg that have been consulted for inspiration, information, and models of interpretation include *The Night Battles: Witchcraft and Agrarian Cults in the Sixteenth and Seventeenth Centuries*, trans. John and Anne C. Tedeschi (Baltimore: The Johns Hopkins UP, 1992) and *Ecstasies: Deciphering the Witches' Sabbath*, trans. Raymond Rosenthal (Chicago: U of Chicago P, 1994). Walter Stephens, *Demon Lovers: Witchcraft, Sex, and the Crisis of Belief* (Chicago: U of Chicago P, 2003) provides another example of innovative historicism from which the study at hand has benefited.

[36] Michel Foucault, *Madness and Civilization*, trans. Richard Howard (New York: Vintage, 1965).

[37] Michel Foucault, *The Order of Things*, trans. Alan Sheridan (New York: Vintage, 1970), 387.

[38] See, among other recent studies, N. Katherine Hayles, *How We Became Posthuman: Virtual Bodies in Cybernetics, Literature, and Informatics* (Chicago: U of Chicago P, 1999); and Bruce Clarke, *Posthuman Metamorphosis: Narrative and Systems* (New York: Fordham UP, 2008).

[39] Jacques Lacan, "The Function and Field of Speech and Language in Psychoanalysis," *Écrits. A Selection*, trans. Alan Sheridan (New York: W. W. Norton, 1977), 72.

40 René Girard, *The Scapegoat*, trans. Yvonne Freccero (Baltimore: Johns Hopkins UP, 1986), 33; *Le bouc émissaire* (Paris: Grasset, 1982), 51.

41 Girard, *Scapegoat*, 33.

42 Girard, *Scapegoat*, 33.

43 See also the essays collected in *Monster Theory: Reading Culture*, ed. Jeffrey Jerome Cohen (Minneapolis: U of Minnesota P, 1997); Cohen's introduction offers methodological considerations (e.g., "the monster's body is a cultural body," "the monster dwells at the gates of difference") with which the present study is in basic agreement.

44 Chris Baldick, *In Frankenstein's Shadow: Myth, Monstrosity, and Nineteenth-Century Writing* (Oxford: Clarendon, 1987), 14.

45 Baldick, 15.

46 Carl Schmitt, *The Nomos of the Earth in the International Law of the Jus Publicum Europaeum*, trans. G. L. Ulmen (New York: Telos, 2003), 95; this work originally appeared in 1950. See also Walter Benjamin's gloss on Parisian police reports during revolutionary upheaval, when "the flâneur completely distances himself from the time of the philosophical promenader, and takes on the features of the werewolf restlessly roaming a social wilderness." *The Arcades Project*, trans. Howard Eiland and Kevin McLaughlin (Cambridge: Harvard UP, 1999), 417–18.

47 Michael Hardt and Antonio Negri, *Multitude: War and Democracy in the Age of Empire* (New York: Penguin, 2004), 10–11.

48 Incidentally, this approach follows the principles of Lacanian psychoanalysis, which seeks to chart the displacements of libidinal energies as they form and deform relations between subjects of desire and their objects of investment; sexuality is properly understood as a structure, not as an etiology; see, for example, Bruce Fink, *A Clinical Introduction to Lacanian Psychoanalysis: Theory and Technique* (Cambridge: Harvard UP, 1999), 165–204.

49 Jean-Paul Roux, *Le sang: Mythes, symboles et réalités* (Paris: Fayard, 1988). Caroline Walker Bynum, *Wonderful Blood: Theology and Practice in Late Medieval Northern Germany and Beyond* (Philadelphia: U of Pennsylvania P, 2007), while focusing on Germany, explores the broader European context of blood symbolism. See also David Biale, *Blood and Belief: The Circulation of a Symbol between Jews and Christians* (Berkeley: U of California P, 2007).

50 The works of Avital Ronell are representative of this approach. See, for example, *The Telephone Book: Technology, Schizophrenia, Electric Speech* (Lincoln: U of Nebraska P, 1991). A similar critical orientation may be found in Laurence A. Rickels, *Aberrations of Mourning: Writing on German Crypts* (Detroit: Wayne State UP, 1988). Both authors derive their concerns from the writings of Derrida; the latter's *Specters of Marx: The State of the Debt, the Work of Mourning, and the New International*, trans. Peggy Kamuf (New York: Routledge, 1994) coins the term "hauntology" (10) — a pun between languages — to name the problem.

51 Hence the premise of the 2000 film *Shadow of the Vampire* (directed by E. Elias Merhige) that Schreck really was a vampire.

52 This trend does not, of course, prevent the monster from ultimately thriving in other environments, also to be discussed.

[53] Franz Kafka, *Die Erzählungen* (Frankfurt am Main: Fischer, 2002), 96; *The Metamorphosis*, translated and edited by Stanley Corngold (New York: W. W. Norton, 1996), 3.

[54] Kafka, 96/3.

[55] Richard Hunter, *The Shadow of Callimachus: Studies in the Reception of Hellenistic Poetry at Rome* (Cambridge: Cambridge UP, 2006) discusses the poetic principle at work.

[56] See, for example, the classic studies by Georg Lukács, *The Theory of the Novel* (Cambridge: MIT Press, 1971); and Mikhail Bakhtin, *The Dialogic Imagination: Four Essays*, ed. Michael Holquist (Austin: U of Texas P, 1982).

[57] Ian Watt, *Myths of Modern Individualism: Faust, Don Quixote, Don Juan, Robinson Crusoe* (Cambridge: Cambridge UP, 1997).

[58] Stephen Greenblatt, *Renaissance Self-Fashioning: From More to Shakespeare* (Chicago: U of Chicago P, 1984).

[59] The most profound meditation on this topic remains that of Elias Canetti, who in *Crowds and Power*, trans. Carol Stewart (New York: Farrar, Straus, and Giroux, 1984), diagnoses an epochal malady (e.g., "as the crowd grows, its units become weaker and weaker" [186] — an observation that leads into the discussion of totalitarianism and madness concluding the essay). At the same time — and especially in view of gender dynamics that will be analyzed throughout the following pages — it is important to note a modernist tendency to feminize mass culture, also implicit in Canetti's work, which reads as a symptom; see the influential essay by Andreas Huyssen, "Mass Culture as Woman: Modernism's Other," in *After the Great Divide: Modernism, Mass Culture, Postmodernism* (Bloomington: Indiana UP, 1986), 44–64.

[60] See, e.g., Vincent Descombes, *Modern French Philosophy*, trans. L. Scott-Fox and J. M. Harding (Cambridge: Cambridge UP, 1981).

[61] Needless to say, these efforts are not always successful (see, in particular, chapter 4).

[62] Eric Hobsbawm, *The Age of Revolution: 1789–1848* (New York: Vintage, 1996).

[63] Jean-Michel Rabaté, arguing for the "ineluctability of spectral returns" in modern culture, shows how literary works are "systematically 'haunted' by voices from the past" (*The Ghosts of Modernity* [Gainesville: The UP of Florida, 1996], xvi). For further exploration along these lines, see Julian Wolfreys, *Victorian Hauntings: Spectrality, Gothic, the Uncanny, and Literature* (New York: Palgrave, 2002).

[64] Strictly speaking — as Summers observes — "the Vampire was not generally known to Gothic lore" (278). That is, this monster does not feature in the works of Horace Walpole, Matthew "Monk" Lewis, and Ann Radcliffe, the eighteenth-century originators of this kind of literature. However, *Metamorphoses of the Vampire* occasionally follows the established critical convention of using the word "Gothic" to include the vampire, if only for convenience. Whenever necessary, appropriate distinctions are drawn.

Part I: The Rise of the Vampire

1: Vampire Country: Borders of Culture and Power in Central Europe

FOR ABOUT TWENTY YEARS in the early half of the eighteenth century, parts of Europe caught vampire fever. The etiology and epidemic nature of the phenomenon are not well known today, and, at first glance, the matter has little to do with the forms that vampirism subsequently assumed. This chapter does not discuss the aristocratic and refined creatures that emerged at later stages of the vampire's career. Instead, it examines peasants who, once they had died, would not stay dead and buried, but instead rose from the grave to kill their former family and friends. This chapter's attention then turns to the mystified reactions of military men and city folk who wished to make sense of the incredible events occurring in the hinterlands for, without the violent acts generated by group panic among members of rural communities fearing collective destruction through supernatural predation, the vampire would never have had the chance to extend its grasp to threaten and thrill the rest of the world. Serbian vampirism threw the spark igniting the flames in which the vampire we know was born.

The history of the vampire began as an enigma. In 1725, a medical officer of the Austrian army named Frombald wrote a letter from the imperial backwaters to the central administration in Vienna. Frombald reported that the Serbian *hajduks* (peasant-soldiers) under his supervision had exhumed a corpse, transfixed it with a stake, and burned it to ashes. They did so, he explained, because they believed that the dead man had returned from the grave at night, climbed atop sleepers, throttled them, and thereby caused them to die after twenty-four hours of illness. The report, which is otherwise written in German, contains a parenthetical remark in which Frombald notes the name that villagers have for "persons of this sort": *vampyri*.[1] Frombald, who in all likelihood did not share a language with his informants, made his report in German; his use of Latin, the international language of science and learning, attempted to conceal from superiors his resourcelessness when confronted with a situation that caught him unawares.

The first time the word "vampire" entered historical record, then, it designated a site of uncertainty where languages and cultures met in mutual incomprehension. The name, whose etymology is still disputed,[2] refers to a being that has died, been resurrected, and now spreads death among the living. Such an occurrence is, of course, a logical impossibility. Moreover, in addition to violating the rules of conventional understanding and discourse, the vampire disrupts ontology, i.e., the notion that words, things, and persons fit into a balanced symbolic order. "Vampire," both as a signifier and as a signified, moves between the categories of self and other, the familiar and the strange, and the temporal and the eternal.

Frombald's document attracted little immediate attention, and seven years of incubation elapsed before busy tongues and pens amplified the feeble, nearly incoherent word *vampyri* into something resembling a roar. In 1732, another medical officer, *Regimentsfeldscher* Flückinger, drew up a protocol documenting the "execution" of another vampire in another Serbian village. Flückinger submitted his account, superscribed "Visum et repertum" (a matter seen and verified), to authorities in Belgrade; from there, it rapidly reached all the European capitals.[3] In German-speaking Central Europe, journals such as the *Wiener Diarium, Vossische Zeitung, Leipziger Zeitung,* and *Breßlauische Sammlungen* spread the monster's fame to Vienna, Nuremberg, Leipzig, Tübingen, Berlin, and other centers of learning.[4] Translations of the Flückinger report also appeared in Paris and London. Twelve books and four dissertations on vampirism appeared 1732 and the following year. Talk of vampires was suddenly everywhere, and for roughly two decades afterwards additional newspaper pieces and scholarly treatises on incidents of vampirism in the Balkans were published.

In the early twenty-first century, we are accustomed to hearing and reading about vampires, which abound in all forms of media — from "old-fashioned" print to digital entertainment and communications technology. Significantly, the vampire's success in the media goes all the way back to the monster's riddling beginnings, when whispers and rumors that had long passed from mouth to ear were transposed into print and, having now received a kind of official recognition, penetrated the cultural capitals of Western Europe. For all its international celebrity, however, the vampire made the biggest impact in the Habsburg-dominated "Holy Roman Empire of the German Nation"; as we will see in the course of this study, the association with a "greater Germany" proved exceptionally long-lived.

The cultural dynamics of the Central European Counter-Reformation explain much of the virulence of the vampire phenomenon. The religious and social upheavals that began with Luther in sixteenth-century Germany, compounded by the rise of France to the position of preeminent Continental power in the seventeenth century, created a climate fraught with tension for the Habsburg elite. Church and crown, faced with the decline of both spiritual and temporal authority, sought to enforce the observation of orthodoxy in the general population in the decades that preceded the vampire reports. As R. J. W. Evans has shown, the uneducated were progressively denied the right to engage in activities that, according to secular and religious authorities, ill-befitted their station and might foment disorder in the body politic.[5]

When authorities attacked popular attempts to harness magical forces, however, they did not do so because they thought that the beliefs underlying such practices were wrong; many in the Catholic Church, after all, held that Satan himself had spurred reformers to apostasy and revolt.[6] The political and intellectual order of the Counter-Reformation acknowledged another universe existing alongside the world of everyday affairs, and it granted that learned individuals might uncover cryptic correspondences and exploit mysterious sympathies. In the proper context and pursued by the proper parties, such activities strengthened the status quo. As Evans observes, "Catholic Central European philosophy presents us with a pervasive habit of mind which invested even commonplace phenomena with 'magical' workings" (342). What was at issue were the governance and administration of supernatural powers. In an effort to quash popular occultism, the Counter-Reformation reasserted the "holy magic of ancient Mother Church" (386) by restoring liturgy and ritual and invoking the power of the saints. In particular, the cult of the saints relied on promoting belief in miracles, which formed, in Evans's words, "the fundamental category of Counter-Reformation magic" (388). A further form of such magic involved the conjuring of souls of the dead from Purgatory (387).[7]

Reports of *vampyri* — creatures that did not fit into established demonological categories, parodied the incorruptible bodies of the saints, and perverted the idea that the souls of the dead had a definite location in the divine plan — commanded the notice of Habsburg intellectuals schooled in Counter-Reformation theology because disorder in the spiritual realm implied disorder in the material realm. Vampires generated interest and discussion because they threatened to disturb the dominion of church and state over the unknown.

Reformed Christians shared their opponents' view of the earth as a realm rife with supernatural powers. When Luther decried the Pope as the Antichrist in the 1500s, he was being quite serious. His followers in the following centuries likewise saw the Devil and his agents as real forces. Protestants, as much as Catholics, based their claims for organizing human affairs on metaphysics. The vampire reports offered them, too, an opportunity to argue theology and politics. Thus, after reviewing a copy of the Flückinger document, the members of the Prussian Academy of Sciences shared the following sarcasm with their patron, King Friedrich Wilhelm I:

> Es ist gewiß, daß die ERscheinung [*sic*] dieser Blutsauger, auch worinne selbige bestanden, [im Bericht] mit nichts dargethan und wir keine Spuren davon in der Historie, und in den hiesigen so wenig als andern Evangelischen Landen iemahls gefunden.

[It is certain, that the Apparition of these blood-suckers, and the account of their substance, is not demonstrated [in the report], and we have no traces thereof in history, in our own or in other Protestant lands, ever.][8]

The distinction the academicians made between "here," in the Protestant North — where nobody claimed to have encountered vampires — and "there," in the Catholic South, where the belief was apparently rife, implied that the vampire superstition was the result of a fallacious spiritual regime. All the nonsense about living corpses provided proof to the Protestant academicians that proper religion guarded against error.

The vampire reports reminded both Catholics and Protestants of points of uncertainty in what a later German philosophical idiom would call the "world picture." Theologians had to fit the prodigies into God's creation or else account for a new sphere of influence for the Devil. "Physics" argued that a humoral or chemical disequilibrium accounted for the undead state. Other academics invoked Cartesian models for malfunctions of the bodily machine. Finally, proponents of occultist theories, especially the followers of Paracelsus, welcomed the reports of the undead because they seemed to substantiate their master's teachings, according to which the event of death does not mark immediate departure from this world.[9]

Among other things, then, the vampire represents a crisis within Christendom, the faith supposedly uniting Europe. The three forms of Christianity in question are Eastern Orthodoxy, Roman Catholicism, and Protestantism, each of which, like all social groupings, is subject to further, internal division. Claims based on different interpretations and versions of the Bible are ultimately more important for the vampire becoming an item of fascination than what rustics thought. Yet Old Testament prohibitions concerning blood and New Testament equations of Christ's blood and the substance of divinity were not at issue. Rather, concerns involved formal categories of interpretation; it went without saying that villagers' activities were an abomination, and certainly it occurred to no one to ask them about their reasoning.

Vampire debates reflected the anxieties of elites seeking to affirm their mastery, both conceptually and politically, over a world that apprehensive minds considered ready to slide into chaos. The long-winded discussions focused on an object that was, in the eyes of all but the most esoterically minded participants, an illusion. Catholic vampirologists looked down the social ladder, at the lowest estate in cultural backwaters. Protestant vampirologists looked down the map, at Catholics. If Paracelsians avoided the tone of obloquy employed by their more orthodox contemporaries, they purchased their "explanation" of the vampire phenomenon with esoteric doctrines that consigned them to a kind of marginality resembling that of

Serbian rustics — the only others who seemed to believe in the reality of the undead.[10]

"Seemed to believe" is the best formulation because vampires, although they posed an interpretive challenge in their own right, offered a pretext for bringing up other matters. The phenomenon of vampirism cannot be abstracted from the social, religious, and political issues that gave it its specific discursive and performative contours.

The vampire reports, to which we now turn, reveal both confusion and the effort to counter it among villagers and officialdom alike. From Frombald's dispatch there emerges the picture of a man invested with imperial authority who stands dumbfounded and amazed by the strangeness of the people and practices in his jurisdiction.

Nachdeme bereits vor 10 Wochen ein in dem Dorf Kisolova, Rahmer-District, gesessener Unthertan nahmens Peter Plogojowiz, mit dem Tod abgegangen, und . . . zur Erden bestattet worden, hat sichs im ermeldtem Dorf geäusseret, daß innerhalb 8 Tagen 9 Personen, sowol alt als junge, nach überstandener 24-stündiger Kranckheit also dahingestorben, daß als sie annoch auf dem Todt-Beth lebendig lagen, offentlich ausgesaget, daß obbemeldet vor 10 Wochen verschiedener Peter Plogojowiz zu ihnen im Schlaf gekommen, sich auf sie gelegt und gewürget, daß sie nunmehro den Geist auffgeben müsten. [. . .] Sintemahlen . . . bey dergleichen Personen (so sie Vampyri nennen) verschiedene Zeichen, als dessen Cörper unverwesen, Haut, Haar, Bart und Nägel an ihme wachsen zu sehen seyn müsten, als haben sich die Untherthanen einhellig resolviret, das Grab des Peter Plogojowiz zu eröffnen, und zu sehen, ob sich würcklich obbemeldete Zeichen an ihm befinden. . . . Ich möchte thun, was ich wolte, allein wofern ich ihnen nicht gestatten werde, . . . mit dem Cörper nach ihrem Gebrauch zu verfahren, müsten sie Haus und Gut verlassen; weilen . . . wohl das gantze Dorf (wie schon unter türckishen Zeiten geschehen seyn solte) durch solchen üblen Geist zu Grund gehen könte. . . . Da dann solche Leute weder mit Guten noch mit Betrohungen von ihrer gefasten Resolution abhalten könte, habe ich mich mit Zuziehung des Gradisker Poppen in benanntes Dorf Kisolova begeben, den bereits ausgegrabenen Cörper des Peter Plogojowiz besichtigt und gründlicher Wahrheit gemäß folgendes befunden: daß Erstlich von solchem Cörper und dessen Grabe nicht der mindeste sonsten der Todten gemeiner Geruch verspüret; der Cörper ausser der Nasen, welche etwas abgefallen, gantz frisch; Haar und Bart, ja auch die Nägel. . . . an ihme gewachsen; . . . das Gesicht, Hände und . . . Füße, und der gantze Leib waren beschaffen, daß sie in . . . Lebzeiten nicht hätten vollkommener seyn können. In seinem Mund hab nicht ohne Erstaunung einiges frisches Blut erblickt, welches, der gemeinen Aussag nach, er von denen,

durch ihme umgebrachte, gesogen. [. . .] Nachdem nun sowol der
Popp als ich dieses Spectacul gesehen, der Pövel aber mehr und mehr
ergrimter als bestürtzter wurde, haben sie gesamte Unterthanen in
schneller Eil einen Pfeil gespitzet, solchen, dem Todten-Cörper zu
durchstechen . . . ; sie haben endlich oftermeldeten Cörper, in hoc
casu gewöhnlichem Gebrauch nach, zu Aschen verbrennet.[11]

[After a subject by the name of Peter Plogojowitz had died, ten
weeks past — he lived in the village of Kisilova, in the Rahm district — and had been buried . . . , it was revealed that in this same
village of Kisilova, within a week, nine people, both old and young,
died also, after suffering a twenty-four-hour illness. And they said
publicly, while they were yet alive, but on their deathbed, that the
above-mentioned Plogojowitz, who had died ten weeks earlier, had
come to them in their sleep, laid himself on them, and throttled
them, so that they would have to give up the ghost. [. . .] Since
with such people [which they call vampires] various signs are to be
seen — that is, the body undecomposed, the skin, hair, beard and
nails growing — the subjects resolved unanimously to open the grave
of Peter Plogojowitz and to see if such above-mentioned signs were
really to be found on him. . . . I could do what I wanted, but if I did
not accord them the viewing and the legal recognition to deal with
the body according to their custom, they would have to leave house
and home, because . . . the entire village — and this was already supposed to have happened in Turkish times — could be destroyed by
such an evil spirit. . . . Since I could not hold such people from the
resolution they had made, either with good words or with threats,
I went to the village of Kisilova, taking along the Gradisk pope,
and viewed the body of Peter Plogojowitz, just exhumed, finding,
in accordance with thorough truthfulness, that first of all I did not
detect the slightest odor that is otherwise characteristic of the dead,
and the body, except for the nose, which was somewhat fallen away,
was completely fresh. The hair and beard — even the nails . . . — had
grown on him. . . . The face, hands, and feet, and the whole body
were so constituted, that they could not have been more complete
in his lifetime. Not without astonishment, I saw some fresh blood
in his mouth, which, according to the common observation, he
had sucked from the people killed by him. [. . .] After both the
pope and I had seen this spectacle, while the people grew more outraged than distressed, all the subjects, with great speed, sharpened a
stake — in order to pierce the corpse of the deceased with it. . . . Finally, according to their usual practice *in hoc casu*, they burned the
often-mentioned body to ashes.][12]

Frombald cannot understand what he has witnessed. Here, in a remote
village, the world seems to have been turned on its head: with his own

eyes, the officer has seen a corpse that does not display the usual signs of putrefaction, and rustics have told him, with absolute conviction, that this body has sucked blood from the living and thereby caused victims to die. Moreover, these same informants, who have disregarded the officer's entreaties not to do anything inappropriate, have "executed" the putative monster in a ritual of collective violence. Although Frombald stresses his disbelief and disapproval of what villagers have said and done, genuine mystification has compelled him to refrain from intervening.

The dispatch from Flückinger, some years later, also displays befuddlement.

Nachdem die Anzeig beschehen, daß in dem Dorf Medvegya die sogenannte Vampyrs einige Persohnen durch Aussaugung des Bluts umgebracht haben sollen, als bin ich auf hohe Anordnung eines allhiesig Löblichen Obercommando, umb die Sach vollständig zu untersuchen, nebst darzu commandirten Herrn Officirn und 2 Unterfeldscherern dahin abgeschicket, und gegenwärtige Inquisition in Beyseyn des . . . ältesten Heydukhen des Dorfs, folgendermassen vorgenohmen, und abgehört worden.

Welche dan einhellig Aussaag, daß vor ohngefahr 5 Jahren ein hiesiger Heydukh, nahmens Arnont Paule, sich durch einen Fahl von einem Heüwag den Hals gebrochen; dieser hat bey seinen Lebszeiten sich öfters verlauten lassen, daß er bei Cossowa in dem Türckischen Servien von einem Vampyren geplagt worden sey. . . . In 20 oder 30 Täg nach seinem Todtfahl haben sich einige Leüth geklaget, daß sie von dem gedachten Arnont Paule geplaget würden; wie dan auch würcklich 4 Persohnen von ihme umbgebracht worden. [. . .] Ferners sagen obgedachte Leüthe aus, daß alle diejenige, welche von denen Vampyrs geplagt, und umbgebracht wurden, ebenfalls zu Vampyrs werden müssen. [. . .] Deme fügen sie auch hinzu, daß dieser Arnont Paule nicht allein die Leüthe, sondern auch das Vieh angegrifen, und ihnen das Blut ausgesauget habe. Weilen nun die Leüth das Fleisch von solch Vieh genutzet, so zeiget sich aufs neüe, daß sich wiederumben einige Vampyrs befinden; allermassen in Zeit 3er Monahten 17 jung und alte Persohnen mit Tod abgegangen.

[After it had been reported that in the village of Medvegya the so-called vampires had killed some people by sucking their blood, I was, by high decree of a local Honorable Supreme Command, sent there to investigate the matter thoroughly, along with officers detailed for that purpose and two subordinate medical officers, and therefore carried out and heard the present inquiry in the company of the . . . oldest *hajduk* of the village, as follows: who unanimously recount that about five years ago a local *hajduk* by the name of Arnont Paule broke his neck in a fall from a hay wagon. This man

had, during his lifetime, often revealed that, near Gossowa in Turkish Serbia, he had been troubled by a vampire. . . . In twenty or
thirty days after his death some people complained that they were
being bothered by this same Arnont Paule; and in fact four people
were killed by him.

These same people say further that all those who were tormented
and killed by the vampires must themselves become vampires. [. . .]
They also add that this Arnont attacked not only the people but also
the cattle, and sucked out their blood. And since the people used the
flesh of such cattle, it appears that some vampires are again present
here, inasmuch as, in a period of three months, seventeen young and
old people died. . . .][13]

This time, the vampire has already created other vampires; in addition to
what we read above, Flückinger presents the results of the sixteen autopsies he performed, which confirm the existence of ten bodies of men,
women, and children "im Vampyrenstande" (in a condition of vampirism).[14] More than anything else, the clinical details register the officer's
confusion — the peasantry's unease as a collective, now transposed into a
detailed, but rambling account of the observer's experience.

The medical terminology used to describe the state of the corpses'
organs stares from the page as an indicator of the strangeness of the phenomenon. For example:

> Nach Eröfnung des Cörpers zeigete sich in Cavitate Pectoris eine
> Quantität frisches extravasirtes Geblüeth; die Vasa als Arteriae
> et Venae nebst denen Ventriculis Cordis waren nicht, wie sonst
> gewöhnlich, mit coagulirten Geblüeth impleiret; die sambtliche
> Viscera als Pulmo, Hepar, Stomachus, Lien et Intestina waren dar-
> bey ganz frisch, bleich bey einen gesunden Menschen; der Uterus
> aber befand sich ganz groß, und externe sehr inflammiret . . . da-
> hero selbiger putredine ware. Die Haut an Händen und Füssen,
> sambt den alten Näglen fiellen von sich selbsten herunter; herent-
> gegen zeigeten sich nebst einer frischen und lebhafften Haut ganz
> neüe Nägl.

> [After the opening of the body there was found in the *cavitas pecto-
> ris* a quantity of fresh extravascular blood. The *vasa* of the *arteriae*
> and *venae,* like the *ventriculi cordis,* were not, as is usual, filled with
> coagulated blood, and the whole *viscera,* that is, the *pulmo, hepar,
> stomachus, lien et intestina* were quite fresh as they would be in a
> healthy person. The *uterus* was however quite enlarged and very
> inflamed externally. . . . wherefore the same was in complete putre-
> faction. The skin on her hands and feet, along with the old nails, fell
> away on their own, but on the other hand completely new nails were
> evident, along with a fresh and vivid skin.][15]

On the one hand, the Latin employed by the officer signifies exactness and precision, attaching a scientific label to each part of the problematic body under examination. Latin is also the language of the Catholic Church — the privileged medium of revelation for the Christian faith. Yet the words that are supposed to clarify matters also mark points of embarrassment, for they underscore how the writer, unable to uncover the deeper principles at work, remains ensnared by mystifying appearances. The profusion of physical detail serves as a kind of screen that diverts attention from whatever is really going on with these bodies — and whatever else is really occurring among the people who have taken these strange signs for wonders. The report, which its first twentieth-century commentator called "barely comprehensible,"[16] is a document of acute personal and cultural alienation.

The imperial officials Frombald and Flückinger could make no sense of what they witnessed. In their reports, they seemingly throw up their hands in despair of ever understanding the "backward" ways of rustics. But whatever Frombald and Flückinger's personal exasperation may have been, their protocols of the Serbians' activities elicited fascination and commentary elsewhere. That is, the "negative" side of the officers' accounts — their incomprehension of the vampire phenomenon — was soon complemented by a more "positive" reaction, when others took up the documents as a challenge to their ability to explain the world in which they lived. A mystery, perhaps, had just been revealed.

Jean-Claude Aguerre has cast eighteenth-century vampirism in the following terms:

> At the moment . . . when, for the first time in the history of Christianity the unquestionable certainty of divinity weakened, when the promise of the resurrection of the flesh as a glorious body on the day of the Final Judgment . . . risked not to occur and corpses, after rotting in the grave . . . risked to experience no afterlife, be it in a Garden of Eden or in infernal flames — at this very moment a cadaver rejected putrefaction, . . . left the tomb, and . . . passed its demonic state on, thereby perpetuating the idea of eternity.[17]

Aguerre's overwrought and melodramatic formulation captures the scandal and shock that the vampire reports provoked, inasmuch as they pointed toward the spiritual disequilibrium of a time when secularization and confessional disputes challenged religious certainties of long standing. Nor could medical training do anything to help matters. Vampirism was a prodigious event, upsetting established categories of knowledge.

Therefore, the officers' mystified reports were no dead letter when they fell into the hands of others. They encrypted confusion and acted as vehicles of unease, if not disease, and they demanded interpretation for this reason. The documents, carrying information for which metropolitans had no theoretical antibodies, infected the learned academic host and produced a feverish rash of speculation, a graphomaniacal outpouring of learned conjecture.[18]

The metaphysical convulsions to which Aguerre draws our attention corresponded to a state of tenuous imperial health. The reports of vampires at the outskirts of Habsburg dominions provided grist for the ready mills of divisive intrigue. Since late-medieval times, the form of Austrian control over its many, ethnically diverse territories had been summed up by the slogan: *Bella gerant alii, tu felix Austria, nube* (Let others wage wars. You, happy Austria, wed). That is, the House of Habsburg supposedly held together its many dependencies by means of marriage alliances instead of more overt kinds of domination. The motto continues: *Nam quae Mars aliis, dat tibi diva Venus* (For what Mars gives to others, is given to you by godly Venus).[19] Orest Subtelny, a noted historian of the Ukraine, casts a sideways glance at the Habsburgs and writes:

> Austria . . . was an imperial organization, not a country. [. . .] Because no nationality represented an absolute majority of the empire, no one culture molded Habsburg imperial society to the extent that Russian culture did in the tsarist empire. [. . . The Habsburg dynasty] lacked the strong, centralized institutions necessary to standardize administration. Therefore, well into the eighteenth century, their empire was a ramshackle, uncoordinated conglomerate, which was frequently in a state of crisis because of internal discord or external pressure.[20]

Serbian vampirism suggested the vulnerability of the House of Habsburg, whose imperial credo claimed (however disingenuously) a soft, feminine approach to rule.

The Thirty Years' War, in the preceding century, had not resolved the fractiousness of Central Europe, where the Habsburgs had their seat of power.[21] As remarked, the stories about vampires provided polemicists in the Protestant principalities of the German-speaking world — especially Prussia — with ample munitions for attacks on competitors for power in the Catholic South. The War of Austrian Succession (1740–48), which began on the pretext that Maria Theresa, as a woman, could not legitimately inherit the Habsburg throne, marked the emergence of Prussia as an international force of note. The theater of fighting rapidly expanded from Silesia to Bohemia and Moravia; seeking to obtain a balance of power favorable to their interests, all the major European states were soon involved. Thus, in both an immediate and a broad historical perspective, the vampire debates reflected past political problems, nascent conflicts, and crises yet to emerge. Besides mirroring inherited dilemmas within the Holy Roman Empire of the German Nation, vampirological disputation anticipated nineteenth-century, Bismarckian *Kulturkampf* (the struggle for political control against the Catholic Church) and the renewal of warfare between Prussia and Austria.

The final collapse of the Habsburg Monarchy would not occur until the twentieth century, when the desire for nationhood among the various peoples nominally united under Austrian rule fractured the realm irrevocably and sparked the First World War — and at the instigation of a Serbian nationalist, no less! However, already in the eighteenth century, the territory was culturally and linguistically divided in a fateful way. Reports of perversely miraculous events at the outskirts of the empire reminded those at the summit of Habsburg power that corrupting forces undermining their authority also lurked inside their own realms. Even if most learned discussions of vampires concluded that the epidemics were the result of overactive peasant imaginations and not to be credited, these instances of mass panic (and, as we will see in further detail in a moment, collective defiance of imperial authority) suggested that the hold of *Felix Austria* on its territories could not possibly be eternal. The foregoing explains why, in many of the texts to be discussed later in this study, vampire fictions display not only the Slavic coloration that is common knowledge, but also a less frequently remarked "German" tinge. Understood loosely — as things often are by writers and filmmakers — vampires belong to territories under the rule of German-speakers. The vampire, like its host, Germany/Austria, will, time and again, represent the other, "uncivilized" side of Europe.[22]

With these eschatological images of political, religious, and ethnic tension in mind, we now turn to what vampire epidemics meant to the inhabitants of actual vampire country, that is, the *hajduks* of Serbia. Paul Barber has argued that the vampire phenomenon represents an early and partially successful attempt to account for biological processes that nineteenth- and twentieth-century medicine finally came to explain more completely. He seeks to use Serbian vampirism to show "how people in pre-industrial cultures look at . . . phenomena associated with death and the dissolution of the body." "As it happens," Barber continues,

> their interpretations . . . , from our perspective, are generally quite wrong. What makes them interesting, however, is that they are also usually coherent, cover all the data, and provide the rationale for some common practices that seem, at first glance, to be inexplicable.[23]

In effect, Barber suggests that the victims of vampirism in Serbia were amateur scientists who theorized death and decay much as any other "primitive" people would.[24] Interesting though this possibility may in fact be, Barber's analytical angle overlooks the most exciting and unsettling aspects of vampirism: the collective determination and single-mindedness of the peasants when faced with what they knew to be supernatural intruders, as well as their bold declarations that they would pursue the proper course of action, no matter how their overlords might object.

Behind the stumbling prose of Frombald and Flückinger, in the conflicted no-man's-land between East and West, a wrathful chorus can be heard. The villagers "unanimously" decide to open the vampire's grave in Frombald's report, and they speak "unanimously" in Flückinger's dispatch, as well. Frombald's informants allege a connection between their present affliction and "Turkish times"; likewise, the villagers whom Flückinger observes associate the vampire with "Turkish Serbia." In both cases, the vampire represents an outside contaminant that has lodged in a member of the social body and now stands to sicken the whole populace. The presence of one vampire portended (in 1725), or supposedly had already caused (in 1732), the arrival of more undead. The perception that universal extinction threatened the communities — Serbian vampires destroyed family, friends, and more distant acquaintances in villages without discrimination — forged solidarity between potential victims, who joined forces to face their destiny together. Thus, when villagers united to do away with one of their own — a party who had become not just someone but *something* else through pollution from outside — they affirmed that they would not allow foreigners to incorporate them, a fate even worse than death.

The delicate position of Serbian *hajduks* between Habsburg and Ottoman powers, combined with a religious mythology of former greatness and a reasonable measure of de facto independence, provide, to borrow Fredric Jameson's terminology, the "political unconscious" of vampire epidemics.[25] Jameson's phrase refers to latent and diffuse social tensions that find expression, in condensed and displaced form, in the symbolic productions of a culture. Like the dreams that Freud proposed to analyze as cryptograms of conflicting desires in the individual, works of art channel the hopes and fears that circulate in the real world into an imaginary one, where they can be examined in a state of suspension. To take Jameson's example, the characters and plots comprising Balzac's *Comédie humaine* are all fiction, but the underlying social situations that the stories explore are absolutely true to life; the hypothetical space of the page provides a laboratory of sorts, where a series of controlled experiments reveals the properties of historical reagents. Serbian vampire executions also admit interpretation as a kind of text: they have a background story (an unlucky individual tainted by a disease of foreign origin), a conflict (which transpires between the vampire and the community it menaces), and a resolution (the action undertaken by the collective to eliminate the threat).

The energies channeled by the Serbian vampire "drama" came from political decisions originating, ultimately, in Istanbul and Vienna — most recently, the Ottoman invasion of Austrian possessions in the seventeenth century.[26] Needless to say, the rustics did not in the least understand the historical forces that shaped their destiny; living at subsistence level and without access to news from the outside world (or the capacity to process it), they only saw their communities in disarray. Since the actors were illiterate and left no records of the reasoning behind their actions, our attempt to explain the vampire executions relies in large part on conjecture. However, the reports of Frombald and Flückinger provide a basis for studied speculation; the essential congruity of accounts by two observers operating independently of one another amounts to something near fact. Additionally, the traditional songs of the *guzlars* (itinerant bards), whose voices ethnographers could still hear and record in the twentieth century, provide further corroborating data inasmuch as they document the long life of the Serbian political mythology that permitted a strong sense of cultural identity to survive centuries of foreign domination.[27]

In the Middle Ages, the Serbs had possessed power and prestige.[28] Their foremost family, the Nemanjas, built an empire. By the death of its greatest scion, Dusan (1307–55), the borders of Serbian lands described a circuit from the Peloponnese to the Danube and down to the Aegean Sea. By 1459, however, the Turks had conquered all Serbian territories. At the end of the seventeenth century, the Austrians successfully fought to claim these lands for themselves. In the shuffle, the Serbs, having lost their empire and popular sovereignty, were demoted from being a fully autonomous people to the lowly station of border guards along the Croatian frontier, serving first Ottoman, then Habsburg, masters. As Tim Judah succinctly puts it, the Serbian *hajduks* "simply switched sides"[29] when the Austrians took over.

> The border came to be organized in such a way that land was owned not by those who farmed it but by the authorities, who granted it to . . . extended family units who in turn were obliged to provide the army with a fixed number of soldiers. This made the average peasant soldier inordinately proud of his status as a free man rather than a serf on a feudal state.[30]

Caught between greater powers to the West and the East, the Serbs were loyal to neither — independent, but without much real control over their lives.

Just as Serbian vampire country was made up of shifting political borders and changing alliances, it also was a site of religious instability. At the time of the vampire epidemics, as is still the case now, the Serbian Orthodox Church existed in a space with Catholicism on one side and Islam on the other. The *Grenzer* (border-people), as the Austrian overlords called the *hajduks*, found themselves threatened from the East and the West by competing empires and different faiths. Long-standing rivalries between Byzantium and Rome, Eastern Orthodoxy and Western Catholicism, which arose following the medieval split of Christendom,[31] further complicated matters. Some Serbs had converted to Islam, which created even more fault lines within the territory and its communities.[32]

In the glorious past, Rastko Nemanja (1175–1235) — better known as Sava (the name he assumed when he took monastic vows) — had obtained autonomy for the Serbian national church from the Byzantine emperor and the Orthodox patriarch, and he canonized his father, Stefan (1132–1200), as the first Serbian saint. Sava's sanctification of his father (which paved the way for the canonization of other Nemanjas, including Sava himself) inscribed the royal family into church liturgy and forged a sense of cultural identity predicated on religion. However, religious independence, like political self-determination, later became a tenuous matter for the border people.

The vampire appeared at the frontier between Islam and Christianity, where the latter was also internally conflicted, in a strategically sensitive region where the regime was prone to sudden and violent change. The Habsburgs subjected the border zone to severe martial law between 1718 and 1739. Nominally, there existed a Kingdom of Serbia for the first time in centuries, yet political control still lay in foreign (that is, Austrian) hands. Rustics' belief that a vampire preyed on them reflected uncertainty about who they were, both as individuals and as a collective. The creature attacked victims with impartiality and threatened to make them a soulless shadow of life, like itself. Thus, the vampire can be read as a symptom of doubts about cultural identity produced by the conflict of different political and religious interests and systems — a transfigured expression of profound fears concerning the reality of appearances, the order of the temporal world, and the arrangement of the heavens. Rustics whose destinies were controlled by political machinations invisible to them hallucinated a demonic agent responsible for their terror. The horrifying prodigy was a baneful impostor: the likeness of a known person, yet one devoid of humanity and bent on destruction. Vampire epidemics expressed the *hajduks'* fear that they would all vanish, devoured by the evil forces that emerged in their midst when the world fell out of joint.

By executing vampires, *hajduks* sought to steer the life of the collective, which tottered on the brink of collapse, back onto the stable ground of tradition. "It is impossible," Judah writes, "to overestimate the historical role of the church in keeping alive the idea of Serbia and its notion that one day the old state would, Christ-like, be resurrected."[33] If vampire executions did not revive the Nemanja dynasty, they solidified the group identity of participants. A kind of religious ceremony that exorcised tensions afflicting the collective, the destruction of vampires affirmed subjective unity against objective disarray. The dynamics of mass hysteria were at play in villagers' allegations that corpses were killing them; this does not preclude, however, that communities experienced acute disorder in a way that was wholly real.[34] There is also no reason to question the imperial officers' statements that calm returned to the upset villages after the vampires had been eliminated. The executions reestablished the balance of life by enabling the villagers to dispel the specter of extinction and to demonstrate to themselves that the collective bonds that had united them in the past still held strong.

Such are the dynamics of vampire executions within Serbian communities.[35] In addition to the inward-directed function of group consolidation, these acts of collective violence had another, outward-directed side. The *hajduks'* destruction of the vampire was also a blow aimed at Austrian authority figures. The amazement that Frombald and Flückinger record stemmed in large part from the insubordination of the peasants. The former states in his account that "the people grew more outraged than distressed" when he attempted to intervene: the officer feared that the villagers might turn their rage on *him* if he did not permit them to destroy the vampire. For the duration of the vampire extermination ritual, relations of power between *hajduks* and imperial officers were reversed: rustics brushed aside the representatives of the Habsburgs and professed an understanding of events to which Frombald and Flückinger, however reluctantly, deferred.

In anthropological perspective, Serbian vampirism may be viewed in terms of René Girard's theory of violence and the sacred. Human beings, Girard observes matter-of-factly, owe their individual traits to acts of "acquisitive mimesis,"[36] that is, copying what others around them do. At the same time, they are always subject to equally important prohibitions, which vary from person to person according to parentage, order of birth, gender, and the like.[37] These restrictions are especially pronounced in homogeneous communities with a strong sense of tradition, where they demarcate spheres of activity, ranks within hierarchies, and social roles. As conservative wisdom would have it, a society risks falling into disarray whenever people do not "know their place": the result is excessive competition for material objects and symbolic positions, and such rivalry can all too easily lead to physical conflicts.[38] Violence arises when the possible outcome of events is not adjudicated in advance by common laws and/or conventions of behavior implicitly accepted by all parties, determining licit and illicit forms of desire. To prevent the eruption of violence, it is necessary to make sure that conflicts are unlikely to emerge in the first place. Religion exists to channel and regulate "man's inhumanity to man," which, while perhaps inevitable, can certainly be controlled.

"Violence," Girard observes, "is a great leveler," for it abolishes the differences and deferential attitudes that prevail in situations of calm. When animated by hatred and aggression, "everybody becomes the double, or 'twin,' of his antagonist,"[39] and particularizing qualities disappear. Violence strips those caught up in it of the ability to see the enemy's humanity — which implies their own loss of the same.

In villagers' minds, the vampire was an uncanny[40] double: a member of the community whose non-identity threatened and undid their sense of who they were. Putative vampires served as scapegoats for communities suffering from what Girard calls a "mimetic crisis."[41] Endemic uncertainty about the material conditions of existence in the poor societies of rural Serbia produced a fractious environment. People looked upon their neighbors in suspicion and sought to account, in some way, for their generally unhappy lot. The vampire represented an agent — however imaginary — within the community, upon whose responsibility all might agree. In a drastic formulation with a bearing on the present context, Girard writes:

> any community that . . . has been stricken by . . . catastrophe hurls itself . . . into the search for a scapegoat. Its members instinctively seek an immediate and violent cure . . . and strive desperately to convince themselves that all their ills are the fault of a lone individual who can be easily disposed of. Such circumstances bring to mind the forms of violence that break out spontaneously in countries convulsed by crisis: lynchings, pogroms, etc.[42]

Forsaking sideways glances at each other, the rustics focused their ambient discontent and personal aggression upon an enemy recognized by everyone in the village as a fitting target for righteous violence.

The ritualized extermination of the vampire, an embodiment of social chaos and contagion, offered the salutary illusion that there was a cause of problems within the community that might be eliminated to the benefit of all — a view preferable to admitting that everyone was powerless. The destruction of a common, domestic enemy who had been contaminated by foreign influence promised a return to normal. Now, villagers might resume the ways of life that had been interrupted, reassured that the proper order once again governed their lives.

To resume psychoanalytic parlance, vampire epidemics were overdetermined occurrences. On the one hand, they were fueled by pervasive anxieties about cultural continuity and, indeed, survival itself; although these fears found expression in forms that were utterly fanciful, their political substrate was entirely factual. On the other hand, by localizing the troubles that afflicted them in a body within their own community, and hence subjecting them to control, villagers achieved a measure of symbolic mastery over their situation and moreover managed, momentarily, to overturn their condition of subjection. The vampire mediated between "here" and "beyond," the temporal and the eternal, the familiar and the strange. Closing down the portal incarnated by the vampire reestablished the balance between realms. Serbian villagers' actions manifested superstition and panic. However, they also provided a form of collective catharsis and allowed a fractured society to maintain its integrity in the face of threats from without.

Because the topic has a bearing on the subsequent development of the vampire myth (as we will see in later chapters), and for methodological reasons that allow us to understand eighteenth-century vampirism more fully, it is worth mentioning a different, but analogous matter: associations between Jews, sacrificial murder, and magic in medieval and early-modern Europe. The first documented case of "blood libel," or the claim that Jews had slaughtered a Christian for ritual purposes, occurred in 1148 in Norwich, England. Numerous, similar charges were repeated throughout Europe for hundreds of years. They reached a height in the fifteenth and sixteenth centuries in the territories of the Holy Roman Empire. R. Pochia Hsia has observed that a key factor in this concentration of accusations in German-speaking territories at this time was the earlier expulsion of Jews from England and France.[43] Terribly, blood libel in "Germany" resulted when official policies of toleration were challenged by popular beliefs under conditions of social stress.

According to Hsia, two roughly contemporaneous, if independent, developments in Christian and Jewish cultures of the Middle Ages set the stage for allegations of ritual murder. On the one hand, the doctrine of transubstantiation, which decreed that the bread and wine offered to worshippers actually became the body of Christ, opened the way for practices of magic that declared blood a mystical substance.[44] "One of the most popular uses of the Eucharist," Hsia observes, "was in love magic"; conversely, "put to evil use in black magic, the Host could cause the destruction of life."[45] The Eucharist cemented long-standing associations between blood and the supernatural. On the other hand, Jews, who had already "acquired a firm magical reputation" in the ancient world, strengthened this image through mystical beliefs and practices in the Middle Ages.[46] In particular, Jews and Christians alike ascribed occult powers to Hebrew amulets, whose presumed efficacy rested on the view that the world teemed with demons, portentous dreams, diseases of supernatural origin, and similar phenomena.

In times of unrest and disaster, Christians faced with inexplicable events turned against the same parties from whom they otherwise sought magical protection. Hsia argues that charges of blood libel and the resultant trials "often revealed major political conflicts within the empire,"[47] especially in the tumultuous period of the Reformation: Jews were blamed for misfortunes that arose not only from natural causes (e.g., epidemic illnesses), but also from religious strife among Christians themselves, whose political course often depended on "invisible" decisions at faraway seats of power. Thus, the phenomenon of ritual murder accusations represents a simplified, popular response to the complexities of historical events.[48] Though they have no basis in actual fact — Jews have never killed Christian babies to use for magical purposes — blood libel accusations and trials reveal a cultural logic that makes a horrible kind of sense. Those who brought the charges against Jews, as well as the juridical instances that evaluated them, were concerned with finding an answer to unsolved mysteries by locating culprits within the community in crisis.[49]

At this point, the association between vampires and Jews remains theoretical and is meant primarily to illustrate crowd mentality and the dynamics of persecution in distressed communities. Vampires are infiltrators. Because Jewish and Gentile societies remain largely segregated until the nineteenth century, vampires must wait until later to assume Jewish traits. Emancipation, which did away with restrictions on the movement and activities of Jews, while opening a world of possible gains, also had the unfortunate effect of creating new conditions of rivalry and ethnic/religious enmity. The latter half of this study (chapters 4, 5, and 6) will explore the situation in detail.

To sum up, then, the emergence of vampires into historical record depended on a very particular political situation. Serbian peasant-soldiers who had had to obey both Austrian and Turkish masters in the space of a few generations reacted to the shocks of their abruptly reorganized political "allegiance" first by panicking, when they envisioned the mass extinction of their communities through a monstrous invader, and then, in a second step, by besting the intruder before the eyes of those who governed their destiny.

The hysterical process repeated itself in a different matrix with the dissemination of vampire news in German-speaking territories. Here, academics and metropolitans remained agnostic about the existence of the undead, yet an astonishing number of them participated in discussions on the subject. The rapid proliferation of writings on vampires resembled the frenzied rumors that circulated among peasants in the hinterlands. The anxieties in cities and at universities were substantially different from those of Serbian villagers, but they too stemmed from an endangered sense of cultural identity. The Habsburg Monarchy had sought to strengthen its grip by means of a campaign against popular superstition; however, the measures introduced by the Counter-Reformation, like all remedies for unrest, pointed toward faltering power. The weakness of the political order in the Austrian Empire corresponded to a debilitated state of spiritual and ecclesiastical authority. In the Protestant North, vampiromania also fed off the insecurities bred by a changing world; here, vampire debates deepened, rather than bridged, confessional differences in the sprawling and internally conflicted Holy Roman Empire of the German Nation. The vampire was terrible not because it meant the resurgence of the primitive, but because it was the harbinger of things to come.

Subsequent chapters will explore how, as the legend of the vampire spread over the world from its Central European point of origin, the monster assumed many new forms. However, later works featuring the vampire still feature a combination of elements that occurred in the first phase of its history, which this chapter has chronicled and analyzed. The vampire displays a parasitic nature that thrives on the unhealthy constitution of its host and threatens to assimilate victims to a state in which outward characteristics of vitality are preserved, but the inner flame of the soul is extinguished. Vampirism, which denatures from the inside out, reverses standing definitions of identity and difference. This subversive quality, which expresses itself in the vampire's impossible condition of "living death" (a state mirroring the "death in life" that victims experience), is — again to borrow psychoanalytic terminology — a condensed and displaced projection onto an imaginary agent of real forces whose true nature is unknown to the parties who believe themselves to be under vampiric attack. A vague intuition of the politico-sociological underpinnings of vampirism is apparent in the fact that victims readily switch from talking about one vampire to complaining about multiple vampires: one agent of unwelcome change is as good — or, more appropriately, bad — as the next. Finally, vampirism presents itself in the context of unsettled and destabilized Christianity, parodying and perverting the religious idea of resurrection.

* * *

In closing this chapter — and as a kind of overture to those that follow — it is worth remarking how, whether by accident or design, subsequent articulations of the vampire myth bear traces of the creature's first appearance on the stage of history.

The foreign accent of Bela Lugosi, the Hungarian actor who brought Bram Stoker's Dracula to life in Tod Browning's 1931 film of the same name, unsettles moviegoers in the same way that his direct stare into the camera (which reverses the subject-object relationship between watcher and watched) unnerves them. Lugosi was born in the Banat, a region now divided between Romania, Hungary, and Serbia; he left his native land for Germany in 1919 and emigrated to the United States two years later.[50] Though this biographical trivia seems just that — trivia — the details of Lugosi's birth and subsequent career hint at more than mere chance.

If Lugosi's name has become virtually synonymous with the otherworldly villain Dracula, this conflation has occurred because Lugosi's onscreen performance and the attributes of his off-screen person combined to forge a fateful identity in the shadowy realm of Hollywood image making.[51] The "Easternness" that Lugosi conveys in his performance is disturbing because it makes the familiar strange without rendering it wholly unfamiliar. For this reason, the actor's screen presence has long been considered an exemplary embodiment of the vampire's uncanny nature. The vampire *is* this foreign appearance and accent — something that not only occurs at the borderlands but also always transgresses them.

The pattern of confusion between East and West recurs again and again in vampire fictions. To take the most obvious point of reference, Bram Stoker's novel *Dracula* (1897) makes the eponymous monster at home in a "district . . . just on the borders of three states," in "one of the wildest and least known portions of Europe."[52] The novel situates vampire country in territories that belong to Austria, and hence to Europe; equally, however, these lands mark the outer limits of Europe, where civilization bleeds gradually into the unfamiliar. On his train journey to Castle Dracula from Budapest, Jonathan Harker (the character whose diary entries comprise the first chapter of Stoker's novel) observes: "The impression I had was that we were leaving the West and entering the East; the most western of splendid bridges over the Danube, which is here of noble width and depth, took us among the traditions of Turkish rule."[53] The same type of landscape appears in numerous other works by writers of the period, who connected the vampire theme with exoticized representations of foreign terrain.[54]

Vampires, until well into the twentieth century, for the most part came from Central Europe, where the borders of Europe and the "Orient" become confused. Sheridan Le Fanu set his vampire story, "Carmilla" (1872), in Styria. The tale concerns an adolescent girl who unwittingly entertains a vampire from parts unknown, just over the border, in "Hungary" — a territory far greater and more vaguely defined than the modern state with this name. Vampire country in Friedrich Wilhelm Murnau's *Nosferatu* (1922) is likewise, as intertitles inform viewers, a "land of ghosts and shadows" in the eastern sector of Central Europe; here, on his native soil, the vampire who will bring the plague to the West wears a Turkish-looking turban and possesses features that connote an alien bloodline.

Christoph Martin Wieland's *Schach Lolo oder das göttliche Recht der Gewalthaber* (1778), Robert Southey's *Thalaba the Destroyer* (1801), and Jan Potocki's *Manuscript Found in Saragossa* (circa 1805–15)[55] freely extend the territory of vampirism to a loosely conceived Arab world, which still, however, is too close for comfort. And in Byron's *Giaour* (subtitled "A Fragment of a Turkish Tale," 1813), a dying Muslim imprecates his killer:

> But first, on earth as vampire sent,
> Thy corse shall from its tomb be rent:
> Then ghastly haunt thy native place,
> And suck the blood of all thy race.[56]

Western authors and filmmakers have repeatedly portrayed the vampire as something that comes from the East. To the extent that vampire stories are set in "Austrian," "German," or "Hungarian" territories, which adjoin and include lands historically in Ottoman possession, their subjects receive a Turkish coloration. The monster represents a threat at the frontiers of the civilized world that intrudes upon European homelands.

Artistic fantasy, whatever detours it takes in its flights, correlates with historical fact when it places the vampire in a geographical and cultural space between Europe and Asia Minor. The territories of the Habsburg Monarchy provide the generative matrix of the vampire myth, and the monster represents real and imaginary confusion as to what belongs to "us," and what to "them." Though at pains to mark the foreignness of the vampire, authors implicitly acknowledge the monster's uncanny familiarity when they set their stories in Balkan territories.

One more example will suffice. The French novelist Paul Féval's *La ville-vampire* (1874) appeared almost exactly midway between the eighteenth-century Austrian vampire bulletins and our own day. Féval's work, to employ the language of structural anthropology, reveals a concentration of "mythemes" that are repeated time and again in vampire stories. "Chaque vampire est un groupe" (Each vampire is a collective),[57] Féval writes. "[C'est] la langue serbe, dont les vampires font généralement usage entre eux" (It is the Serbian language that vampires generally use between themselves);[58] a "fact" affirms the monsters' ties to Central Europe. Indeed, the "vampire city" that gives the novel its title is located in a mysterious place known only to "les gens qui habitent la sauvage campagne de Belgrade" (the people who inhabit the barbarous lands around Belgrade).[59] Féval also connects the vampire and German erudition in the person of one Dr. Goetzi — PhD Tübingen and undead monster.

Read allegorically, "Serbia" and "German erudition" form two functions rather than two fixed reference points. In the chapters to follow, Poland or another "backward" country (e.g., Ireland, the provincial, Catholic country nearest to metropolitan England) will take the place of Serbia; alternately, vampirism will be defined along "vertical" class lines rather than "horizontal" national ones. "German erudition" will occasionally be replaced by "French rationalism" or "Dutch science"; sometimes religion will offer answers to the problem of the undead, sometimes it will represent the cause of the affliction. The word "vampire," as Gilles Deleuze and Félix Guattari have observed, does not designate a state of being so much as one of becoming.[60] The social and epistemological structuring of vampirism, however one "fills in the blanks," will not display much variation. The next chapter, which explores the vampire's entry into explicitly political and literary discourse, discusses the monster's aptness for embodying differently inflected — but wholly analogous — perceptions of crisis in a variety of new cultural contexts.

Notes

[1] Klaus Hamberger, *Mortuus non mordet: Kommentierte Dokumentation zum Vampirismus 1689–1791* (Vienna: Turia & Kant, 1992), 8. This volume collects and commentates archival material pertaining to vampires in their "native" context.

[2] E.g., Peter Mario Kreuter, "The Name of the Vampire: Some Reflections on Current Linguistic Theories on the Etymology of the Word *Vampire*," *Vampires: Myths and Metaphors of Enduring Evil*, ed. Peter Day (Amsterdam: Rodopi, 2006), 57–63.

[3] Antoine Faivre, in "Du vampire villageois aux discours des clercs" (in *Les vampires* [Paris: Albin Michel, 1993], 46–53), charts the travel of the vampire reports in the eighteenth-century press.

[4] Milan V. Dimic, "Vampiromania in the Eighteenth Century: The Other Side of Enlightenment," in *Man and Nature/L'Homme et la Nature: Proceedings of the Canadian Society for Eighteenth-Century Studies* 3, ed. R. J. Merrett (Edmonton: The Society, 1984), 1–22; here 3.

[5] R. J. W. Evans, *The Making of the Habsburg Monarchy, 1550–1700: An Interpretation* (Oxford: Oxford UP, 1984); hereafter cited parenthetically in the text.

[6] For a survey and discussion of an "apocalyptic age," see Andrew Cunningham and Ole Peter Grell, *The Four Horsemen of the Apocalypse: Religion, War, Famine, and Death in Reformation Europe* (Cambridge: Cambridge UP, 2001).

[7] Caroline Walker Bynum, in *The Resurrection of the Body in Western Christianity, 200–1336* (New York: Columbia UP, 1995), offers a thorough account of lay ideas and theology concerning the soul and the body, death and resurrection, until the High Middle Ages. These beliefs and teachings provided a reserve of arguments for justifying decisions in the period under discussion.

[8] Hamberger, 112.

[9] Faivre, 53–60, enumerates and discusses the various discourses engendered by the vampire scandal. Alexandre Koyré's study of early-modern German mysticism illuminates the Paracelsian line of reasoning: "The physical body dissolves in the tomb, but . . . it takes some time before its elements return to chaos; similarly, the spirit animating the body subsists for a certain time after death, and it is entirely natural that this spirit, which is, in a sense, the motor . . . of the body, continue to 'operate' for a while (by inertia or habit, so to speak), and that, as a result, it haunt the places it inhabited while alive and perform the likeness of gestures that it performed in life. . . ." (Alexandre Koyré, *Mystiques, spirituels, alchimistes du XVIe siècle allemand* [Paris: Armand Colin, 1955], 56).

[10] Stefan Hock, *Die Vampyrsagen und ihre Verwertung in der deutschen Literatur* (Berlin: Alexander Duncker, 1900), 44–48.

[11] Hamberger, 43–45.

[12] Translation in Paul Barber, *Vampires, Burial, and Death* (New Haven: Yale UP, 1988), 5–7.

[13] Hamberger, 49–50; Barber, 16.

[14] Hamberger, 52; Barber, 17.

[15] Hamberger, 51; Barber, 17.

[16] Hock, 38.

[17] Jean-Claude Aguerre, "Résistance de la chair, destitution de l'âme," *Les vampires* (Paris: Albin Michel, 1993), 87. Cf. Dieter Sturm and Klaus Volker, *Von denen Vampiren* (Frankfurt am Main: 1994), 544.

[18] See chapters 4 and 5, as well as the section of chapter 6 devoted to Fritz Lang's *Das Testament des Dr. Mabuse*, where the connection between vampires, writing, and medicine reemerges.

[19] On the slogan and the Habsburg rise at the turn of the sixteenth century, see Norman Davies, *Europe: A History* (Oxford: Oxford UP, 1996), 524–25; and Joachim Leuschner, *Deutschland im späten Mittelalter* (Göttingen: Vandenhoeck & Ruprecht, 2000), 209–15.

[20] Orest Subtelny, *Ukraine: A History* (Toronto: U of Toronto P, 1994), 212.

[21] Charles W. Ingrao, in *The Habsburg Monarchy, 1618–1815* (Cambridge: Cambridge UP, 2002), 23–177, presents an overview of the Thirty Years' War, its legacy, and the subsequent of orientation of Habsburg political concerns (toward Turkey from 1648 to 1699, and toward Prussia from 1700 to 1740).

[22] Wolf Lepenies, in *The Seduction of Culture in German History* (Princeton: Princeton UP, 2006), assesses the "culture-civilization" split between Germany and France that Norbert Elias, in a classic study published in 1939, first made an object of critical inquiry; Elias's book has been translated as *The Civilizing Process: Sociogenetic and Psychogenetic Investigations*, trans. Edmund Jephcott (Oxford: Blackwell, 2000).

[23] Barber, 1.

[24] Abnormalities of decomposition in the region, decades before the word "vampire" was recorded, had in fact been items of interest since the seventeenth century (Hock, 43); however, the overall social significance of debates was not great.

[25] Fredric Jameson, *The Political Unconscious: Narrative as a Socially Symbolic Act* (Ithaca: Cornell UP, 1982).

[26] A thorough account of culminating events is found in John Stoye, *The Siege of Vienna: The Last Great Trial between Cross and Crescent* (London: Collins, 1964).

[27] See the documents transcribed from the original (with accompanying translation into German) collected in Friedrich S. Krauss, *Slavische Volkforschungen: Abhandlungen über Glauben, Gewohnheitrechte, Sitten, Bräuche und die Guslarenlieder der Südslaven* (Leipzig: Wilhelm Heims, 1908), 177–403.

[28] Sima M. Cirkovic, *The Serbs* (Oxford: Wiley-Blackwell, 2004).

[29] Tim Judah, *The Serbs: History, Myth, and the Destruction of Yugoslavia* (New Haven: Yale UP, 1997), 14.

[30] Judah, 15; see also Cirkovic, 146–61.

[31] Mikhail Emmanuelovich Posnov, *The History of the Christian Church until the Great Schism of 1054*, trans. Thomas Herman (Bloomington: AuthorHouse, 2004), 450–88.

[32] Sima Cirkovic notes that under Turkish rule "urban communities were the center of islamization" (125); in this respect, vampire epidemics represent a conflict between city and country populations.

[33] Judah, 46.

[34] "Hysteria" is a loaded term, not least because it derives from the Greek word for "womb." While long understood as a "female malady," hysteria has in recent

decades been subject to intense critical scrutiny by scholars who have pointed out the economic and sociological basis of conditions that have received this diagnosis. Helen King has pointedly asked whether hysteria is not, in fact, "a name without a disease" ("Once upon a Text: Hysteria from Hippocrates," in *Hysteria beyond Freud*, Sander L. Gilman et al. [Berkeley: U of California P, 1993], 3) — that is, a label for phenomena that fundamentally escape the province of medicine. Elaine Showalter, *Hystories: Hysterical Epidemics and Modern Media* (New York: Columbia UP, 1998), explores the continued timeliness of this problematic designation in late-twentieth-century America. Cf. Juliet Mitchell, *Mad Men and Medusas: Reclaiming Hysteria* (New York: Basic Books, 2001) for a carefully argued case for retaining the terminology.

[35] The underlying mentality and ideas proved enduring. Discussing nineteenth-century vampirism, John V. A. Fine Jr. concludes: "Vampire beliefs were widespread in Serbia. . . . They were not limited to the ignorant peasantry but were also widespread among the clergy. Among Serbs the main issue was not whether or not there were vampires . . . but how was one to deal with them; should one use traditional village methods [i.e., the means of eighteenth-century forebears, recorded by Frombald and Flückinger] or should one take a more spiritual approach and call on the clergy to eliminate them through prayers?" "In Defense of Vampires," in *The Vampire: A Casebook*, ed. Alan Dundes (Madison: U of Wisconsin P, 1998), 65.

[36] René Girard, *Things Hidden since the Foundation of the World*, trans. Stephen Benn and Michael Metteer (Stanford: Stanford UP, 1987), 7–10, 26–27.

[37] René Girard, *Violence and the Sacred*, trans. Patrick Gregory (Baltimore: Johns Hopkins UP, 1979), 147.

[38] Girard, *Things*, 183–98.

[39] Girard, *Violence*, 79.

[40] See introduction.

[41] Girard, *Things*, 19–30.

[42] Girard, *Violence*, 79–80.

[43] R. Po-chia Hsia, *The Myth of Ritual Murder: Jews and Magic in Reformation Germany* (New Haven: Yale UP, 1988), 3.

[44] David Biale, "God's Blood: Medieval Jews and Christians Debate the Body," in *Blood and Belief: The Circulation of a Symbol between Jews and Christians* (Berkeley: U of California P, 2007), 81–122. The excellent study by Caroline Walker Bynum, *Wonderful Blood: Theology and Practice in Late Medieval Northern Germany and Beyond* (Philadelphia: U of Pennsylvania P, 2007), focuses on the Christian perspective.

[45] Hsia, 10.

[46] Hsia, 5.

[47] Hsia, 12.

[48] The fourteenth century, Hsia notes, had relatively few blood accusations because of "the massive pogroms associated with the Black Death of midcentury, during which entire Jewish communities . . . were destroyed" (3).

[49] Discussing a case that occurred in 1900, Helmut Walser Smith, in *The Butcher's Tale: Murder and Anti-Semitism in a German Town* (New York: W. W. Norton, 2003), documents the persistence of the belief into modern times.

[50] Arthur Lennig, *The Immortal Count: The Life and Films of Bela Lugosi* (Lexington: UP of Kentucky, 2003); for a discussion of Lugosi's native soil and historical episodes of vampirism, see Hamberger, 20–21, 87–88.

[51] See Nina Auerbach, *Our Vampires, Ourselves* (Chicago: U of Chicago P, 1995), 112–13.

[52] Bram Stoker, *Dracula*, ed. Glennis Byron (Ontario: Broadview, 1998), 32.

[53] Stoker, 31.

[54] The foundational and most influential work on the topic is Edward Said, *Orientalism* (New York: Vintage, 1979). See also his subsequent study, *Culture and Imperialism* (New York: Vintage, 1994). Although Said offers many insights on Europeans' construction of an "Oriental other," his work has been critiqued for preserving a dichotomous perspective; cf., for example, David Cannadine, *Ornamentalism: How the British Saw Their Empire* (Oxford: Oxford UP, 2002).

[55] The uncertainties surrounding the composition of the work are discussed in Jan Potocki, *Manuscript Found in Saragossa*, trans. Ian Maclean (London: Penguin, 1995), xii-xiv.

[56] Byron, *Poetical Works*, ed. Frederick Page (Oxford: Oxford UP, 1970), 259 (ll. 755–58).

[57] Paul Féval, *Le chevalier Ténèbre, suivi de La ville-vampire* (Verviers: Marabout, 1972), 158; *Vampire City*, trans. Brian Stableford (Encino: Black Coat Press, 2003), 66.

[58] Féval, 168/76.

[59] Féval, 200/120.

[60] Gilles Deleuze and Félix Guattari, *A Thousand Plateaus*, trans. Brian Massumi (London: Continuum, 2004), 261, 266–68.

2: Vampires and Satire in the Enlightenment and Romanticism

IN CHAPTER 1, WE SAW HOW, in the earliest stages of the vampire's history — that is, first among Balkan *hajduks* and then for German and Austrian academicians — the name of this monster marked sites of troubled cultural continuity. Enlightenment sensibilities quickly dispelled the earnest speculation of early academic vampirologists. After the rash of vampire treatises in the 1730s and early 1740s, the monster ceased to provide an object of serious contemplation. In Vienna, at midcentury, the royal adviser Gerard van Swieten, a Dutchman exemplifying the sober mindset of his native country, prevailed upon Maria Theresa to regard the outbreaks of undead activity with the same levelheadedness with which she viewed the persecution of supposed witches. In 1755, the Empress issued two decrees forbidding witch hunting, the "execution" of vampires, magic, fortune telling, and digging for treasure.[1]

We now turn to the social tensions that the vampire incarnated elsewhere, when the featureless, yet striking invader came to represent injustice, greed, and corruption in political and monetary economies. France faced its own problems (to be discussed in a moment), but the troubles of Versailles were not those of Vienna. France did not produce much in the way of vampire commentary, except for the dismissive remarks of Jean-Baptiste de Boyer, Marquis d'Argens, who ascribed vampire beliefs to overactive imaginations in the 137th installment of the Montesquieu-inspired *Lettres juives* (1737), and Dom Augustin Calmet (whom we have already encountered), who described vampirism and witchcraft as equally ridiculous forms of "illusion, superstition, and prejudice."[2] Likewise, in Italy, the response was muted. Giuseppe Davanzati, in his *Dissertazione sopra i vampiri* (1744), maintained that "l'apparizione de' Vampiri non [è] altro che puro effetto di Fantasia" (the appearance of vampires is nothing other than purely an effect of fantasy).[3] His views were shared by his countryman Lodovico Antonio Muratori.[4]

Across the Channel, away from Continental hubbub, the phlegmatic English had reacted with lofty scorn from day one. As soon as the news from Serbia was reported, the London journal *The Craftsman* printed a satirical dialogue on the subject. Composed as the account of a dispute between "a grave *Doctor of Physick* and a beautiful young *Lady*," "Poli-tickal Vampyres" granted that both parties were right.

> I must agree with the learned Doctor, that an inanimate Corpse can-not perform any vital Functions; yet, agree with the Lady that there are Vampyres. This account, you'll observe, comes from the Eastern Part of the World, always remarkable for the *Allegorical Style.* The States of *Hungary* are in *Subjection* to the *Turks* and *Germans,* and govern'd by a pretty hard Hand; which obliges them to couch all their Complaints under *Figures.* [. . .]
> These *Vampyres* are said to torment and kill the Living by sucking out all their Blood; and a *ravenous Minister,* in this part of the World, is compared to a *Leech* or a *Blood-sucker,* and carries his Oppressions beyond the Grave, by anticipating the *publick Revenues,* and entail-ing a perpetuity of *Taxes,* which must gradually drain the Body Poli-tick of its Blood and Spirits.[5]

The article cleverly remarks that vampires are not such a big deal at all: according to the anonymous author, the creatures represent a disempow-ered people's protest against rulers; the life-stealing power that vampires manifest in "Hungary" is identical to the parasitic governance of the Whigs in England, as well as the activities of "Private Persons" such as "Sharpers, Usurers, and Stockjobbers, fraudulent Guardians, unjust Stew-ards, and the dry Nurses of great Estates."[6]

This pronouncement of journalistic *sprezzatura* raised the vam-pire to a second life as a figure of political satire. Aribert Schroeder, who has compiled early references to the undead, observes: "The arti-cle . . . founded a literary tradition that consisted of using the vampire motif to perform criticism of all sorts, especially concerning political and social affairs."[7] A text by Charles Forman published in 1733, the year after the *Craftsman* piece, also used "vampire" as a metaphor to attack Robert Walpole for his plan to raise taxes. Oliver Goldsmith's Orien-talist satire, *The Citizen of the World* (1762), featured parasitic military courtiers named "Colonel Leech" and "Major Vampire." Robert Burns, in a poem to his patron Sir Graham of Fintry (1791, published 1793), lamented the travails of poor writers at the mercy of profiteers when he complained of "Vampyre booksellers."[8] Thomas Moore, in *Corruption and Intolerance* (subtitled "Poems . . . addressed to an Englishman by an Irishman," 1808), indicted:

> That greedy vampire, which from Freedom's tomb
> Comes forth with all the mimicry of bloom
> Upon its lifeless cheek, and sucks and drains
> A people's blood to feed its putrid veins![9]

France, too, knew the vampire above all in satirical form. Louis Sebastien Mercier's *Songes d'un hermite* (1770) mocks social parasites as "vampires."[10] Voltaire, in his *Questions sur l'Encyclopédie* (1772; later appended to the *Dictionnaire philosophique*), reports having witnessed, in London and Paris, "des agioteurs, des traitants, des gens d'affaires, qui sucèrent en plein jour le sang du people" (speculators, tax officials, and businessmen who sucked the blood of the people in broad daylight).[11] As opposed to the creatures of provincial backwaters, Voltaire writes, "ces suceurs véritables ne [demeurent] pas dans des cimetières, mais dans des palais fort agréables (these true bloodsuckers [do] not live in cemeteries, but prefer beautiful palaces).[12] And when, at the beginning of *The 120 Days of Sodom* (written in 1784; unpublished until 1904), the Marquis de Sade fulminates against the very *sangsues* (leeches) whose cruelty he then celebrates over hundreds of pages, he presents his interminable narrative as a kind of vampire story; *sangsue* is the word Calmet had used to translate "vampire" into French.[13] In Sade's *Juliette* (a work most likely antedated to 1797), the atheistic nun who initiates the protagonist into the "prosperities of vice" mocks those of Christian faith for believing in "l'existence du *vampire* qui fait leur félicité" (the existence of the vampire that is the author of their felicity)[14] — in other words, God. The great Swedish naturalist Linnaeus and his contemporary, the Comte de Buffon, paid tribute to the monster's celebrity by naming different bloodsucking bats in Asia and South America *vampyri* — an association destined for great fortune in visual culture.[15]

Klaus Hamberger has observed that the vampires of the late eighteenth and early nineteenth centuries, for all their many appearances in literature, are "poor in images."[16] Compared to the flashy vampires in aristocratic guise that emerged later, after John Polidori's Lord Ruthven (to be discussed in the next chapter), Hamberger's statement is certainly accurate. However, the undead monster's lack of a distinct profile in the period between serious-minded vampirology and Romanticism made the vampire a uniquely dynamic allegory for the depersonalizing aspects of modernization; in this light, its imagistic poverty possesses a paradoxical richness. Whether stock-jobber, military officer, Whig politician, or publisher, the monster presented a caricature of life in an age of unprecedented social mobility. The vampire's facelessness correlated with the unclear pedigree of newly ascendant parties in political and economic affairs.

Beginning with *The Craftsman,* writers invoked the vampire to indict abuses of power on the part of governments and private parties, both in the context of domestic business and the arena of international relations. Thus, in the age of the French and Industrial Revolutions, the vampire retained the unsettling core energy it possessed both in Serbian instances of collective panic and the German and Austrian academic debates they triggered in the 1730s and 1740s.

The vampirism of "men without qualities" (to adapt a phrase from Austrian novelist Robert Musil) will quite likely continue to provide the stuff of artistic creation for so long as profit-hungry governments and parasitic privateers upset traditional ways of life. The poverty Hamberger attributes to the vampire — its lack of an authentic substance and violation of "proper," "just," and "natural" orders — has in fact insured the monster's long life. Thus, in cartoons from the nineteenth and twentieth centuries, one encounters vampires that caricature virtually every great power and established interest, as dictated by the political allegiances of artist and publisher.[17] Vampires constantly renew their lease on life and escape exposure and justice because they cannot definitively be located and arraigned for their crimes. Although the names attached to vampirism change from one context to another, the sinister darkness remains. Indeed, the vampire, inasmuch as it is a faceless, featureless, and anonymous usurper, is a shadow without a body — a force without a genuine being of its own.

The image of the shadow warrants a brief excursus. As a signature of visibility, the shadow confirms the reality of objects and the life of the subjects who exist among them. Victor Stoichita has studied the symbolism of the shadow in the European arts, where it serves the purpose of signifying immaterial, spiritual reality. He draws attention to the physiognomic theory of the Swiss poet and pastor Johann Kaspar Lavater (1741–1801), which exercised considerable influence on late-eighteenth- and early-nineteenth-century literature. Lavater claimed that physical features, properly interpreted, could reveal otherwise invisible aspects of personality and character. He developed his ideas through the study of silhouettes. Like the subsequent pseudoscience of phrenology, physiognomy posited the outward visibility of inner essence; instead of bumps on the head, however, it examined the composition of the face. For Lavater, the silhouette — a shadow given "concrete" form — revealed a person's true nature inasmuch as it put into relief a hidden side of the body, which he understood as an image of the party's soul.[18]

Just as astrology seeks the secrets of an individual's destiny in the stars, physiognomy locates the mysteries of his or her being in the arrangement of eyes, ears, nose, mouth, and other facial features. The silhouette, or shadow, puts this portentous "constellation" into relief; accordingly, though it verges on material nonexistence, it is the most precious of possessions. Stoichita argues that Lavater's theory offers a key to understanding, among other works, *Peter Schlemihls wundersame Geschichte* (1814) by French-German author Adelbert von Chamisso. In this story, the protagonist sells his shadow to the Devil. The transaction enriches him materially, but he soon finds himself an outcast, unable to enjoy his wealth or the company of others. Schlemihl loses the defining feature of his humanity when he forfeits his dark double.[19]

As all vampire aficionados know, legend holds that the undead are invisible in mirrors. This attribute of vampires — like much of vampire lore — is the invention of Bram Stoker.[20] However, this sign of vampirism follows from the logic underlying Lavater's theory, which in turn fits into the tradition (reaching back to antiquity) that represents the spirit through ephemeral, material appearances. Like shadows, reflections "prove" that something or someone is really there and fits into the chain of being extending to the sun in the heavens, without which neither shadows nor reflections — indeed, nothing at all — would exist. A man without a shadow lacks a connection with the natural world and is therefore not fully human. Similarly, the vampire, which also lacks this connection, represents a kind of virulent shadow, seeking human life in the quest to fill its empty core. The conflicted vampiric condition points back toward the lack that constitutes the human being: the desire for worldly possessions, social standing, and all the other "accidents" promising a completed existence.[21] A missing reflection is functionally identical to a missing shadow — that is, a missing soul.

Thus, we can understand why the vampires of satire traffic, above all, in money. Gold and other items of exchange represent potential happiness, even if they do not guarantee it (and, indeed, often stand in its way). Karl Marx's oeuvre can be read as a nineteenth-century transposition, onto the world of objects, of Lavater's concern for revealing the hidden substance of the soul. Marx's distinction between "exchange value," which makes things functionally the same, and "use value," which refers to the factual uniqueness of goods concealed by commerce, posits that capitalism, by imposing an ever-expanding array of imaginary equivalencies between objects, is a demonic enterprise.

Focusing on the human cost of this economic system, Marx writes: "Capital is dead labor that, vampire-like, only lives by sucking living labor."[22] Terrell Carver has observed that in *Capital* (1867), the "vampire motif" appears alongside references to "witchcraft, animism, tribal religions, spiritualism, magic, . . . ghosts, . . . alchemy, . . . raising of the dead, conjuring tricks, levitation, and perpetual motion machines."[23] Like the more famous example of the commodity fetish, the vampire occupies what Carver calls "a kind of unholy Chartres Cathedral"[24] where the icons of modern and primitive societies commingle:

> Vampires are well known as creatures of the night, an attribute Marx exploited when he wrote that "the prolongation of the working day beyond the limits of the natural day, into the night . . . only slightly quenches the vampire thirst for the living blood of labour." Capitalist production, [Marx] concluded, has an inherent drive "towards the appropriation of labour throughout the whole of the 24 hours in the day." The vampire will not let go "while there remains a single muscle, sinew or drop of blood to be exploited."[25]

Marx's references to vampires reveal the capitalist system's viciousness and bad faith; the vampire stands for inauthenticity and alienation. His polemic, though elaborated in supernatural terms, has a solid basis in fact. Especially in its early, unregulated stage, industrial capitalism worked people to the bone and made them miserable. Still today, the division of labor means, as Marx puts it in *The German Ideology*, that "man's own deed becomes an alien power opposed to him."[26] Marx's vampires represent the relations of production that kill both body and soul.[27]

Marx, who never abandoned a Romantic phraseology in his polemics against the mystifications produced by capitalism, continued the iconoclastic project of Enlightenment. In fact, there is greater continuity between the dominant intellectual currents of the eighteenth and nineteenth centuries than conventional, thumbnail sketches of history admit. Milan Dimic notes in his discussion of a Enlightenment-era vampirism:

> The "Age of Reason" was not only the time of philosophers, neoclassical rules and certified traditions. It was also the era of rococo decoration and architecture, Piranesi's "Prisons"; of gloomy nights, haunted churchyards, and desolate ruins in the poetry of Young, Gray, Thomson, and Gessner; of the tortured sensibility of Richardson's novels, the anguish of *Manon Lescaut,* the *Nouvelle Héloïse* and *Werther;* of the integral originality of the *Sturm und Drang* group . . . ; of the "crisis of laughter" which began with the black humour of Swift's *Modest Proposal;* of Macpherson's "Ossian" and the rediscovery of genuine ballads, tales, and legends of folklore; of nightmarish Gothic romances, . . . tales of brigandism . . . ; of Germanic pietism, Wesley's Methodism . . . ; and it was also the time of esotericism and . . . secret societies.[28]

The cultural movement conventionally called "Enlightenment" abolished neither superstition among the general European population nor the supposedly backward ways of its rulers. Indeed, the term is misleading inasmuch as it suggests a monolithic endeavor, when in fact the phenomenon consisted of many separate lights. Though they often burned brightly, these points of luminescence could only shine against an enduring background of darkness.

The "coronation" of Voltaire at the Théâtre Français in 1778, when clamoring Parisian crowds reached out to touch the archenemy of the Catholic Church as if he were a saint, reveals just how little *philosophie* managed to illuminate the minds of its popular adherents.[29] Conversely, Romanticism, though fascinated by solitude, sublimity, and irrational, elemental forces, did not simply reject the supposed optimism of the preceding epoch. Instead, following the dialectical movement its great thinkers so prized,[30] Romanticism negated the facile suppositions of universality that often resulted from Enlightenment-era understandings of "man" and the world "he" inhabits. From such an interplay of light and darkness come the riotous fantasies of E. T. A. Hoffmann, whose undead automata (most famously, Olympia in "The Sandman") poke fun at the idea that one might explain the complexity of human life on the model of the machine; here, too, is the reason for the garish costumes and the scandalous public provocations of a Byron or *les Jeunes-France*.[31]

Romanticism sought a more flexible and fuller picture of human life, one that took into account the powers of imagination in the individual, as well as the correlates of these energies in varying human cultures. If there is a dark side to Enlightenment, there is also an illuminist thrust to Romanticism. Both movements were fascinated by the vampire, which embodied their respective moments of self-doubt. Before discussing the Romantic vampire, then, a few words about the cultural atmosphere in which it flourished are in order.

The work of the great French historian, Jules Michelet, proponent of the Revolution and heir to its project of mass enlightenment, illustrates the productive contradictions of the Romantic mind. Instead of viewing history as a river on whose banks one encounters a series of discrete settlements, Michelet pictures the collective life of humanity as an ocean.[32] The tides provide a model of order, but the sea is composed of elemental forces that surge up from and return down to the deep after whirling and eddying on the surface. If rationalists understand the path of human fortune as a movement that follows freely made decisions in a more-or-less-straight line, another perspective reveals that matters are considerably more complex: mankind's many vessels describe trajectories leading to many harbors, and safe arrival depends on the conditions of the skies above and the depths below. Enlightenment views human affairs at sea level, whereas Romanticism favors the view from the air and the water. The two perspectives do not stand in necessary contradiction.

It would be anachronistic at best, and perilous at worst, to follow Michelet too far in his understanding of history as a kind of Wagnerian symphony of cosmic elements, yet his Romantic conception of the world reminds us that whatever clarity we may observe in the past appears in an optic that those who were contemporary with events never possessed. Michelet also commands our attention because another set of metaphors he employs suggests a necromantic art not far removed from the topic of vampirism.

For Michelet, Roland Barthes has observed, "Blood is the cardinal substance of History,"[33] and its flow governs the lives of men and nations. The ruddy cheeks of peasants hard at work and the virginal blush of maidens are suffused with its vivifying force, as are the liberating political events of 1789, and even the Terror of 1793. This energy must be summoned from the sepulchral stillness of the past. Michelet writes:

Jamais dans ma carrière je n'ai perdu de vue [le] devoir de l'historien. J'ai donné à beaucoup de morts trop oubliés l'assistance dont moi-même j'aurai besoin.

Je les ai exhumés pour une seconde vie. Plusieurs n'étaient pas nés au moment qui leur eût été propre. D'autres naquirent à la veille de circonstances nouvelles et saisissantes qui sont venues les effacer, pour ainsi dire, étouffer leur mémoire. . . .

L'histoire accueille et renouvelle ces gloires déshéritées; elle donne vie à ces morts, les ressuscite. Sa justice associe ainsi ceux qui n'ont pas vécu en même temps, fait réparation à plusieurs qui n'avaient paru qu'un moment pour disparaître. Ils vivent maintenant avec nous qui nous sentons leurs parents, leurs amis. Ainsi se fait une famille, une cité commune entre les vivants et les morts.[34]

[Never in my career have I lost sight of [the] duty of the Historian. I have given many of the too-forgotten dead the assistance which I myself shall require.

I have exhumed them for a second life. Some were not born at the moment suitable to them. Others were born on the eve of new and striking circumstances which have come to erase them, so to speak, stifling their memory. . . .

History greets and renews these disinherited glories; it gives life to these dead men, resuscitates them. Its justice thus associates those who have not lived at the same time, offers reparation to some who appeared so briefly only to vanish. Now they live with us, and we feel we are their relatives, their friends. Thus is constituted a family, a city shared by the living and the dead.][35]

The office of seer-priest assumed by Michelet transposes to the historian's office the role claimed by increasing numbers of poets at the turn of the nineteenth century and afterward. Paul Bénichou calls this Romantic turn "the consecration of the writer" — a self-elevation that attributes to literary artists the powers formerly invested in men of the cloth.[36] Discussing the English counterpart of what Bénichou explores in France, M. H. Abrams has written of "supernatural naturalism" (a phrase he adapts from the "natural supernaturalism" that Thomas Carlyle half-seriously, half-mockingly advocated in *Sartor Resartus* [1831]). As Abrams observes, "inherited theological ideas and ways of thinking" shaped the language of Romantic authors. The latter reformulated "traditional concepts, schemes, and values which had been based on the relation of the Creator to his creature and creation." This reworking occurred in the new, secularized framework of "subject and object, ego and non-ego, the human mind or consciousness and its transactions with nature."[37] Romantics sought to preserve the past even as they transformed it, and the models of understanding the cosmos that resulted are rife with productive paradox.

In Romantic fictions, the vampire embodies the rift between the world and the atomized subject, who, though often commanding great powers, nevertheless finds himself dwarfed both by the universe within and the one without. In Percy Bysshe Shelley's *Prometheus Unbound,* to be a "vampire" is to be a plague to oneself as well as others ("A soul self-consumed . . . the wretch crept a vampire among men").[38] In Byron's *Giaour,* when a dying Muslim lays the curse of vampirism upon his slayer, he means for his killer to feed off the grief he will cause himself by destroying his family.[39] The eponymous hero of Mary Shelley's *Franken-stein* describes his state of mind upon learning that his brother has fallen victim to the monster he created:

> No one can conceive the anguish I suffered. . . . My imagination was busy in scenes of evil and despair. I considered the being whom I had cast among mankind, and endowed with the power to effect purposes of horror, such as the deed which he had now done, nearly in the light of my own vampire, my own spirit let loose from the grave, and forced to destroy all that was dear to me.[40]

"Vampire" refers to part of Victor Frankenstein's most intimate self — a subjective nightmare doubling the objective evil of his monstrous creation.

The English Romantics' vampire was split in two and tortured itself just as much as it preyed on others. Its own soul had been annihilated, and it wandered through the world spreading a private hell to all with whom it came into contact. The poets' identification with the monster gave literary form to a despairing but strangely giddy intuition: it is impossible to exorcise the demon once it has become the secret sharer of one's humanity — a part of the self whose appetites are impossible to understand fully.

James B. Twitchell observes that the Romantic vampire's predations illustrate psychological energy exchange. For early-nineteenth-century writers, the monster embodies the pathological aspects of every imaginable mental and interpersonal dynamic — e.g.,

> the forces of . . . incest (Byron's Manfred), oppressive paternalism (Shelley's Cenci), adolescent love (Keats's Porphyro), avaricious love (Poe's Morella and Berenice), the struggle for power (Emily Brontë's Heathcliff), sexual suppression [*sic*] (Charlotte Brontë's Bertha Rochester).[41]

Vampirism is a term Twitchell applies from without to most of these texts, but it is not one foreign to their internal logic.[42] Later in the century, in France, Baudelaire employed the figure of the vampire to express the same sense of fateful conflict with life. His poem, "L'héautontimoroumenos" (The Self-Tormentor), concludes:

Je suis de mon coeur le vampire,
— Un de ces grands abandonnés
Au rire éternel condamnés,
Et qui ne peuvent plus sourire!

[I am my own heart's vampire
— One of the great lost number
Condemned to eternal laughter,
Who can never smile again!][43]

Like Victor Frankenstein, Baudelaire's self-tormentor is divided against himself and therefore also stands at odds with God, the creator of mankind.[44]

The fissure within motivates an aggressive turn outward, from the fractures in the subject to an illusorily whole object. Hence the abundant examples of vampiric eroticism, e.g., the explosion of desire in a letter from German author Clemens Brentano to fellow Romantic and poet, Karoline von Günderode:

Öffne alle Adern deines weissen Leibes, dass das heisse, schäumende Blut aus tausend wonnigen Springbrunnen spritze, so will ich dich sehen und trinken aus den tausend Quellen, trinken, bis ich berauscht bin und deinen Tod mit jauchzender Raserei beweinen kann.

[Open all the arteries of your white body, that the hot, frothing blood streams from a thousand blissful fountains, that's how I want to see you and to drink from the thousand springs, to drink until I am intoxicated and can bewail your death with shouts of madness.][45]

Novalis's *Hymnen an die Nacht* (*Hymns to the Night*) contains a fantasy that the poet's child bride, Sophia, does not lie eternally in her grave, but instead returns to die again and again "in heiliger Glut" (in holy fervency).[46] And Heinrich Heine, parodying versions of the *Faust* story in which the magician summons the most beautiful woman of antiquity from the shadows, explores the same dynamic in "Helena":

Preß deinen Mund an meinen Mund,
Der Menschen Odem ist göttlich!
Ich trinke deine Seele aus,
Die Toten sind unersättlich.

[Press your mouth on my mouth,
Mankind's breath is divine!
I drink up your soul,
The dead are insatiable.][47]

Friedrich Hebbel's remark, cited in the introduction, that all dear parties become vampires after death — "Jeder Tote ist ein Vampir, die ungeliebten ausgenommen" (All dead are vampires, except the unloved ones) — generalizes the personal lyricism of his countrymen and locates the undead in the ground of hidden affective investment that Freud, some fifty years later, would call the Unconscious.[48]

Despite the intensely personal inflection of the foregoing reveries, the Romantic vampire possesses an explicitly political dimension in the works of Heine. Stefan Hock, in an early study of the vampire in German literature, observes that "Heine employs the word as a matter of preference."[49] The poet does not do so only when his subject is love and sexuality. For example, in *The Romantic School,* a presentation of his countrymen's works to a French audience, Heine describes the way things are in his native Germany, where "das Mittelalter . . . nicht, wie bei euch, gänzlich tot und verwest ist" (medievalism is not completely dead and putrefied, as it is in France).[50]

> Das deutsche Mittelalter liegt nicht vermodert im Grabe, es wird vielmehr manchmal von einem bösen Gespenst belebt, und tritt am hellen, lichten Tage, in unsre Mitte, und saugt uns das rote Leben aus der Brust. . . .
> Ach! seht ihr nicht, wie Deutschland so traurig und bleich ist? [. . .] Seht ihr nicht, wie blutig der Mund des bevollmächtigten Vampirs, der zu Frankfurt residiert, und dort am Herzen des deutschen Volkes so schauerlich langsam und langweilig saugt?

> [German medievalism is not lying mouldered in its grave; on the contrary, it is often animated by an evil spirit and steps into our midst in bright, broad daylight and sucks the red life from our hearts.
> Alas, don't you see how sad and wan Germany is? [. . .] Don't you see how bloody is the mouth of the fully authorized vampire that resides in Frankfurt and there sucks so horribly slowly and protractedly at the heart of the German people?][51]

Here, the "vampire" is the Bundestag, the confederate government council whose antidemocratic policies corresponded to the antimodern sensibilities of so many German poets to whom Heine objected.[52]

Whether drawn to the left or the right, Romantics were attracted to radicalism of all sorts. Thus, if Baudelaire's poem mentioned above ("L'héautontimoroumenos") ultimately derives its title from a play by the Roman dramatist Terence, it owes a more immediate debt to Joseph de Maistre (1754–1821), who used the ancient playwright's language to describe the torments of a sinful soul in distress. Baudelaire, who professed admiration for the revolutionary Louis-Auguste Blanqui (1805–81) in his youth, said that the arch-reactionary Maistre had "taught [him] how to reason."[53] Shelley and Byron were social utopians who looked to future improvement. Samuel Taylor Coleridge, the author of "Christabel"

(1797) — a poem that tells of a young woman's encounter with a vampiric stranger — was conservative, if idiosyncratically so.[54] Whatever their convictions, when poets wrote about vampires, they expressed a sense of dislocation and alienation resulting from political transformations.

* * *

Since the vampire thrives on upsetting strict chronology — among other orders — we should not be too surprised to find, earlier than expected, an example or two of the monster appearing in a form that points to its later, Romantic guise. A poem by Heinrich August Ossenfelder from 1748 offers not only the first example of a literary use of the vampire figure, but also the first case in which the monster serves to represent a psychological state. Ossenfelder's work concerns a lover and a girl who resists his advances. The opening lines reveal that the beloved follows her mother's moral precepts strictly:

> Mein liebes Mägdchen glaubet
> Beständig steif und feste,
> An die gegebenen Lehren
> Der immer frommen Mutter.

> [My sweet girl believes
> Steadfastly, firmly, and deeply
> In the teachings she has received
> From her always-pious mother.] [55]

The girl's modesty assimilates her body to an asexual maternal order. Her name "Christianchen" (little Christine) reinforces the idea of her dutiful adherence to the religious rules set forth by the older generation. Because she will not accommodate her suitor, his love takes a sinister turn:

> Du willst mich gar nicht lieben;
> Ich will mich an dir rächen. . . .
> Und wenn du sanfte schlummerst,
> Von deinen schönen Wangen
> Den frischen Purpur saugen.
> Alsdenn wirst du erschrecken,
> Wenn ich dich werde küssen
> Und als ein Vampir küssen:
> Wann du dann recht erzitterst
> Und matt in meine Arme,
> Gleich einer Todten sinkest
> Alsdenn will ich dich fragen,
> Sind meine Lehren besser,
> Als deiner guten Mutter?

[You do not want to love me;
I want to revenge myself on you. . . .
And when you gently slumber,
From your pretty cheeks
Drink the fresh red.
Then you'll get a fright,
When I kiss you
And kiss you like a vampire:
Then, when you really tremble
And sink into my arms,
Pale as a corpse,
Then I want to ask you
Are my teachings better
Than your good mother's?][56]

When the lover threatens to force the girl to acknowledge his carnal "teachings," he means to thrust himself between mother and daughter. The desire to join his body with his beloved's goes along with the wish to tear apart a chaste and pious relationship. It implies assimilation of a different sort. The girl will "sink into [the lover's] arms/pale as a corpse." The "little death" she experiences in her lover's embrace will make her resemble the man whose lust is so strong that it dehumanizes him and makes him act like a body without a soul.

In the second part of *Faust,* a work he completed in 1831, Goethe expressed his disdain for the lascivious vampires that took European letters by storm after John Polidori's "Vampire" (1819) had become an international success and produced a spate of melodramas featuring undead intruders preying on youthful innocents.[57] In the first act of *Faust II,* just as an unnamed *Satiriker* takes the stage, "die Nacht- und Grabdichter lassen sich entschuldigen, weil sie soeben im interessantesten Gespräch mit einem frisch entstandenen Vampyren begriffen seien, woraus eine neue Dichtart sich vielleicht entwickeln könnte" (the night-poets and graveyard-poets excuse themselves on account of their being presently involved in a most interesting discussion with a freshly risen vampire, from which perhaps a new form of poetry could emerge).[58]

Notwithstanding his contemptuous attitude in later years toward the vampire vogue, Goethe referred to his own "Bride of Corinth" (1797) as a "vampirisches Gedicht" (vampiric poem).[59] The "Bride of Corinth" sharpens the social critique implicit in Ossenfelder's earlier poem by confronting pagan sensuality with life-hating Christian asceticism. Once again, a mother stands in the way of a young couple's union, only this time the girl is the party whose lust assumes preternatural proportions. She returns from death in an effort to consummate her desire, but this appetite exceeds the satisfaction that one lover can provide:

Aus dem Grabe werd ich ausgetrieben,
Noch zu suchen das vermißte Gut,
Noch den schon verlorenen Mann zu lieben
Und zu saugen seines Herzens Blut.
Ists um den geschehn,
Muß nach anderen gehn,
Und das junge Volk erliegt der Wut.[60]

[From the grave betimes I have been driven,
I seek the good I lost, none shall me thwart,
I seek his love to whom my troth was given,
And I have sucked the lifeblood from his heart.
If he dies, I will
Find me others, still
With my fury tear young folk apart.][61]

This vampire loves life sincerely, and the destruction she will wreak (when she "tear[s] young folk apart") stems not from her own wishes, but from the mortifying prohibitions imposed on the young by an older generation that has lived only to die in an odor of false sanctity. Goethe makes fun of a superannuated moral code in his ballad, and the work falls in line with Enlightenment polemics against arranged marriages and parents forcing children into cloisters.[62] The vampire girl is a pathetic figure, not a threatening one; her mother is the true fiend.

The vampire in its myriad guises signals fissures between appearance and reality. *The Craftsman* made this allegorical function explicit when it posited the ubiquity of vampirism in the English social body and pointed out gaps between seemingly respectable figures' public personae and the self-interested actions they pursued in private. Voltaire's vampires performed a similar function, and Marx made the same equation — only he ascribed monstrosity to an entire economic system instead of individual parties. In none of these instances does the vampire fill the points of rupture where it appears with an authentic substance. As occurred when the monster assumed the form of a Serbian revenant and caused academic scandal in the early eighteenth century, the Enlightenment vampire signified negatively: marking a line beyond which identities and categories lost their stability, where the contradictions of the host culture became painfully manifest. In a more properly literary dimension, that of narrative fiction and poetry, the vampire represented split levels of consciousness and mediated historical presence. Romantic authors employed the monster to stage the torments and thrills of a mind divided against itself: clear, waking life as preyed upon by memory, regret, desire, and, more generally, events that somehow would not go away with the passing of time.

The artistic revolt of the Romantics did not necessarily amount to a political stance.[63] However, the antibourgeois aesthetic that developed after 1800, if it did not amount to class consciousness or produce genuine historical insight, registered, besides a subjective attitude, a fault line running through the social order. Already in early-modern Europe, the notion of an international *respublica litteraria* had expressed intellectual and artistic dissatisfaction with the political organization of the world, which, because it served dynastic interests, was implicitly provincial and "backwards." A republican ideal of the literary kind informed the Romantic milieus of Germany, England, and France (although, it should be noted, this did not necessarily amount to republican political convictions on the part of writers).

This oppositional stance could degenerate into an aestheticizing pose. Dolf Oehler has passed a damning judgment on the *littérateurs* of France after the Restoration:

> When Hugo, in 1831, defined Romanticism as *le libéralisme en littérature,* liberalism had already fossilized into a counter-revolutionary doctrine. In the July Monarchy, "liberal Romanticism" turned into amusement for court and salon: Victor Hugo became a *pair de France* and member of the Académie de France, Lamartine a fashionable speaker for the dynastic opposition, Vigny likewise an *académicien.* A good part of the classically oriented bourgeois public may not have liked it, but their fear of supposed "literary sans-culottism" had disappeared; contraventions of the *dictionnaire* and Aristotelian rules did not shock them anymore, and certainly did not connote social upheaval. After 1840, all that remained of the period when Romantics like Hugo, Lamartine, Sainte-Beuve, Gautier, and Balzac had flirted with the early-socialist thought of Saint-Simon and Fourier or the socialist Catholicism of Lamennais were the self-contradictory stereotypes of the "social mission of the artist," on the one hand, and *L'art pour l'art,* on the other. This was the logical consequence of the wholly abstract positions of social criticism espoused by the two Romanticisms — the petty bourgeois humanitarianism of Hugo and George Sand and the art-intoxication of the *Jeunes-France,* even during their "Storm-and-Stress" phase.[64]

Oehler's evaluation of the literary culture of "Art for Art's Sake" follows Marx's assessment of contemporary French economists like Proudhon: "[sie] spielen sich als blasierte Fatalisten auf und werfen von der Höhe ihres Standpunktes einen stolzen Blick der Verachtung auf die menschlichen Maschinen, die den Reichtum erzeugen" (they present themselves as blasé fatalists and cast, from their lofty position, a proudly contemptuous gaze down upon the human machines who produce wealth).[65] Supposedly radical art, as anyone familiar with the transgressive posturing of heavy metal or hip hop in our own day will have observed, need not amount to more than a quest for distinction in the commercial market.

Notwithstanding such literary bad faith, Théophile Gautier's short story, "La morte amoureuse" (The Dead in Love, 1836), uses the vampire motif to thematize false consciousness in post-Restoration France. Whatever the author's politics may have been at the time of its composition or afterwards — and whatever the self-deception of which he may be guilty — the narrative structure of his work gives "The Dead in Love" a trenchant irony that transcends the superficial cult of Beauty, even if it does not, in the manner of Heine or Baudelaire, cut to core contradictions maintaining social illusions.[66]

"The Dead in Love" begins in mid-conversation, when the narrator and protagonist of the story, a "poor country priest" named Romuald, is asked by a fellow clergyman whether he has "ever loved."[67] The old man — he is now sixty-six — responds that he led a "double vie" (double life; 148/115) for three years:

> Le jour, j'étais un prêtre du Seigneur, chaste, occupé de la prière et des choses saintes; la nuit, dès que j'avais fermé les yeux, je devenais un jeune seigneur, fin connaisseur en femmes, en chiens et en chevaux, jouant aux dés, buvant et blasphémant. [. . .] De cette vie somnambulique il m'est resté des souvenirs . . . dont je ne puis pas me défendre.

> [During the day, I was a priest of the Lord, chaste, absorbed in prayer and holy things; each night, as soon as I closed my eyes, I would become a young nobleman, a subtle connoisseur of women, dogs, and horses, who gave himself up to gambling, drink, and blasphemy. [. . .] From this somnambulistic existence I have retained memories . . . against which I am powerless still.] (117/91)

Reading after Freud, one feels inclined to interpret this passage, and indeed the entire tale, in terms of dream logic and psychosexual repression. Romuald, after all, says that he led an exuberant life of the senses "each night, as soon as I closed my eyes." His nocturnal existence embraced everything that days spent in devotion to God and His works shut out.

We should note, however, that the breakaway narrative technique suggests that the time when Romuald speaks is contemporaneous with the time when Gautier published his tale. If one admits the possibility that the story takes place in 1836, then the priest was in his late teens and early twenties when the story-within-the-story took place — that is, it coincides perfectly with the beginning of the Revolution in France. Romuald's dual existence reproduces the split of the French social body in 1789, just as his haunting memories mirror the specter of past historical events. "The Dead in Love" transforms the conflicts faced by a nation into a personal struggle.

In dreams — whether personal, political, or, as is the case here, both — fears and desires assume a new guise. "The Dead in Love" contrasts love for God and things spiritual, on the one hand, with love for a woman and material goods, on the other. History, which is accessible only through symbolic representations, appears in the topos of death and rebirth, as it does in Michelet. "The Dead in Love" does not show a path to God, even for a man of the cloth. It therefore grants ascendancy to the confusion of the sublunary world, fraught both with the tensions of the late eighteenth century and those of the July Monarchy, whose leader, Louis-Philippe, received a title — "Citizen King" — that encoded the political paradoxes of the French nation. One of the characters in Gautier's tale exclaims fittingly: "Dans quel siècle vivons-nous, bon Dieu!" (Good God, what a century is ours!; 137/107).

Despite Romuald's assertion that he formerly led a life of incomparable dissipation, the nocturnal scenes of debauchery he recounts do not fully support this claim. The young man's behavior is certainly unbecoming for a priest, but it is not wanton, cruel, or particularly perverse. Thus, "The Dead in Love," like Goethe's "Bride of Corinth," suggests that religious prohibitions are the true evil. In Clarimonde, the supernatural beauty with whom Romuald consorts, "la femme me répondait du vampire" (the woman made answer for the vampire; 147/114). Gentle and kind, she simply possesses too much sensuousness for a mortal body. Her death and resurrection are due to the passion she conceives for Romuald, a forbidden lover. She pines away and expires when she cannot realize her love — "Je t'ai attendu si longtemps, que je suis morte" (I waited so long for you, that I died of waiting; 135/105), she tells him — and then comes back to life when he, in his second, secret existence, yields to his stifled emotions and visits her crypt.

In contrast to the fulfillment offered by Clarimonde, service to the church presents a morbid task:

> Je comprenais toute l'horreur de ma situation, et les côtés funèbres et terribles de l'état que je venais d'embrasser se révélaient clairement à moi. Être prêtre! c'est-à-dire chaste, ne pas aimer, ne distinguer ni le sexe ni l'âge, se détourner de toute beauté, se crever les yeux, ramper sous l'ombre glaciale d'un cloître ou d'une église, ne voir que des mourants, veiller auprès de cadavres inconnus et porter soi-même son deuil sur sa soutane noire, de sorte que l'on peut faire de votre habit un drap pour votre cerceuil!

> [I grasped the full horror of my situation, and saw with utter clarity the funereal ghastliness of the profession I had embraced. To be a priest! — that is, to be chaste, never to love, to make not the slightest distinction of sex or age, to turn one's back upon all beauty, to put out one's eyes, to creep along in the icy darkness of church or cloister, to see only the dying, and to shroud oneself in a black cassock as in one's own funeral pall.] (124/97)

The phrase "somnambulistic existence" with which Romuald qualifies his nightlife applies much more readily to his service in the church, for it connotes automatism, a dormant mental state, and life tinged with lifelessness. In contrast, Clarimonde, whose name means "bright world," provides an escape from the "tomb" (124/97) of the priesthood.

When Romuald first sees Clarimonde, he is taking his vows. At the threshold of sanctity, he experiences an epiphany:

> A mesure que je la regardais, je sentais s'ouvrir dans moi des portes qui jusqu'alors avaient été fermées; des soupiraux obstrués se débouchaient dans tous les sens et laissaient entrevoir des perspectives inconnues; la vie m'apparaissait sous un aspect tout autre; je venais de naître à un nouvel ordre d'idées.

> [As I gazed, doors that hitherto had been closed began to open within me. Windows that had been blocked were unplugged, yielding glimpses of unknown vistas; life appeared to me in an entirely different light; I had been reborn to a new order of ideas.] (121/94)

The vampire, as a portal to another world, does not have a positive identity; instead, Clarimonde offers a shifting screen for fantasy:

> Avoir Clarimonde, c'était avoir vingt maîtresses, c'était avoir toutes les femmes, tant elle était mobile, changeante et dissemblable à elle-même; un vrai caméléon! Elle vous faisait commettre avec elle l'infidélité que vous eussiez commise avec d'autres, en prenant complètement le caractère, l'allure et le genre de beauté de la femme qui paraissait vous plaire.

> [To possess Clarimonde was to possess twenty mistresses, so mobile and changeable was she, and so dissimilar from herself — a veritable chameleon! She would make you commit with her the infidelity that you might have committed with others, so thoroughly did she assume the nature, appearance, and style of beauty of the woman who had stolen your fancy.] (144/112)

Ironically, Clarimonde's protean nature, which molds itself to the movements of fantasy, contains and limits erotic excess, whence her appearance of "chasteté mélancolique" (melancholy chastity; 134/104) and her "air de complaisance maternelle" (air of maternal indulgence; 142/111). She is every woman to Romuald and actually prevents greater inconstancy on his part.

"The Dead in Love," like the greater part of the other works we have examined in this chapter, stages an encounter with the undead to satirical ends. Religiosity and dogmatism provide the most obvious target, but by implication Gautier also takes aim at bourgeois mediocrity, which is content to take the sunlit world of waking life for the whole of reality. In addition, Clarimonde, who embodies the percolating rhythms of memory shaped by longing and pain, refutes the positivist notion of linear time. Romuald's narrative foregrounds the persistence of the past in the present and, in the process, conjures up unresolved conflicts haunting the nineteenth century.

However, in the same breath, "The Dead in Love" underscores how a kind of emptiness pervades Romantic vampires just as it does their Enlightenment forebears, "poor in images." Clarimonde has no real being independent of Romuald. As Mario Praz observes, "the thirst for the infinite . . . animates the lines of the Romantics,"[68] and vampires' constitutive lack in Romantic fictions makes them coterminous with desire. Since desire shuns cold, hard facts in favor of undisclosed potentialities, vampires reveal, through their chameleon-like metamorphoses, the material conditions of life that generate symbolic compensations in fantasy. The instability and mutability of the vampire play out as a dialectic between true and false, latent and manifest, visible and invisible. Although vampires are fictional, the tensions and contradictions that they move between are real. When, in a literary space, vampires infract norms and rules and defy established systems and balances of power, their imaginary sovereignty negates the material constraints in place in the societies where their representations circulate.

This is why, for Gautier and his contemporaries, vampires are often associated with faraway lands and/or times. The scene of Charles Nodier's "Smarra" (1821) is Thessaly, the classical *locus* of witchcraft.[69] Eugène Sue's *Mystères de Paris* (1842–43) likens to a vampire a "grande créole à la fois svelte et charnue, vigoureuse et souple comme une panthère, . . . le type de la sensualité brûlante qui ne s'allume qu'aux feux des tropiques" (large Creole woman, both svelte and full, vigorous and supple like a panther, . . . the embodiment of the burning sensuality that only takes flame in the fires of the tropics).[70] In *Fortunio* (1836), Gautier himself makes a similar comparison, with a similar set of foreign associations:

> Soudja-Sari avait . . . des passions violentes comme les parfums et les poisons de son pays. Elle était de la race de ces terribles Javanaises, de ces gracieux vampires qui boivent un Européen en trois semaines et le laissent sans une goutte d'or ni de sang, plus aride qu'un citron dont on a fait de la limonade.

> [Soudja-Sari had . . . passions as strong as the perfumes and poisons of her country. She belonged to the race of those fearsome Javanese women, those graceful vampires, who drink up a European man in three weeks and leave him with neither a drop of gold nor of blood, drier than a lemon that has been turned to lemonade.][71]

These examples of fantastic literature tend to place descriptions of supernatural beings within elaborate frameworks of storytelling or the papers of a vanished party. Such a design places vampires at a remove from the reader and his/her world. However, the distancing techniques also bring the vampires closer. The probability of the tales' veracity increases to the extent that they refer to things that cannot be readily verified by the reader's experience. Since protagonists as a rule have the same nationality as the readers to whom the works are addressed, the fictions "automatically" inspire confidence.

Descriptions of encounters with vampires escort the foreign and strange into familiar territory. Romanticism answers the Enlightenment by taking figural gibes literally and fleshing out the vampires that writers of a more purely rationalist sensibility used only in passing. In this game of rhetorical escalation, Romantic authors satirize the satirists, engineering boundless (because self-reflecting) irony.[72] The *mise-en-scène* amounts to a *mise-en-abyme*. To quote Marx (whose authority on vampires has been established), "all that is solid melts into air."[73] The vampire is the specter of history risen.

* * *

A look at a work by a popular author who inherited the literary conventions and political problems outlined above will allow us to close this chapter of our "vampire chronicles" and open the next. *Les Mille et Un Fantômes* (The Thousand and One Ghosts, 1849), by Alexandre Dumas, who also composed a vampire melodrama,[74] presents an explicitly political framework for his fantastic tales. The framed narratives that comprise the novel are told by parties assembled, we read, on a September evening in 1831. The time between the telling of tales in the fiction and their publication in actuality coincides almost exactly with the duration of the July Monarchy.

In his introduction, Dumas admits his ambivalence about the course of recent French history:

> Tous les jours nous faisons un pas vers la liberté, l'égalité, la fraternité, trois grands mots que la Révolution de 1793, . . . l'autre, . . . a lancés au milieu de la société moderne comme elle eût fait d'un tigre, d'un lion et d'un ours habillés avec des toisons d'agneaux; mots vides, malheureusement, et qu'on lisait à travers la fumée de juin sur nos monuments criblés de balles.

> [Every day we take a further step toward liberty, equality, and fraternity — three great words that the Revolution of 1793, . . . the other one, . . . cast into the middle of modern society as it would have released a tiger, a lion, and a bear dressed in sheep's clothing — empty words, unfortunately, as one read through the smoke of June on our monuments riddled with bullets.][75]

On the one hand, Dumas writes that he has supported the Republican cause; as he puts it a little further on: "Moi, je vais comme les autres; moi, je suis le mouvement" (As for me, I go the way of everyone else; I, too, follow the general movement; 243). On the other hand, he is no political radical. Dumas, through his reference to "la fumée de juin," expresses his disapproval of the massacre that took place in 1848, when the state violently suppressed the workers' uprising that followed the closing of the *Ateliers nationaux*. However, the remark that precedes this phrase, in which Dumas compares revolutionary slogans to beasts of prey let loose upon the social body, suggests that he does not consider the fallen wholly innocent. Indeed, to mark the "other" revolution — the "big one" of the eighteenth century — Dumas chooses 1793, the year of the Terror.

The framed narratives of *The Thousand and One Ghosts*, which for the most part revolve around events alleged to have taken place in the tumult of revolutionary upheaval, culminate in a story told by a "dame pâle" (pale lady; 384/116). Her silent presence while others related their tales has heightened the uncanny atmosphere of the evening. Madame Gregoriska's story describes an encounter she herself claims to have had with a vampire — an experience accounting for her ghostly complexion.

Madame Gregoriska begins by evoking the everyday reality of the supernatural in her native land and its presence from time immemorial:

> Je suis Polonaise, née . . . dans un pays où les légendes deviennent des articles de foi. . . . Pas un de nos châteaux qui n'ait son spectre, pas une de nos chaumières qui n'ait son esprit familier. Chez le riche comme chez le pauvre, on reconnaît le principe ami comme le principe ennemi.
>
> [I am Polish, I was born . . . in a country where legends become articles of faith. . . . There's not one of our castles that doesn't have its ghost, not one of our cottages that doesn't have its familiar spirit. Rich and poor, in castle and in cottage, all recognise the existence of the friendly principle and the hostile principle.] (384–5/117)

However, as the "pale lady" continues her story, she reveals that Poland is not, in fact, an unchanging realm of simple "faith" governed by the elementary distinction between "friend" and "foe" without history. Instead, Madame Gregoriska's tale takes place in modern times — a mere six years before she recounts it to her French auditors. "L'année 1825 vit se livrer entre la Russie et la Pologne une de ces luttes dans lesquelles on croirait que tout le sang d'un peuple est épuisé comme souvent s'épuise tout le sang d'une famille" (The year 1825 witnessed a conflict between Russia and Poland — one of those struggles in which one might believe that the lifeblood of a whole nation is exhausted, just as the lifeblood of a family often finally fails; 385/117, translation modified).

The story of the pale lady is as follows. After both her brothers have fallen in combat with the Russians, the narrator's father decides that his daughter (the future Madame Gregoriska) should be placed in a convent for her own safety. On a journey through the Carpathian Mountains, a band of robbers kills her companions. Their leader — "un jeune homme de vingt-deux ans à peine, au teint pâle, aux longs yeux noirs, aux cheveux tombant bouclés sur ses épaules" (a young man of twenty-two at most, with a pale complexion, slanting black eyes, and hair that fell in curls on his shoulders; 391/122) — claims the young woman for himself. Before the bandit can subject her to any outrage, a second man, the brigand's brother, appears — "tombé, pour ainsi dire, du ciel" (fallen, as it were, out of the sky; 393/124).

The two brothers share a common mother, a scion of the noble Brankovan family (393/124). Their bloodlines diverge on their fathers' sides. Gregoriska, the elder, is a blond-haired, blue-eyed Slav, the legitimate son of a nobleman raised in Vienna. His father, before he died, saw to it that his son learned to appreciate "the advantages of civilization" in order to become a true "European" (398/127). Kostaki, the younger, is a bastard, born of his mother's "relations coupables" (illicit relationship; 398/128) with a half-Greek, half-Moldavian count; he now commands men "vêtus de peaux de mouton" (dressed in sheepskins), each carrying "un long fusil turc" (a long Turkish rifle; 391/122). The half-breed prowls the forest with his accomplices, living by theft and murder; until this point, however, he (Kostaki) has grudgingly deferred to the authority of his older sibling (Gregoriska), who has kept the younger brother's lawlessness in check.

In the Carpathians, Occident and Orient, civilization and barbarism, clash in two brothers' rivalry for the affections of a Polish girl who speaks French as "une langue presque maternelle" (practically her mother tongue; 396/126, translation modified). Gregoriska (the elder, blond, "European" brother) wins her heart, but not without committing fratricide — upon provocation, of course. Kostaki, the robber, comes back from the grave as a vampire and preys upon the bride-to-be. A timely marriage to Gregoriska saves her, but her husband now belongs to death; as he lies dying, he enjoins his young wife to leave the land, which she promptly does, for France.

Though set in Central Europe — a region unlike any other, the narrator claims[76] — Madame Gregoriska's tale concerns France. In 1848 — just one year before *The Thousand and One Ghosts* was published — French revolutionaries clamored for the independence of Poland, in whose destiny they saw the reflection both of their own national fortunes and those of Europe as a whole. The struggle for Polish independence concerned the very same issue for which the French, too, were willing to spill their blood ("là aussi deux principes plus terribles, plus acharnés, plus implacables encore, sont en présence: la tyrannie et la liberté" [two even more terrible principles are to be found in my land, even more determined and implacable: tyranny and freedom; 385/117]). Madame Gregoriska's weakened state, evident in her preternatural pallor, mirrors not only the condition of her country, but also that of those who listen uneasily to her story.

Like other framed narratives (e.g., Boccaccio's *Decameron,* which unfolds against the backdrop of the plague), the storytelling in *The Thousand and One Ghosts* takes place with disaster perilously close at hand. The tales recounted by the various figures in *The Thousand and One Ghosts* are meant as a diversion. This word is intended in a twofold sense. On the one hand, the diversion is an end unto itself: "distraction" or "entertainment" that draws attention away from the looming social chaos. On the other hand — but in a sense that complements the first meaning — the diversion occurs through turning (the etymological sense of the word *divert,* which has as its root the Latin verb *vertere*) real unrest and upheaval into flights of imagination. To take up again Michelet's elemental imagery of history as a vast ocean: the stories in *The Thousand and One Ghosts,* like canals or other works of human artifice, break up and redirect the raw matter of fear coursing in the "general movement" that Dumas invokes in his preface into smaller streams — little babbling brooks of discourse without apparent connection to their turbid and violent source.

A hermeneutic of suspicion[77] reveals the connections between historical fact and narrative fancy. Besides the presence of the political rhetoric of French revolutionaries ("liberty" and "tyranny") in Madame Gregoriska's story, there is at least one other feature of the Polish woman's tale that links the fantastic narrative set in the wilds of Central Europe to Paris. Madame Gregoriska tells her auditors that when her betrothed came back to the house after killing his savage brother, the mother of the two Carpathian siblings asked Gregoriska, "Où est ton frère?" (Where is your brother?). "Je songeai que c'était la même question que Dieu avait faite à Caïn" (I reflected that this was the same question that God had asked Cain; 411/139), the pale lady comments. The Biblical reference, while conjuring up mankind's most distant origins, also echoes the discourse with which nineteenth-century writers and politicians described events in their own day. Oehler, writing about the political slogans and polemics of midcentury France, remarks:

> The June Massacres irrevocably marked the end of the drunkenness and "cant" (Marx) about brotherhood. [. . .] It became common to speak of *fraternité bourgeoise,* which culminates in fratricide. In place of republican brotherliness, warning-images of siblings who were mortal enemies, such as Cain and Abel, appeared. At the same time, the Biblical example received different interpretations: for

those on the Right, Abel was always the innocent victim; for those on the Left, it was more commonly Cain, who on the one hand commits the murder, but on the other hand does so as one who has been placed in a position of gross disadvantage, who represents the archetype of the disinherited and the damned, the pariah.[78]

Deep in the Carpathians, where French political reality is darkly reflected, lies an age-old drama that modern history simply repeats. The ancient story of bloodshed calls into question the modern myth of progress.[79]

The Thousand and One Ghosts, which contains truth in the folds of fiction, generates narrative interest through a game of concealment and ruse. In closing this chapter, and to prepare for the discussion of vampiric imposture to follow in the next, it is worth noting that textual evidence suggests that Madame Gregoriska falsifies the information she presents to her auditors (and the reader). In her narrative, the mysterious pale lady recalls the song of the guide who conducted her through the Carpathian Mountains until the brigands appeared:

Dans le marais de Stavila,
Où tant de sang coula,
Voyez-vous ce cadavre-là?
Ce n'est point un fils d'Illyrie;
C'est un brigand plein de furie,
Qui, trompant la douce Marie,
Extermina, trompa, brûla.
[. . .]
Ses yeux bleus pour jamais ont lui,
Fuyons tous, malheur à celui
Qui passe au marais près de lui,
C'est un vampire! Le loup fauve
Loin du cadavre impur se sauve,
Et sur la montagne au front chauve,
Le funèbre vautour a fui.

[In the marshes of Stavila,
Many warriors shed their blood.
You see that body near the wood?
That's no son of proud Illyria,
That's a brigand filled with ire
Who deceived Mary: hateful liar!
And massacred with sword and fire.
[. . .]
His blue eyes now no more will gleam.
Let's all take flight; and woe to him
Who walks the marshes near to him.
He is a vampire! The wild wolf

Flees that dread corpse to save himself.
The ghastly vulture, too,
Has fled to the mountain bare and grim.] (389–90/121, translation
modified)

This song, which serves the narrative purpose of adding "local color" and
a genuine air to the story the pale lady tells, is a plagiarized document.
Madame Gregoriska does not, as she claims, quote "un de ces hommes des
montagnes" (one of those men of the mountains; 389/121), but rather a
ballad by Prosper Mérimée (1803–70), a contemporary of Dumas! Mérimée's poem appeared in *La Guzla* (1827), a collection of works supposedly
from Central Europe. *La Guzla* was a fake, like the same author's *Théâtre
de Clara Gazul* (1825) from two years earlier.[80] This Restoration-era mystification, inserted in Madame Gregoriska's narrative as a mark of authenticity, raises a question: What if the unearthly-pale Madame Gregoriska, the
declared victim of a vampiric visitation in the Carpathians, is now herself a
vampire, searching for fresh blood in France?

Such an imposture — especially in view of the fact that her listeners
cannot verify what Madame Gregoriska says about who she is — leads us
to the topic of the next chapter. As we have seen, "vampire" was above
all a term of abuse, applied in derision, in the eighteenth century. As the
word came to designate a being with literary personhood, the vampire
became more complex and harder to recognize. This transformation
occurred in parallel to European societies' shift from a hierarchical order
to a form of organization characterized by the possibility of greater movement between social stations. Some thirty years before the publication of
The Thousand and One Ghosts, John Polidori's Lord Ruthven, to whose
career we now turn, performed an elaborate series of deceptions to cast a
web of enchantment that allowed vampire kind to thrive in the capitals of
the nineteenth century.

Notes

[1] Klaus Hamberger, *Mortuus non mordet: Kommentierte Dokumentation zum
Vampirismus 1689–1791* (Vienna: Turia & Kant, 1992), 85–86.

[2] Quoted in Gábor Klaniczay, *The Uses of Supernatural Power: The Transformation of Popular Religion in Medieval and Early-Modern Europe,* trans. Susan Singerman (Oxford: Polity Press, 1990), 181.

[3] Quoted in Montague Summers, *The Vampire* (London: Senate, 1995), 25.

[4] Klaniczay, 177; cf. Hamberger, 38.

[5] E.J. Clery and Robert Miles, eds., *Gothic Documents: A Sourcebook, 1700–1820*
(Manchester: Manchester UP, 2000), 24–25.

[6] Clery and Miles, 26. See Markman Ellis, *The History of Gothic Fiction* (Edinburgh: Edinburgh UP, 2000), 162–68, for a fuller account of the intricacies of

the article; it was written as a response to an item in the *London Journal*, "the mouthpiece of propaganda for the ministry of Sir Robert Walpole" (163), which had introduced vampirism to an English readership. Ellis also discusses the relationship between vampire reports and "the birth of folklore" (168–75).

[7] Aribert Schroeder, *Vampirismus: Seine Entwicklung vom Thema zum Motiv* (Frankfurt: Akademische Verlagsgesellschaft, 1973), 117.

[8] Quoted in Schroeder, 175.

[9] Schroeder, 187. The conflicted relations between England and Ireland provide, at the end of the century, an important subtext for Bram Stoker's *Dracula*; see chapter 4.

[10] Milan V. Dimic, "Vampiromania in the Eighteenth Century: The Other Side of Enlightenment," in *Man and Nature/L'Homme et la Nature: Proceedings of the Canadian Society for Eighteenth-Century Studies* 3, ed. R. J. Merrett (Edmonton: The Society, 1984), 8.

[11] Dimic, 7; translation, 17.

[12] Dimic, 7; translation, 17.

[13] Donatien Alphonse François de Sade, *Les 120 journées de Sodome* (Paris: 10/18, 1993); Dom Augustin Calmet, *Dissertation sur les vampires* (Grenoble: Jérôme Millon, 1998), 30.

[14] Donatien Alphonse François de Sade, *Histoire de Juliette, ou les Prospérités du vice, Oeuvres complètes* VIII, eds. Annie Le Brun and Jean-Jacques Pauvert [Paris: Pauvert, 1987], 84; *Juliette*, trans. Austryn Wainhouse (New York: Grove Press, 1968), 37. The author explains the reasoning of the dissolute nun in a footnote: "Le *vampire* suçait le sang des cadavres, Dieu fait couler celui des hommes, tous deux à l'examen se trouvent chimériques: est-ce se tromper que de prêter à l'un le nom de l'autre?" (The vampire drank the blood from corpses, God causes that of men to be spilt; examination reveals both to be figments of disordered imagination; may we not justifiably call the one by the other's name?; 84/37).

[15] Schroeder, 161–67. In this respect, representations of the vampire fused with medieval depictions of winged devils, e.g., in Dante's *Inferno*. As Friedrich Kittler has observed in *Discourse Networks, 1800/1900*, trans. Michael Metteer with Chris Cullens (Stanford: Stanford UP, 1992), "every imaginable speech disturbance" occurs in Hell, "whereas the blessed [are] with the Word and God" (221); the misshapen nature of demons and the damned, which is expressed in their tormented language, corresponds to the semiotic confusion surrounding both animal and human vampires, which appear at the outer limits of established systems of classification.

[16] Hamberger, 16.

[17] For example, Norbert Borrmann, in *Vampirismus oder die Sehnsucht nach Unsterblichkeit* (Munich: Diederichs, 1999), 147–48, 187, presents political cartoons from various sources that portray the English, Germans, and Japanese as vampires. D. J. Enright, in *The Oxford Book of the Supernatural* (Oxford: Oxford UP, 1994), notes that in the Second World War, the United States Army issued free copies of Bram Stoker's *Dracula* to troops, effectively invoking "the sinister

Count . . . as a German soldier"; subsequently, "during the Cold War," Dracula "came to symbolize 'the fanatical hordes of the East' who threatened to conscript the West into their way of life"; "the vampire," Enright concludes, "can be slotted in practically anywhere, a myth for all seasons" (206).

[18] For a discussion of Lavater's ideas and influence, see Robert E. Norton, *The Beautiful Soul: Aesthetic Morality in the Eighteenth Century* (Ithaca: Cornell UP, 1995), 176–209; and the essays found in Melissa Percival and Graeme Tytler, eds., *Physiognomy in Profile: Lavater's Impact on European Culture* (Newark: U of Delaware P, 2005). In the twentieth century, Walter Benjamin sought to rehabilitate Lavater's theory for dialectical purposes in his writings on modern cityscapes; see Carol Jacobs, *In the Language of Walter Benjamin* (Baltimore: Johns Hopkins UP, 2000) for many leads.

[19] Victor I. Stoichita, *Brève histoire de l'ombre* (Geneva: Droz, 2000), 163–202.

[20] Though Jonathan Harker, the protagonist, remarks that Dracula has "a very marked physiognomy" (48), he finds that it does not appear in the looking-glass: "I had hung my shaving glass by the window, and was just beginning to shave. Suddenly, I felt a hand on my shoulder, and heard the Count's voice saying to me, 'Good morning.' I started, for it amazed me that I had not seen him, since the reflection of the glass covered the whole room behind me. [. . .] Having answered the Count's salutation, I turned to the glass again to see how I had been mistaken. This time there could be no error, for the man was close to me, and I could see him over my shoulder. But there was no reflection of him in the mirror!" (56) Bram Stoker, *Dracula*, ed. Glennis Byron (Ontario: Broadview, 1998).

[21] See Jacques Lacan, "The Mirror Stage as Formative of the Function of the *I*," in *Écrits: A Selection*, trans. Alan Sheridan (New York: W. W. Norton, 1977), 1–6.

[22] Quoted in David L. Macdonald, *Poor Polidori: A Critical Biography of the Author of* The Vampyre (Toronto: U of Toronto P, 1991), 194.

[23] Terrell Carver, *The Postmodern Marx* (University Park: Pennsylvania State UP, 1998), 15–16.

[24] Carver, 16.

[25] Carver, 15.

[26] Karl Marx, *The German Ideology*, ed. C. J. Arthur (London: Lawrence and Wishart, 1974), 54.

[27] See, for example, Terry Eagleton, *Marx* (New York: Routledge, 1999), 32; and Chris Baldick, *In Frankenstein's Shadow: Myth, Monstrosity, and Nineteenth-Century Writing* (Oxford: Oxford UP, 1987), which includes an excellent chapter ("Karl Marx's Vampires and Grave-Diggers,"121–40) on this topic.

[28] Dimic, 1.

[29] Darrin M. McMahon, *Enemies of the Enlightenment: The French Counter-Enlightenment and the Making of Modernity* (Oxford: Oxford UP, 2001), 4.

[30] See Manfred Frank, *The Philosophical Foundations of Early German Romanticism*, trans. Elizabeth Millan-Zaibert (Albany: State U of New York P, 2004).

[31] See Théophile Gautier's reflections on his youth collected in *Les Jeunes France: Romans Goguenards* (Paris: Édition des autres, 1979). For a more detached

description of the French Romantics' milieu and exploits, see Enid Starkie, *Petrus Borel, the Lycanthrope: His Life and Times* (New York: New Directions, 1954).

[32] Jules Michelet, *La mer* (Paris: Gallimard, 1983).

[33] Roland Barthes, *Michelet*, trans. Richard Howard (New York: Farrar, Straus and Giroux, 1987), 119.

[34] Roland Barthes, *Michelet* (Paris: Seuil, 1954), 78–79.

[35] Barthes (1987), 101–2.

[36] Paul Bénichou, *The Consecration of the Writer, 1750–1830*, trans. Mark K. Jensen (Lincoln: U of Nebraska P, 1999).

[37] M. H. Abrams, *Natural Supernaturalism: Tradition and Revolution in Romantic Literature* (New York: W. W. Norton, 1973), 12–13.

[38] Quoted in Schroeder, 189.

[39] Byron, *The Major Works* (Oxford: Oxford UP, 2000), 227–28 [ll. 746–85].

[40] Mary Shelley, *Frankenstein or the Modern Prometheus* (London: Penguin, 1985), 74.

[41] James B. Twitchell, *The Living Dead: A Study of the Vampire in Romantic Literature* (Durham: Duke UP, 1981), 5.

[42] See Twitchell, *The Living Dead*, 39–102.

[43] Charles Baudelaire, *Oeuvres complètes* (Paris: Laffont, 1980), 57. Lautréamont, Baudelaire's heir, gives his antihero Maldoror the sobriquet *vampire*, which is "toujours vivace, toujours hideux, et . . . ne périra qu'avec l'univers" (Isidore Ducasse/Comte de Lautréamont, *Oeuvres complètes*, ed. Hubert Juin [Paris: Gallimard, 1973], 42) (ever enduring, always hideous . . . and will perish only with the universe itself [*Maldoror and the Complete Works of the Comte de Lautréamont*, trans. Alexis Lykiard (Cambridge, MA: Exact Change, 1994), 46]). Of all the names Maldoror receives, "vampire" comes closest to capturing his formless, seething substance. Maldoror's vampirism expresses itself in terms that invert, but preserve, the self-torment of Baudelaire's lyrical "I": "J'ai voulu rire comme les autres; mais cela . . . était impossible. J'ai pris un canif dont la lame avait un tranchant acéré, et me suis fendu les chairs au endroit où se réunissent les lèvres. [. . .] Je regardai dans un miroir cette bouche meurtrie par ma propre volonté! Le sang . . . coulait avec abondance des deux blessures. . . . Après quelques instants de comparaison, je vis bien que . . . je ne riais pas" (20–21) (I've longed to laugh, with the rest, but that . . . was impossible. Taking a penknife with a sharp-edged blade, I slit the flesh at the point joining the lips. [. . .] I saw in the mirror a mouth ruined at my own will! The blood . . . gushed freely from the two wounds. . . . After some moments of comparison I saw quite clearly that . . . I was not laughing; 30). Baudelaire's "self-tormentor" can only laugh and never smile. Maldoror smiles perpetually yet cannot laugh. See Jean Michel Olivier, *Lautréamont: le texte du vampire* (Lausanne: L'Âge d'Homme, 1981).

[44] For a discussion of how Baudelaire's self-annihilating lyricism connects with a conflicted field of social relations, see Eugene Holland, *Baudelaire and Schizoanalysis: The Sociopoetics of Modernism* (Cambridge: Cambridge UP, 1993); the poem in question is treated on pp. 97–98.

[45] Quoted in Stefan Hock, *Die Vampyrsagen und ihre Verwertung in der deutschen Literatur* (Berlin: Alexander Duncker, 1900), 88.

[46] Novalis, *Gedichte/Die Lehrlinge zu Sais* (Stuttgart: Reclam, 1984), 154.

[47] Reprinted in Dieter Sturm and Klaus Völker, *Von denen Vampiren* (Frankfurt am Main: Suhrkamp, 1994), 37.

[48] Tzvetan Todorov, *The Fantastic: A Structural Approach to a Literary Genre*, trans. Richard Howard (Ithaca: Cornell UP, 1975), 157–75. Dorothea von Mücke, *The Seduction of the Occult and the Rise of the Fantastic Tale* (Stanford: Stanford UP, 2003), explores the rise of this literary motif in Germany, its stakes, and its diffusion abroad.

[49] Hock, 57n.

[50] Heinrich Heine, *Die Romantische Schule und andere Schriften über Deutschland* (Cologne: Könemann, 1995), 159; *The Romantic School and Other Essays*, eds. Jost Hermand and Robert C. Holub (New York: Continuum, 1985), 125.

[51] Heine, 159/125.

[52] See Hock, 55–62, for eighteenth-century examples of vampires as means of political critique in Germany.

[53] Walter Benjamin's classic essay, "The Paris of the Second Empire in Baudelaire" (in *Baudelaire: A Lyric Poet in the Era of High Capitalism*, trans. Harry Zohn [London: Verso, 1983]), frames its analysis of the poet's works with discussions of Blanqui. For a study treating the opposite side of the coin, see Daniel Volga, *Baudelaire et Joseph de Maistre* (Paris: José Corti, 1957).

[54] Peter J. Kitson, "Political Thinker," *The Cambridge Companion to Coleridge*, ed. Lucy Newlyn (Cambridge: Cambridge UP, 2002).

[55] Reprinted in Hock, 65.

[56] Reprinted in Hock, 65.

[57] See chapter 3.

[58] Johann Wolfgang von Goethe, *Faust, erster und zweiter Teil* (Munich: Deutscher Taschenbuch Verlag, 1997), 157.

[59] Sturm and Völker, 560; see also Hock, 80.

[60] Reprinted in Sturm and Völker, 15–20; these lines form the antepenultimate stanza of the ballad.

[61] Johann Wolfgang von Goethe, *Selected Poems*, ed. Christopher Middleton (Boston: Suhrkamp, 1983), 142–43.

[62] Hock, 69; well-known examples of the period from England and France include Richardson's *Clarissa* (1748) and Diderot's *La Religieuse* (1760).

[63] See Carl Schmitt, *Political Romanticism*, trans. Guy Oakes (Cambridge: The MIT Press, 1986), especially 78–108, for a withering critique of the "occasionalist structure of Romanticism."

[64] Dolf Oehler, *Pariser Bilder I (1830–1848): Antibourgeoise Ästhetik bei Baudelaire, Daumier und Heine* (Frankfurt am Main: Suhrkamp, 1979), 29–30.

[65] Cited in Oehler, 31.

[66] Oehler explores this thesis further in *Ein Höllensturz der Alten Welt* (Frankfurt am Main: Suhrkamp, 1988), the companion volume to *Pariser Bilder*.

[67] Théophile Gautier, "The Dead in Love," *Demons of the Night: Tales of the Fantastic, Madness, and the Supernatural from Nineteenth-Century France*, ed. Joan Kessler (Chicago: U of Chicago P, 1995), 91. Further quotations are from this translation, preceded by the French text printed in Théophile Gautier, "La morte amoureuse," *Récits fantastiques* (Paris: Flammarion, 1981). Hereafter both texts are cited parenthetically in the text.

[68] Mario Praz, *The Romantic Agony*, trans. Angus Davidson (Oxford: Oxford UP, 1933), 4.

[69] E.g., in the works of Ovid, Lucan, and Apuleius. Diane Purkiss, *The Witch in History: Early Modern and Twentieth-Century Representations* (New York: Routledge, 1996), 250–75, stresses the racial anxieties underlying witches' foreignness.

[70] Quoted in Praz, 207.

[71] Théophile Gautier, *Fortunio et autres nouvelles* (Paris: Garnier, 1930), 160.

[72] See, for example, Winfried Menninghaus, *Unendliche Verdopplung: Die frühromantische Grundlegung der Kunsttheorie im Begriff absoluter Selbstreflexion* (Frankfurt am Main: Suhrkamp, 1987).

[73] On this phrase and the political and cultural logic that underlies it, see Marshall Berman, *"All That Is Solid Melts into Air": The Experience of Modernity* (New York: Penguin, 1988).

[74] See Summers, 297–303.

[75] Alexandre Dumas, *Les Mille et Un Fantômes*, précédé de *La Femme au collier de velours*, ed. Anne-Marie Callet-Bianco (Paris: Gallimard, 2006), 242–43. Translations from the dedication of this work are mine, as it does not appear in the English version of Dumas's work; otherwise, English quotations follow Alexandre Dumas, *The Thousand and One Ghosts*, trans. Andrew Brown (London: Hesperus Classics, 2005). Hereafter both texts are cited parenthetically in the text.

[76] "Nos monts Carpathes ne ressemblent point aux montagnes civilisées de votre Occident. Tout ce que la nature a d'étrange et de grandiose s'y présente aux regards dans sa plus grande majesté. Leurs cimes orageuses se perdent dans les nues . . . ; leurs immenses forêts . . . se penchent sur le miroir poli de lacs pareils à des mers. . . . Là le danger est partout" (Our Carpathian Mountains are not at all like the civilised mountains of your western countries. Nature at her most exotic and grandiose here reveals herself in her fullest majesty. Their stormy peaks are lost in the clouds . . . ; their immense pine forests . . . lean over the polished mirror of lakes that are as big as seas. . . . Here, danger is ever-present . . . ; 386–87/118–19).

[77] See introduction.

[78] Oehler, *Höllensturz*, 75–76.

[79] As do, more explicitly, the words of the Russian revolutionary Alexander Herzen (1812–1870), who, also writing in 1848 from the French capital, lamented: "Paris! How long has this name been a lodestar to people! Who did not love and

worship it? But its time has passed. [. . .] Paris has aged and its youthful dreams no longer become it. [. . .] The horrors of June did not bring about recovery. Where will this decrepit vampire obtain more blood of the just . . . ?" Alexander Herzen, *Selected Philosophical Works* (Moscow: Foreign Languages Publishing House, 1956), 376.

[80] Note that the later "forgery" anagrammatically takes up the name of the earlier one. For a discussion, see Jean-François Jeandillou, *Supercheries littéraires: La vie et l'oeuvre des auteurs supposés* (Geneva: Droz, 2001), 140–82; and Julia Abramson, *Learning from Lying: Paradoxes of Literary Mystification* (Newark: U of Delaware P, 2005), 102–15.

Part II: England and France

3: The Bourgeois Vampire and Nineteenth-Century Identity Theft

E NLIGHTENMENT WORKS THAT EMPLOYED the word "vampire" did not present a creature with much personality; the name was above all a term of ridicule — a pejorative designation for someone who held power abusively. Romantic fictions, on the other hand, made this figure of moral bankruptcy and spiritual destitution the very opposite of what it had been: the vampire became an emblem of anguished consciousness, representing psychological interiority as a kind of bottomless pit of imperfectly disavowed culpability. This chapter examines both the chronological and the symbolic middle ground between the "empty" vampires of Enlightenment polemic and the "overfull" vampires of Romantic lyricism. The key to this transformation, we will see, lies in the rise of a new social class. The vampire's newfound character is a reflection of the bourgeoisie's ascendancy — a fact illustrated by the fortunes and misfortunes of one Lord Ruthven and his ill-starred creator.

A gathering in 1816 on the shores of Lake Geneva, where Percy Bysshe Shelley and his young mistress Mary Godwin joined Lord Byron and his physician John Polidori, has become the stuff of literary legend.[1] Famously, the group whiled away time reading German tales of the fantastic in French translation until Byron proposed that everyone write his or her own supernatural narrative. The celebrity of the figures invented by Shelley's teenage girlfriend and Byron's consort has eclipsed the works that two of the greatest English Romantics wrote on the occasion. The eponymous hero of Mary Shelley's *Frankenstein or the Modern Prometheus* has become the icon of the mad scientist, and his creation — the nameless monster often confused with his maker — a symbol of what results when "man tries to play God."[2] Polidori's invention, the vampiric Lord Ruthven, does not enjoy as much recognition value today. However, the villain of "The Vampyre" enjoyed international popularity in the early nineteenth century, and his status as an aristocrat, a traveler, and a seducer unquestionably provided much of the inspiration for Bram Stoker's Count Dracula, the most notorious vampire of them all.

The success of "The Vampyre" was in large part responsible for Polidori's suicide. The work recorded and escalated tensions between Polidori and Byron, and members of the press, unable to believe that an unknown writer had authored the tale, accused him of plagiarism, which drove the already unstable man to even sharper despair. But the question of inauthentic authorial identity is not just a matter of Polidori's unhappy biography. It surfaces apropos of other vampire stories written around the same time and afterward. This chapter focuses on fictional, real, and wholly imaginary instances of impersonation in vampire legends born in the first decades of the nineteenth century, when the monster first gained many features that are so familiar today.

The nineteenth-century vampire possesses an identity chiefly to the extent that his victims invest him with one. Ruthven and his kind are ambitious monsters who exploit gaps in a destabilized social order. As such, their appearance refracts the uncertainties of the world "open to talents," that is, the world of Napoleon's reformed military in France, the newly industrialized economy in England, and the increasingly autonomous force of markets (including, as we will see, literary ones) throughout Western Europe.

It is instructive to begin with a quick look at *Frankenstein,* for Polidori's "Vampyre" responds to the same unease recorded in Mary Shelley's novel. Both works express anxiety about changes in the social order and threats posed by a pair of emergent classes whose battles with one another — as well as the ancien régime, which often succeeded in recruiting one side or the other for its own purposes — shapes much of nineteenth-century history. In a now-classic reading of *Frankenstein,* Franco Moretti offers a Marxist interpretation of the creature:

> Like the proletariat, the monster is denied a name and an individuality. He is the Frankenstein monster; he belongs wholly to his creator. . . . Like the proletariat, he is a *collective* and *artificial* creature. He is not found in nature, but built. [. . .] Reunited and brought back to life in the monster are the limbs of those — the "poor" — whom the breakdown of feudal relations has forced into brigandage, poverty, and death.[3]

Owing his very life to the machinations of another, the anonymous Frankenstein monster has nothing of his own: even his body is composed of parts taken from elsewhere, which therefore do not truly belong to him. His creator abhors him, a sentient being, because of his ugliness, and denies him human status. The monster's situation mirrors that of the urban masses, who also formed a "collective and artificial" body without refinement or political rights when Shelley composed her tale. *Frankenstein* reflects the predicaments of class society during the Industrial Revolution.

Moretti continues:

> Between Frankenstein and the monster there is an ambivalent, dialectical relationship, the same as that which . . . connects capital with

wage-labour. On the one hand, the scientist cannot but create the monster: "often did my human nature turn with loathing from my occupation, whilst still urged on by an eagerness which perpetually increased, I brought my work near to a conclusion." On the other hand, he is immediately afraid of it and wants to kill it, because he realizes he has given life to a creature stronger than himself and of which he cannot henceforth be free.[4]

Frankenstein does not realize that the changes he has wrought in the world implicate him, the "modern Prometheus." The monster, in contrast, sees this connection quite clearly. He demands inclusion in the Family of Man and, moreover, another being like himself as a companion. Shelley's novel demonstrates Hegel's dialectic: the master's position depends on the slave's acceptance of his power.[5] It follows that the creature's monstrosity, which the fiction casts in aesthetic terms, is in fact a political issue. The slave is unwilling to subordinate himself to the master and accept a manmade situation as a natural — and therefore unchangeable — fact; because his defiance is inadmissibly close to tensions in the "real world," the novel makes him appear as an abomination. The monster represents the insights of the author, who, as the daughter of social reformers and the companion of artistic rebels, was attuned to the transformations affecting society; yet at the same time, the novel distances itself from the historical truths it contains by placing them in a fantastic context that questions their reality.

Mary Shelley's work provides a touchstone for understanding the conflicts faced by Western Europe at a pivotal juncture in modern history — the reconfiguration of the relations of production that inaugurated high capitalism. Polidori's "Vampyre" likewise reflects on the changed world and also disavows the social transformation that has taken place, but it does so in a different way. Instead of focusing on the proletariat, as *Frankenstein* does, "The Vampyre" concentrates on its dialectical counterpart, the bourgeoisie. Ruthven is noble in name only. He represents the menace of barbarism without pedigree — cruelty without civilization.

Polidori's "Vampyre" contrasts modern life in northern, industrialized Europe with the traditional ways of southern, Mediterranean countries. The beginning and the end of the story take place in London society; in between, the action unfolds in Italy and Greece. "The Vampyre" juxtaposes the bustling metropolitan capital of England and a quieter, rustic setting. The vampire circulates in both spheres but prefers an English hunting ground. Here, he enjoys freer movement; no one is able to see him for what he truly is where social change has become the norm.

The vampire chooses a victim who has not yet found his way in life, a "young gentleman." This party, Aubrey, was an orphan left with an only sister in the possession of great wealth, by parents who died while he was yet in childhood. Left also to himself by guardians, who thought it their duty merely to take care of his fortune, while they relinquished the more important charge of his mind to the care of mercenary subalterns, he cultivated more his imagination than his judgment. [. . .] He believed all to sympathize with virtue, and thought that vice was thrown in by Providence merely for the picturesque effect of the scene.[6]

"Attached as he was to the romance of solitary hours" (17), the youth falls under the sway of the vampire when he leaves his rooms and solitary reverie to find his way in society. This influence transforms him. As if incubating a sickness, Aubrey withdraws again and the dreamworld in which he lives turns into a nightmarish stupor:

> For days he remained in state; shut up in his room, he saw no one. . . . At last, no longer capable of bearing stillness and solitude, he left his house, roamed from street to street. . . . His dress became neglected, and he wandered, as often exposed to the noonday sun as to the mid-night damps. He was no longer to be recognized. (35)

Stripped of his illusions after the vampire has insinuated himself into his life by becoming a dark companion the young man cannot avoid, Aubrey dies, at the end of the story, in a nervous paroxysm. It is important to note that the youth suffers no physical violence at all: "bad company" is his undoing. Instead of rising to join the ranks of those "in possession of great wealth" that has been inherited, Aubrey loses his way in self-alienation that is also a form of social alienation.

The vampire is named Lord Ruthven. The villain's title, seductive ways, and destructive effect on others have, since the nineteenth century, caused readers to see in him a stylized representation of Polidori's employer, George Gordon, Lord Byron, and to read the tale as a series of allusions to this notorious libertine's exploits. Byron was reputed to have murdered a mistress and to have had an affair with his half-sister. Bisexual, profligate in his finances, an avowed atheist, and radical in his political beliefs, he journeyed throughout Europe in order to flee rumors and creditors, as well as to seek adventure.[7]

The very picture of a decadent aristocrat, Byron certainly provided a model for Ruthven. Indeed, he was in part responsible for Polidori's creation inasmuch as he not only proposed that the company at Villa Diodati write horror stories, but himself authored a fragment in which a mysterious figure named Augustus Darvell contrives his resurrection after death; Byron's unfinished story served as an immediate inspiration for "The Vampyre." We will return to the conflicted relationship between Polidori and Byron in a moment. The point of greatest significance for our immediate purposes, however, is that Ruthven also bears traits that separate him from Byron and the aristocracy in general, and these features make him a representative of an indeterminate — and therefore threatening — class of new men.

Ruthven is named — that is, identified — only long after the narrative has introduced him. The story first presents a figure shrouded in mystery who radiates fascination:

> It happened that in the midst of the dissipations attendant upon London winter, there appeared at the various parties of the leaders of the town a nobleman more remarkable for his singularities, than his rank. He gazed upon the mirth around him, as if he could not participate therein. Apparently, the light laughter of the fair only attracted his attention, that he might by a look quell it and throw fear into those breasts where thoughtlessness reigned. Those who felt this sensation of awe, could not explain whence it arose: some attributed it to the dead grey eye, which, fixing upon the object's face, did not seem to penetrate . . . ; but fell upon the cheek with a leaden ray. . . . His peculiarities caused him to be invited to every house; all wished to see him, and those who had been accustomed to violent excitement, and now felt the weight of ennui, were pleased at having something in their presence capable of engaging their attention. (15–16)

Ruthven owes his magnetism to the "dissipations" of the society that provides him with a hunting ground; the circles in which he moves are made up of "those . . . accustomed to violent excitement," who fear nothing more than "the weight of ennui." The vampire represents a disease that corrupts the social body, but this body is already unhealthy and predisposed to illness because of its licentiousness and thrill seeking.

Why can Ruthven not participate in the general mirth? The text states that he is a "nobleman," yet it also affirms that he is "more remarkable for his singularities, than his rank." Since no illustrious forebears or ancestral lands are mentioned, it is entirely within the logic of the fiction that Ruthven does not, in fact, possess a title at all. Instead, his self-confident bearing and "reputation of a winning tongue" (16) confer upon him the illusion of an aristocratic pedigree. The "Lord" resembles, more than anything else, a high-stakes mountebank like Mesmer or Cagliostro — careerists who dressed themselves in the trappings of science and nobility in order to advance socially.[8] "[A] man entirely absorbed in himself" (17), Ruthven does not display a poet's — or, for that matter, any real person's — psychological depth. This "extraordinary being" (17) is exceptional because he is *all surface* and therefore provides a screen on which the desires of others take form. Ruthven has no visible fangs, ability to fly by night, or any of the other overtly supernatural attributes that are now commonly associated with vampires. The only real quality that Ruthven has is a propensity to mirror others' wishes and, in so doing, to pervert them. Thus, he seduces Aubrey indirectly, by taking advantage of the youth's capacity for self-deception.[9]

The whirl and confusion of London disguise Ruthven better than could any shape-shifting powers (which, incidentally, this vampire does not possess). The gossip and hearsay that fill the long society evenings make it possible for him to set a trap without lifting a finger.

> [Aubrey] . . . learnt that Lord Ruthven . . . was about to travel. Desirous of gaining some information respecting this singular character, who, till now, had only whetted his curiosity, he hinted to his guardians, that it was time to perform the tour, which for many generations has been thought necessary to enable the young to take some rapid steps . . . towards putting themselves upon an equality with the aged. . . . They consented: and Aubrey immediately mentioning his intentions to Lord Ruthven, was surprised to receive from him a proposal to join him. Flattered [by] such a mark of esteem, . . . he gladly accepted it, and in a few days they had passed the circling waters. (18)

On the continent, Aubrey encounters enchantment in the form of a peasant girl named Ianthe and the rustic world in which she lives. This idyll vanishes abruptly when, late one night during a violent downpour, Aubrey seeks refuge from the elements: "The thunders, for a moment silent, allowed him to hear the dreadful shrieks of a woman mingled with the stifled, exultant mockery of a laugh, continued in one almost unbroken sound" (26). Aubrey rushes to the woman's aid and struggles with her assailant, but in vain. The enemy escapes, and the youth is left with the mortal remains of Ianthe, "Upon her throat . . . the marks of teeth having opened the vein" (27). In a simpler, country setting, Ruthven's predatory nature expresses itself more openly.

"The Vampyre" weaves together the strands of character, plot, and imagery combined to more delicate effect in the novels of sense, sensibility, and sincerity that descend from Rousseau.[10] The rustic world in which Aubrey sees the promise of contentment is a Rousseauian landscape of primitive virtue. In *Julie, or the New Heloise*, Saint-Preux describes the metropolitan vice at the root of all others: "C'est le premier inconvénient des grandes villes que les hommes y deviennent autres que ce qu'ils ne sont, et que la société leur donne pour ainsi dire un être différent du leur" (The main objection to large cities is that men become other than what they are, and society imparts to them, as it were, a being other than their own).[11] Saint-Preux's sojourn in Paris, away from the beneficent influence of Julie, renders him, by his own account, "vil, bas, méprisable" (vile, base, despicable), exposed as he is to what his beloved calls "la contagion des ambitieux" (the contagion of the ambitious).[12] In contrast, provincial Switzerland, like the distant islands Saint-Preux visits on his sea-voyage, offers an earthly paradise.[13] Here, where true hearts discern "le mérite dans tous les rangs" (merit in all ranks), even the "sang à demi glacé" (half-congealed blood)[14] of old men is warmed by the solicitude of the angelic Julie.

"The Vampyre" spills Rousseauian blood of sentiment all over the page.[15] The same pastoral world where Aubrey pursues his ill-starred romance is home to another, equally Romantic, but less wholesome element: robbers. Though he suspects the worst of his companion, Aubrey continues to travel with Ruthven, even after Ianthe's death. On their journeys, the two are waylaid by a band of brigands. The cutthroats wound Ruthven — mortally, it seems — but this act of seeming cruelty and destruction in fact signifies solidarity between the rustic outlaws and the big-city charlatan, for it permits the Lord to extract an oath from Aubrey:

> "Assist me! You may save me — you may do more than that — I mean not life, I heed the death of my existence as little as that of the passing day; but you may save my honor, your friend's honor." — "How? Tell me how? I would do anything," replied Aubrey. — "I need but little, my life ebbs apace — I cannot explain the whole — but if you would conceal all you know of me, my honor were free from stain in the world's mouth — and if my death were unknown for some time in England — I — I but life." — "It shall not be known." — "Swear!" cried the dying man raising himself with exultant violence. "Swear by all your soul reveres, by all your nature fears, swear that for a year and a day you will not impart your knowledge of my crimes or my death to any living being in any way, whatever may happen, or whatever you may see." — His eyes seemed bursting from their sockets; "I swear!" said Aubrey. (30–31)

Ruthven then expires. The same robbers responsible for his death steal the corpse and place it on a mountaintop, "according to a promise they had given his lordship, that it should be exposed to the first cold ray of the moon that rose after his death" (31). When Aubrey returns to England, he finds that a certain Earl of Marsden has received his sister's hand. He recognizes Lord Ruthven in the Earl, but his oath dooms him to silence and, before long, to death.

"The governing body of [Ruthven's] life is lunar," Nina Auerbach has noted.[16] The vampire's "affinity . . . is with the bloodless, the inorganic, [and] the ghostly"; the monster's kin are Shakespeare's "fairies or phantoms,"[17] not human beings. These observations accurately point toward the "occult," seemingly immaterial sources of Ruthven's power. However, the vampire's apparent connection to the imaginary world of the Elizabethans should not conceal this monster's modernity. Ruthven is not only a false aristocrat but also, more fundamentally, a false person — that is, he is not really a person at all. The supernatural strictures that govern him are closer to Rousseau's law of the heart (albeit in an inverted, Satanic form) than to the gentle constraints of Shakespeare's sprites. Ruthven embodies movement and change; he goes from metropolitan salon to rural hovel, destroying the wellborn and the poor alike. Across Europe, he transgresses class lines and upsets the traditional stratification of social life. This mobility, dynamism, and "in-between" status make him a noxious representative of the middle classes that, when Polidori wrote his tale, were on the move throughout Europe, but especially in industrial England.

"Tant de gens veulent monter, qu'il est toujours aisé de descendre" (So many wish to climb, that it is always easy to descend),[18] Julie had warned Saint-Preux in Rousseau's novel. In the context of changing social relations, Aubrey's bond with Ruthven resembles nothing so much as a contract for wage labor. The young man's continental voyage — "the Grand Tour"[19] — is supposed to serve as his induction into adult life as a member of the upper class. Instead, it demotes him in status: besides leading to the splendors of Athens and Rome, the pair's travels take them to the rustic, Balkanized lands into which classical antiquity declined; Ruthven's robber-associates might well be Serbian *hajduks*.[20] Aubrey does not, technically speaking, work for Ruthven, and, in contrast to laborers, he belongs to him not in body but in soul. However, the fiction's transformation of his bondage from a matter of material obligation to one of spiritual constraint — this is what the oath means — makes the vampire's grip even more complete.

The truly monstrous quality of Ruthven lies in the fact that he creates a slave without at all appearing to do so. To all appearances, Aubrey retains his liberty, and his actions are those of a free man. The youth's situation resembles that of workers who are "free" to deny their labor to capitalists, but who dare not do so for fear of the effects this action might have on their dependents and loved ones. Ruthven, that cold, "bloodless," "inorganic," and "ghostly" controller of Aubrey's waking and dreaming life, represents the subtle tyranny of the factory owner, in contrast to the ostentatious displays of power characteristic of the ancien régime. The vampire's lunar rhythms of death and rebirth follow the unnatural patterns of life that, as Marx observed, "[prolong] the working day beyond the limits of the natural day, into the night."[21]

The ending of Polidori's tale explicitly states that the vampire belongs to a *class* of beings with a corrosive effect on the social body. Having surmised from Aubrey's fatal fit of nerves that something is amiss, "The guardians hastened to protect Miss Aubrey; but when they arrived, it was too late. Lord Ruthven had disappeared, and Aubrey's sister had glutted the thirst of a *vampyre!*" (40). The indefinite article "a" before "*vampyre*" means that Ruthven exemplifies a type; further attacks from him and his kind threaten the sons and daughters of England.[22]

In the context of the symbolic economy of the fantastic in literature and drama, on the one hand, and material economies of production and finance, on the other, it is worth remarking that the exploitation of Polidori's tale by cunning manipulators of the market amounted to a kind of vampirism. Critics panned "The Vampyre," but the public loved it.[23] In England, the *New Monthly Magazine* published the story on April 1, 1819; it soon appeared as an independent volume and was translated into French and German. As Montague Summers puts it, "It were [*sic*] not easy to overestimate the astounding sensation."[24] Readers gobbled up the tale in large part because they could read Lord Ruthven's adventures as a series of thinly disguised references to Lord Byron's exploits. Profit-hungry editors across Europe ascribed Polidori's work to the scandalous celebrity, and the author even had to defend himself against the charge of stealing the material. As a result (and as we noted at the outset of the chapter), the man Mary Shelley called "poor Polidori," having reaped no material rewards and indeed having suffered calumny for his talents, killed himself in obscurity not long afterward.

Byron, in turn, was vexed by the undead impostor to no end. "What do I know of Vampires?" he indignantly asked a friend in a letter.[25] His embarrassing association with Polidori and what he considered a mediocre work haunted him. In fact, Byron knew a great deal about the monster. Works from his pen have vampires in them (e.g., *The Giaour* and *Don Juan*), and he called the fragment featuring Augustus Darvell (published in appendix to *Mazeppa* in 1819) upon which Polidori had based his tale "my real 'Vampyre.'"[26] Byron was disingenuous: the English Romantics did not avoid vampires. Both he and Shelley owned books containing references to the monster,[27] and the Countess Potocka in their company at Villa Diodati in Geneva was related to Jan Potocki, the eccentric Polish nobleman who wrote *Manuscript Found at Saragossa* — a work which centers on a young officer's encounter with undead sisters.[28]

There is something of cruel poetic justice in Polidori's misfortune. As Auerbach remarks, "The vampire fragment Byron began at Villa Diodati in 1816 and Polidori's 1819 tale . . . are symbiotic." She continues:

> In his poetry, Byron generally displays himself in all the flair of the first person, but his Darvell has no existence independent of his traveling companion's awe. The real Polidori watched his master's histrionics with diagnostic resentment; the companion Byron creates brims with a tenderness that consecrates the apparent death . . . of his brilliant, strangely debilitated friend. The fragment is less a tale of terror than an account of a romantic friendship which only a vampire could inspire.[29]

Auerbach concludes that Polidori's work "is a sardonic development of Byron's material. The tale is Polidori's own, but it is steeped in Byron and Byronism."[30] Ruthven kills the girl Aubrey loves and costs the young man first his sanity (when it becomes clear that the vampire has claimed — or will soon claim — his sister), then his life. Aubrey falls prey to the monster because of the Lord's charisma and beguilement, and the youth's folly is that he offers friendship to a fiend. "Out of a hating, needing companionship between men," Auerbach concludes, "came. . . . the Romantic vampire."[31]

Yet if Byron and Polidori's vampires embody the forces of psychic interdependence and resentful intimacy, the further career of the Romantic vampire they co-created reveals nothing but cold-blooded calculation. The improbably named French critic Daniel Sangsue has pointed out that Charles Nodier, the impresario of "The Vampyre" in France, played a canny game with the reading public and theater goers. In 1812–13, Nodier spent nine months in Laibach (today, Ljubljana) editing the *Télégraphe*, the official journal of the French administration in the "Illyrian Provinces." During his tenure there, he displayed what Sangsue describes as a *position voltairienne*[32] on the subject of vampires, which he mentioned only once (and briefly) in a discussion of native bardic traditions; moreover, Nodier's knowledge of the undead derived not from investigation conducted on-site, but from a book, the *Voyage en Dalmatie* by the Abbé Fortis (published in 1778). When the tale written by Polidori but attributed to Byron appeared in French translation, Nodier found himself in the ideal position to use a text that belonged to others for his own aims. Perverting a putative review of "The Vampyre" in the anti-liberal *Drapeau blanc* — whose motto of reluctant royalism was "Vive le Roi! . . . quand même" (Long live the King . . . all the same) — for purposes of self-aggrandizement, Nodier, instead of critiquing the "Byronic" tale, discussed at length his own understanding of vampirism, which he claimed was based on firsthand experience. Thereby, as Sangsue puts it, "Nodier established himself, in the eyes of readers and other agents in the field of literature, as an authority on vampires (*maître ès vampires*)."[33]

Nodier's underlying motivation was strictly mercenary. In his false recension, he slyly announced that the subject matter of "The Vampyre" "offrira . . . tout cet attirail de mélodrame à la Melpomène des boulevards; et quel succès alors ne lui est pas réservé!" (will provide . . . all the appurtenances of melodrama to the Melpomene of the boulevards — what success will it not enjoy!).[34] This statement publicized a project of his own. At the beginning of the following year (1820), Nodier oversaw the publication of *Lord Ruthwen* [sic], *ou les Vampires,* by Cyprien Bérard. The subtitle of the book reads: "publié par l'auteur de *Jean Sbogar* et de *Thérèse Aubert*." Nodier, already known for the latter works, thereby assured a greater level of interest for a book by an unknown party (identified only as "C.B.") and, at the same time, avoided direct association with a quickly composed piece of hack writing. This set the stage for Nodier's next move. In June, the Théâtre de la Porte Saint-Martin produced a melodramatic version of "The Vampyre." The authors of the piece were Achille de Jouffroy, Adolphe Carmouche, and Nodier himself; significantly, the latter collaborated anonymously.

Sure enough, Nodier's vampire melodrama was a smash, and within weeks six more vampire plays had appeared.[35] Throughout the 1820s, the European market was flooded by stage productions featuring the undead (the most enduring example of which is August Marschner's 1828 opera *Der Vampyr*).[36] As Sangsue observes,

> The boulevard theater, at this time, offered significant earnings to authors who wrote for it; however, such activity was detrimental to their symbolic prestige. . . . Nodier wanted to profit from the opportunity . . . , but was at the same time careful not to taint, through participation in popular literature, the image of the sophisticated man of letters he was crafting for himself — a pursuit that later led to his induction into the French Academy.[37]

Nodier, parasitically feeding off Byron's celebrity and the work falsely attributed to the notorious Lord, established himself as an authority on vampires and made some quick money, all the while retaining an appearance of sovereign detachment above the vulgar market and unseemly world of popular theater. The coup was worthy of Lord Ruthven himself.

"Positive truths do not flatter the imagination," Nodier wrote in his fake review of Polidori's tale, "We know where we are in politics; in poetry we have reached the age of the nightmare and the vampires."[38] This statement encapsulates the essential concerns of the study at hand. Nightmares and vampires are code words for the uncertainties engendered by modernization.

In his study of fantastic literature, José Monleón draws attention to the fact that the disappearance of estate society and the rise of manufacture in the eighteenth century effaced long-standing markers of class difference: "Within the new economic configuration, it became more difficult to define social relations and to assign the proper images or the appropriate spaces to the different elements of society."[39] Gothic literature, Monleón notes, developed during this key period of modernization. When it showcases confining spaces (castles, abbeys, and ruins) and despots who lord over them (e.g., Matthew Lewis's Ambrosio or Ann Radcliffe's Schedoni), Gothic literature implicitly contrasts an "alien yet proximate world"[40] located in southern, Catholic Europe with the "free" society of the north, especially England.

In the fictional productions of the nineteenth century, Monleón continues, an "internalization of monstrosity"[41] occurred:

> Frankenstein's monster does not need medieval chambers of con-
> finement in order to emerge; he does not require monks and inqui-
> sitions in order to adopt a terrorific image. On the contrary, he
> moves about civilized centers and travels through Europe, retrac-
> ing the Napoleonic invasions. In Polidori's ["The Vampyre"], part
> of the action does occur in Greece, . . . but contemporary London
> salons also make their appearance. . . . Fantastic literature under-
> took . . . a concentric journey which [brought] unreason, through
> time and distance, from the periphery to the center, from barba-
> rism to civilization.[42]

"The Vampyre" trades in the same political currency as *Frankenstein*. The
social conflict in the latter work is much more visible: the Faustian hero
embodies the drive of modernization and his pathos-laden creature the
human cost this process entails. Polidori's tale, in contrast, plays out in
London society and rural Greece; it conspicuously avoids reference to
science, industry, and other forces of change. However, the narrative
framework, which seems pre-Revolutionary — or, better still, entirely
indifferent to Revolution — belies the picture it contains. At its center
are a young man, whose station at the crossroads of life mirrors that of a
society faced with an uncertain future, and a diabolical *parvenu* possessing distinction that, upon closer inspection, has nothing to substantiate it;
this "self-made man" contrives to level social distinctions by promoting
himself and undoing others.

Ruthven's brigand-associates on the European continent do not appear
in London, but the parallels that the tale establishes between overt barbarism in the Balkans and the vampire's more subtle forms of predation in
England (which exact a similarly horrible human cost) point toward a fluid,
criminal element, whose contours are difficult to define. Here, Polidori's
tale connects with a broad web of fictions that explore the mystifications
of modernization. Balzac's *Histoire des Treize* (1833–39, comprised of
the novels *Ferragus, The Duchess of Langeais,* and *The Girl with the Golden
Eyes*), features a shadowy organization called the *Dévorants* made up of parties from the most varied stations in life. The members of this fraternity
(whose number — thirteen — conjures up the idea of a witches' Sabbath)
unite in a conspiracy of self-interest that defies all social order in the years
of the Napoleonic Empire, when the world was being remade along lines
whose ultimate shape no one could foresee. In the twentieth century, silent-
film pioneer Louis Feuillade's serial *Les Vampires* (1915–16) recounts the
exploits of a band of assassins, blackmailers, and thieves so accomplished
in crime that their victims mistake them for supernatural beings. Like these
works, Polidori's "Vampyre" intimates that a society without clear demar-
cations of status breeds lawlessness and terror.

* * *

The melodramatic stage vampires that multiplied after the publication of Polidori's tale did not arise from deeply conflicted interpersonal psychological dynamics. Indeed, they reacted in large measure against such complexities. The term "melodrama" (which is composed of the Greek words for "song" and "theater") originated in the eighteenth century to describe a spoken text accompanied by music.[43] By the early nineteenth century, melodrama had become a fixed form of theatrical entertainment with interludes of song and dance, featuring a starkly delineated opposition between good and evil, dramatis personae that reflected this simplified moral universe, and staging techniques that emphasized spectacle and played to the audience's emotions more than to their intellects.

The melodrama flourished in a disreputable milieu. In Paris, the Boulevard du Temple, where theaters were located, was also called the "Boulevard du Crime."[44] In other European cities, the theaters that produced melodramas were often similarly ill-famed. Roxana Stuart, in her study of stage vampires, quotes a German traveler to London in 1826, who describes a scene that might equally well have been encountered on the Continent:

> The most striking thing . . . is the unheard-of coarseness and brutality of the audiences. Freedom . . . degenerates into the rudest license, and it is not uncommon . . . to hear some coarse expression shouted from the galleries. . . . This is followed . . . either by loud laughter or approbation. . . . Another cause for the absence of respectable families is the resort of hundreds of those unhappy women with whom [the city] swarms. [. . .] Between the acts they fill the large and handsome "foyers" and exhibit their effrontery in the most revolting manner.[45]

At theaters where audiences flocked to see melodramas, the evening's entertainment consisted of sensation, which was to be found in equal measures onstage and off. Vampires thrived inasmuch as their predations mirrored the nightly assaults on virtue that occurred in the wings, among audience members, and on the streets outside theaters. The largely illiterate and impoverished masses beheld a spectacle on the boards that possessed the clarity that real life lacked.

The playbills advertising an evening's entertainment represent visually and in condensed form the air of lurid excitement surrounding productions, and they illuminate the profile the vampire assumed at this historical juncture. Stuart reprints an advertisement publicizing James Robinson Planché's vampire play, which was produced at the English Opera House.[46] "THE VAMPIRE" occupies the center of the announcement, but it is part of a package including other attractions: an operetta ("Woman's Will — A Riddle!"), a farce ("Whang Fong: Or, How Remarkable!"), and a room with exotic decoration (the "Illuminated Oriental Garden"). The author of the piece receives no billing, but the actors and composers do. The emphasis falls squarely on the visual and acoustic images of the drama, as well as the sensational nature of the material:

> THE PIECE IS FOUNDED ON the various traditions concerning THE VAMPIRES, which assert that they are *spirits* deprived of all *Hope of Futurity*, by the Crimes committed in their Mortal State — but, that they are permitted to roam the Earth, in whatever Forms they please, with *Supernatural Powers of Fascination* — and, that they cannot be destroyed, as long as they sustain their dreadful Existence, by imbibing the BLOOD of FEMALE VICTIMS, whom they are first compelled to marry.

The publicity claims an ancient pedigree for the vampire and seeks to legitimate the play with reference to folk beliefs, but the "various traditions" are in fact of extremely recent origin. Nodier invented the conceit that the vampire must marry his victims and that their exsanguination renews the monster's life. Planché borrowed heavily from the French author, just as Nodier had taken freely from Polidori, and Polidori had drawn on Byron. The guise of antiquity in fact signals the piece's modernity. These creatures, which "roam the Earth in whatever Forms they please" and exercise uncanny "*Powers of Fascination*," embody the enchantments of the spectacle itself, and their sinister features refract the dehumanizing social conditions for which the utopian ending (in which vice is punished and virtue rewarded) provides an imaginary antidote.

History surfaces as a vampire in Planché's play. The piece, subtitled "The Bride of the Isles," takes place in an Ossianic setting — that is, in a landscape encoded with the myths of premodern Scottish culture.[47] The action unfolds in "Basaltic Caverns" and a "Gothic" castle.[48] Equally, the scenery calls to mind the world of romance popularized by the works of Walter Scott, with their vivid portrayal of the rugged and valorous citizenry of independent-minded Scotland.[49] The characters, with the exception of the undead interloper, belong to the two classes of a stratified society, the peasantry and the aristocracy. On the one hand, there are the bibulous McSwill and his moralizing wife Bridget, the attendant Robert, and the young couple Andrew and Effie. On the other, the play presents Lord Ronald and his daughter, Lady Margaret. The opening sequence, in which a sleeping Margaret beholds a vision warning her of imminent danger, features spirits with Shakespearean names that further inscribe the play in a fantasy-filled, premodern world.

"Impostor" (79) is the key word in Planché's work. Ruthven surprises Lord Ronald and Lady Margaret when he takes the stage because, earlier, the arrival of the "Earl of Marsden" had been announced. Ronald knew him by another name, as the traveling companion of his departed son, and he believed him dead after an attack by brigands. The patriarch explains:

When called . . . by the sudden illness of my now lost son to Athens,
I found Lord Ruthven, with whom he had contracted an intimacy,
hanging over his sick couch, and bestowing on him the attentions
of a brother. Such behavior naturally endear'd him to me; and after
my poor boy's death, his lordship being, like myself, an enthusias-
tic admirer of the beauties of nature and the works of art, became
the constant companion of my excursions. [. . .] Returning to
Athens, . . . one evening, we were attack'd by some banditti. [. . .]
Ruthven threw himself before me, and receiv'd the ruffian's saber in
his own breast. [. . .] Gallant, unfortunate Ruthven! (64–66)

Margaret has agreed, without meeting the man, to wed the elder brother
of the supposedly deceased Ruthven out of the love she conceived for a
family that showed such kindness to her own. The alibi Ruthven has con-
cocted blurs the distinction between his "real" and "fake" identities. The
question about his "true" self is unanswerable, just as mortals are unable
to combat the evil he embodies. It takes a higher power to stop the vampire, and a higher power to understand his nature. The rightful order
under Heaven prevails only through divine intervention: the curtain falls
after "[a] terrific peal of thunder is heard . . . [and] a thunderbolt strikes
Ruthven" (112).

The characters saved from Ruthven never know exactly what has happened. In historical terms, however, the vampire's supernatural being is
made up of the dangers of social change and the decomposition of a feudal
world. Ruthven wishes to expedite his marriage to Margaret because his
time for renewing the contract that assures his undead existence is running
out. When he concocts a story that "business of the utmost importance
recalls me to London" (73), his words point through the archaizing veil to
their real referent: the world of commerce in the nineteenth century. Likewise, the oath that the vampire extracts from his new company, as in Polidori's tale, has less to do with chivalry and honor than with the economic
calculations characteristic of industry. Perforce, Ruthven must find, marry,
and destroy new victims in yearly intervals. This schedule coincides with
the rotations of the sun and the cycle of the seasons, but it is in fact controlled by the moon, which reanimates the vampire.[50] Here, the unsteady
nighttime planet that has been associated since antiquity with witchcraft
and magic scans as a symbol for the rhythms of the man-made world of
production — a second, artificial "nature."

Ruthven's attack on one family represents an attack on the basic unit
of social order. The "Holy Family," to borrow Marx and Engel's formulation, signifies on two levels: for the newly formed proletariat, it represents
the harmony disrupted by the move from the city to the country, away
from an agrarian life to the unnatural conditions in factories; in a larger,
yet complementary sense, it reads as the continuity between generations

and the security represented by the vanished feudal system (whose vestiges remained in the nineteenth century, if increasingly only in form). The tremendous celebrity that the vampire enjoyed on city stages throughout Europe reflects the hunger of metropolitan audiences for a clear-cut view of the world opposing the confusion of modernization. Lord Ronald, if misguided, is still a good man, and his servants, if also fallible, are good people, too. Ruthven, who embodies the tumults of change, is starkly evil.

The vampire's destruction at the end of melodramas provided wish fulfillment for a world steeped in the nightmare of history.[51] Happy endings substituted light for darkness as a kind of narcotic — "opium for the masses." In a more rarefied, artistic sphere, such an artificial paradise was harder to come by. The work of Charles Meryon (1821–68) is a case in point. The etchings by this contemporary of Baudelaire have been lauded by Walter Benjamin, in a customary tone of melancholy, as "the death mask of old Paris."[52] An image first captured by Meryon is likely to be recognized even by parties lacking all but the most cursory familiarity with art history, namely the sight of the contemplative gargoyle perched atop Notre Dame and overlooking the city in undying contempt. The picture is accompanied by a couplet from the artist: "Insatiable Vampire, l'éternelle luxure/Sur la grande Cité convoite sa pâture" (Eternal Excess, the insatiable vampire/Lusts, above the city, after its prey).[53] Meryon's vampire astride the cathedral embodies perennial vice mocking modernization and the idea of improvement. Though dead, the past lives on.

* * *

Few readers today, in a media landscape teeming with the undead, will have the patience to make it to the end of *Varney the Vampire* (1847)[54] — at over 850 double-columned pages, it is the mid-nineteenth century's equivalent of Gothic soap opera. However, this Victorian "penny dreadful," besides providing an important relay between Polidori and Bram Stoker, illustrates the political nature of the vampire with exceptional clarity, for the fiction presents Varney's "birth" as the result of civil war.

After 196 chapters in which he preys on a seemingly endless array of young beauties, "Varney opens the vast store-house of his memory" to a "liberal-minded but anxious clergyman" (847–48).[55] The vampire, whose undead career has consisted of repeated acts of imposture, reveals that he first became what he now is when universal strife gripped England:

> In the reign of the First Charles, . . . I was a well-paid agent in some of the political movements which graced and disgraced that period.
> [. . .]
> I took no prominent part in the commotions . . . , but I saw the head of a king held up in its gore at Whitehall as a spectacle for the multitude.

There were thousands of persons in England who had aided to bring about that result. . . . Among these were many . . . men, who had been quite willing to shake the stability of a throne so far as the individual occupying it was concerned; but who certainly never contemplated the destruction of monarchy. . . .

They had raised a spirit they could not quell again, and this was a fact which the stern, harsh man, Cromwell, with whom I had many interviews, was aware of.

My house was admirably adapted for the purposes of secrecy . . . , and I became a thriving man from the large sums I received for aiding the escape of distinguished loyalists. (854)

Varney — or "Mortimer" (857), as he was then known — exercised no clear profession. Instead, he enriched himself parasitically on the disorder besetting his country. Happy to help royalists for personal gain, he just as readily assisted "His Highness" (855), Oliver Cromwell.

Vaguely intuiting the metaphysical stakes of political events, the vampire speaks of a "spirit" the English "could not quell again." However, the date at which Varney reports that he first rose from the grave leaves no room to doubt the historical dimensions of his vampiric condition:

I staggered to my feet, the scene around me was a churchyard, . . . my clothes hung about me in tattered remnants. The damp smell of the grave hung about them, I met an aged man. . . . He looked at me with a shudder. . . . A peal of bells came . . . upon the night air.
"What means that?" said I.
"Why, this is the anniversary of the Restoration." (858)

Varney describes how he wandered off into darkness, now bearing the curse of the undead: "I had not yet fully awakened to all the horror of what I was" (858). By implication, the twilight state of the vampire is also that of the land whose misfortunes his violently interrupted — and abruptly resumed — life reflects.

Significantly, and as if the author of *Varney the Vampire* were unwilling to admit the reality of the historical horror, the protagonist's "vampirization" is attributed to an action that nothing in the story seems to motivate. Enticed by Cromwell's offer of even more money if he betrays a man he has promised to smuggle to Holland, the future vampire kills his own child for no apparent reason. To underscore the incongruity of this shocking occurrence, the passage is worth citing at length:

It [Cromwell's request to hand over the fugitive] was not a very agreeable affair, view it in whatever light I might; but as regarded Cromwell, I knew my jeopardy, and it would be perceived that I had not hesitated a moment in obeying him. Moreover, I considered, . . . I should have a good round sum by the transaction, which added to the fifty pounds I had received from the royalists, made the affair appear to me in a pleasant enough light. Indeed, I was revolving in my mind as I went along, whether it would not be worth while, almost entirely to attach myself to the protector.

"If," I reasoned with myself, "I should do that, and still preserve myself a character with the royalists, I should thrive."

But it will be seen that an adverse circumstance put an end to all those dreams.

When we reached the door of my house, the first thing I saw was my son wiping his brow, as if he had undergone some fatigue; he ran up to me, and catching me by the arm, whispered to me. I was so angered at the moment, that heedless of what I did, and passion getting the mastery over me, I with my clenched fist struck him to the earth. [. . .] I had murdered him. (856)

From an aesthetic viewpoint, this narrative jump — like the many other twists and turns in the story — is a mark of bad writing. In terms of the political logic at work in *Varney the Vampire,* however, this fault in the novel's design shows the vampire for what he is: a figuration of the self-divided English Commonwealth and its legacy, where the bonds uniting men — brother with brother, father with son — have been destroyed.

Varney's apparently gratuitous murder of his son also makes perverse sense in light of the fact that *nothing* he is does is inherently meaningful. Just as the vampire will serve one employer as willingly as another, the emotions of one moment are as good as those of the next in determining his actions. Varney's fateful act of infanticide represents the sheer arbitrariness of a life with no loyalties. His existence as a vampire, in which he assumes a series of inauthentic identities to impose upon succeeding generations of English, renews itself through betrayal. Thus, Varney, who also commands a silver tongue,[56] could be yet another name for Ruthven, or vice versa. These two vampires are lost in the game of predatory impersonation to the point that any identity they may once have possessed is now just as insubstantial and weak — and just as eerily powerful — as the light in the night sky. The paradoxically luminous darkness with which they surround themselves is not supernatural, as the conventions of fiction would have it, but an emanation of the earth and human affairs.

The integrity of the United Kingdom — in both a spiritual and a material sense — provides the core concern of the work explored in the next chapter, Bram Stoker's *Dracula.* Although the English Civil Wars had been over for more than three hundred years, British imperialism was at its zenith. Stoker's vampire surpasses Ruthven and Varney because his wily command of international affairs rivals the collective intelligence of those in the land he invades. *Dracula,* written on the eve of the twentieth century, augurs the sunset of British power over the globe.

Notes

[1] For the facts and discussion, see David Lorne Macdonald, *Poor Polidori* (Toronto: U of Toronto P, 1991).

[2] Hollywood film adaptations, most famously the one by James Whale in 1931, have brought out this aspect of the tale; see Susan E. Lederer, *Frankenstein: Penetrating the Secrets of Nature* (New Brunswick: Rutgers UP, 2002), 31–51. The first cinematic adaptation of the material, curiously enough, was made under the patronage of none other than master inventor Thomas Edison in 1910. The sixteen-minute film, which was directed by J. Searle Dawley, portrays the monster's "birth" (out of a vat of steaming chemicals) as decay in reverse: first a mass of bones, then an articulated skeleton, and finally a flesh-and-blood body.

[3] Franco Moretti, *Signs Taken for Wonders: Essays in the Sociology of Literary Forms,* trans. Susan Fischer, David Forgacs, and David Miller (London: Verso, 1983), 85.

[4] Moretti, 85.

[5] See the immensely influential (and, given its subject, surprisingly lucid) book by Alexandre Kojève, *Introduction to the Reading of Hegel: Lectures on the Phenomenology of Spirit,* trans. James H. Nichols (Ithaca: Cornell UP, 1980).

[6] John Polidori, *Polidori's Vampyre* (Doylestown: Wildside Press, 2002), 16–17; hereafter cited parenthetically in the text.

[7] Fiona MacCarthy, in *Byron: Life and Legend* (New York: Farrar, Straus and Giroux, 2004), offers an excellent biography and concludes with a discussion of "The Byron Cult" (525–74).

[8] See chapter 6.

[9] "[A]llowing his imagination to picture everything that flattered its propensity to extravagant ideas, [Aubrey] soon formed this object into the hero of a romance, and determined to observe the offspring of his fancy, rather than the person before him" (17–18).

[10] This literary parentage in turn connects with that of Frankenstein. See David Marshall, *The Surprising Effects of Sympathy: Marivaux, Diderot, Rousseau, and Mary Shelley* (Chicago: U of Chicago P, 1988), 178–234.

[11] Jean-Jacques Rousseau, *Julie ou la Nouvelle Héloïse,* ed. R. Pomeau (Paris: Garnier, 1960), 251; *Julie or the New Heloise,* trans. Philip Stewart and Jean Vaché (Hanover: University Press of New England, 1997), 223.

[12] Rousseau, 273, 283/240, 249.

[13] The comparison is made most explicitly in Part IV, Letters X and XI (Rousseau, 422–72/363–401), in particular when Saint-Preux likens the Helvetian "Elysium" at Clarens to Tinian and Juan Fernandez: "Julie, le bout du monde est à votre porte!" (Julie, the ends of the earth are at your gate!; 454/387).

[14] Rousseau, 541, 540/454.

[15] That said, for all his apparent frankness, Rousseau remains an elusive thinker. Christopher Frayling and Robert Wokler have argued for a reappraisal of his works on the basis of less well-known remarks, particularly his *Lettre à Christophe de Beaumont* (1762); they conclude: "[Rousseau's] main contribution to social anthropology stems not so much from his praise of primitive peoples as from his account of [a] form of animal transfiguration — . . . that of a civilised man into a vampire, that is, into a beast created, nurtured, and bred by man himself. . . . [Rousseau's] boldest and most imaginative ideas about mankind pertain . . . to the connections he perceived between the animal and the human essence of both our physical form and our social behaviour. . . . [H]is anthropology revolved . . . around the double metamorphosis from natural beast to man to beast of our own making." "From the orang-utan to the vampire: towards an anthropology of Rousseau," in *Rousseau after Two Hundred Years: Proceedings of the Cambridge Bicentennial Colloquium*, ed. R. A. Leigh (Cambridge: Cambridge UP, 1978), 109–110.

[16] Nina Auerbach, *Our Vampires, Ourselves* (Chicago: U of Chicago P, 1995), 24.

[17] Auerbach, 27.

[18] Rousseau, 282/248.

[19] James Buzard, in "The Grand Tour and After (1660–1840)" (*The Cambridge Companion to Travel Writing*, eds. Peter Hulme and Tim Youngs [Cambridge: Cambridge University Press], 37–52), discusses the origins and social role of the practice; see also the documents collected in Paul Fussell, *The Norton Book of Travel* (New York: W. W. Norton, 1987), 127ff.

[20] See chapter 1.

[21] See the preceding chapter.

[22] Like the cadaverous Falkland in William Godwin's *Caleb Williams* (1794), Polidori's vampire is obsessed with outward appearances; however, whereas Falkland is a squire who embodies the established order of chivalry, Ruthven represents a new constellation of power that impersonates the old distinctions Godwin's villain would preserve. On Godwin's politics and poetics, see Gary Kelly, *The English Jacobin Novel 1780–1805* (Oxford: Oxford UP, 1976), 179–260.

[23] Macdonald, 188–90.

[24] Montague Summers, *The Vampire* (London: Senate, 1995), 289.

[25] Quoted in Macdonald, 184.

[26] Quoted in Aribert Schroeder, *Vampirismus: Seine Entwicklung vom Thema zum Motiv* (Frankfurt am Main: Akademische Verlagsgesellschaft, 1973), 200.

[27] Schroeder, 193.

[28] Schroeder, 205.

[29] Auerbach, 15–16.

[30] Auerbach, 16.

[31] Auerbach, 16.

[32] Daniel Sangsue, "Nodier et le commerce des vampires," in *Nodier*, ed. Georges Zaragoza (Dijon: Éditions universitaires de Dijon, 1998), 102.

[33] Sangsue, 106.

[34] Sangsue, 106–7.

[35] Roxana Stuart, *Stage Blood: Vampires of the Nineteenth-Century Stage* (Bowling Green: Bowling Green University Popular Press, 1994), 55; see also Sangsue, 109.

[36] For an overview of these plays, see Summers, 303–11; and Stefan Hock, *Die Vampyrsagen und ihre Verwertung in der deutschen Literatur* (Berlin: Alexander Duncker, 1900), 97–108. See also Dieter Sturm and Dieter Völker, *Von denen Vampiren* (Frankfurt am Main: Suhrkamp, 1994), for a discussion of the "Vampirmode" (vampire fashion; 554) in Germany.

[37] Sangsue, 109.

[38] Quoted in Stuart, 46.

[39] José B. Monleón, *A Specter Is Haunting Europe: A Sociohistorical Approach to the Fantastic* (Princeton: Princeton UP, 1990), 55.

[40] Monleón, 34.

[41] Monleón, 63.

[42] Monleón, 52–53.

[43] One of the first examples, curiously enough, is Jean-Jacques Rousseau's *Pygmalion* (written in 1762 and produced in 1770), with music by Horace Coignet. *Imitations of Life: A Reader on Film and Television Melodrama*, ed. Marcia Landy (Detroit: Wayne State UP, 1991), besides a discussion of twentieth-century melodrama in the mass media, contains essays on the theatrical and literary origins of what Peter Brooks calls the "melodramatic imagination." For more on this term, see Brooks's book of the same title, *The Melodramatic Imagination: Balzac, Henry James, Melodrama, and the Mode of Excess* (New Haven: Yale UP, 1976).

[44] Marcel Carné dramatizes the milieu in his 1945 film, *Les enfants du paradis*.

[45] Stuart, 71–72.

[46] The theater, originally called the Lyceum, would reassume this name in 1834, after being rebuilt following a fire; Bram Stoker was later its business manager.

[47] James Macpherson's publication of his own works as those of an ancient bard remains one of the most successful hoaxes of literary history; it is only fitting, then, that his images be taken up in a play dealing with fraud and impersonation. See Thomas M. Curley, *Samuel Johnson, the Ossian Fraud, and the Celtic Revival in Great Britain and Ireland* (Cambridge: Cambridge UP, 2009); and the discussion of Mérimée's *Guzla* at the end of chapter 2.

[48] James Robinson Planché, *The Vampire, or The Bride of the Isles*, in Polidori, 43, 51; hereafter cited parenthetically in the text.

[49] Ian Duncan, in *Scott's Shadow: The Novel in Romantic Edinburgh* (Princeton: Princeton UP, 2007), shows how the author used his works to define national identity; the study is also noteworthy for its discussion of Scott's significance for international letters and the history of the novel.

[50] Auerbach, 23–27.

[51] See David Worrall, "The Political Culture of Gothic Drama," in *A Companion to the Gothic*, ed. David Punter (Oxford: Wiley-Blackwell, 2001), 94–106.

[42] Walter Benjamin, *The Arcades Project*, trans. Howard Eiland and Kevin McLaughlin (Cambridge: Harvard UP, 1999), 23.

[53] Quoted in Heinz Brüggemann, *"Aber schickt keinen Poeten nach London!" Großstadt und literarische Wahrnehmung im 18. Und 19. Jahrhundert* (Hamburg: Rowohlt, 1985), 141–42.

[54] The authorship of *Varney* is disputed; the work is attributed both to James Malcolm Rymer and Thomas Preskett Prest. References follow the text presented in *Varney the Vampire, or, The Feast of Blood*, ed. Devendra P. Varma (North Stratford, NH: Ayer, 1998), 3 vols. (hereafter cited parenthetically in the text).

[55] "We must recollect," says the generous man of the cloth, "that even he, dreadful existence as he is, was fashioned by the same God that fashioned us" (851).

[56] Many observations on Varney's suave nature occur throughout the book, e.g., when a party just introduced to the vampire remarks: "His manners are easy and polished; he has evidently mixed in good society, and I never, in all my life, heard such a sweet, soft, winning voice" (103).

4: *Dracula:* Vampiric Contagion in the Late Nineteenth Century

Sᴏᴏᴏᴛʟʏ ʙᴇғᴏʀᴇ ʜɪs ᴅᴇᴀᴛʜ, Bram Stoker published *Famous Impostors* (1910). In this work, the author admits that he has set himself a task potentially limitless in scope:

> Impostors in one shape or another are likely to flourish as long as human nature remains what it is, and society shows itself ready to be gulled. [. . .] So numerous are instances [of imposture], indeed, that the book cannot profess to exhaust a theme which might easily fill a dozen volumes.[1]

Imposture, as Stoker understood it, is a phenomenon of vast dimensions spanning all times and places. His book surveys actual cases in which parties "masqueraded in order to acquire wealth, position, or fame," the history of legendary figures (e.g., the Wandering Jew), instances of mass hysteria (witch trials), and contemporary hoaxes.[2] The topic of imposture, which vacillates between "facts . . . real and authentic" and "the field of fiction,"[3] invites polygraphy — a single volume could "easily" become "a dozen."

As previous chapters have shown, the history of vampires fits within Stoker's (admittedly broad) definition of imposture. Among Serbian *hajduks* in the early eighteenth century, the vampire was a deceased member of the community who impersonated life and spread death. The erudite vampirology that thrived soon thereafter at academies and among the learned in Central Europe yielded no tangible results; instead, the participants in these debates, while purportedly discussing epidemics of undead activity among rustics, competed to discredit their rivals' confessional prejudices and "errors." In the spirit of these polemics, by the end of the 1700s, "vampire" had come into wide circulation as a pejorative term for those who abused power: the true identity of the monster was now to be found by unmasking financiers and politicians. Finally, the vampires in works by Romantics and the playwrights of nineteenth-century melodrama embodied imposture outright, inasmuch as they readily changed character to prey upon victims. The vampire's history is one of mass hysteria, obfuscation, and smoke and mirrors.

This chapter explores Stoker's *Dracula* (1897) as a point of culmination for the vampire-impostor.[4] The novel, though composed by an otherwise undistinguished author, achieves greatness by featuring a villain who operates almost exclusively by means of impersonation and falsification. Though the namesake of *Dracula* nowadays evokes a stable set of characteristics owed, in large part, to the many cinematic adaptations of the material, the word "Dracula" in Stoker's novel designates not only a literary personality, but also a creeping process of invasion and corruption. The Transylvanian Count displays much more fluidity and ambiguity than familiar film images might lead one to believe. This dynamism — the ability to shatter his own form in order to reconstitute himself in new guise for unexpected attack — makes the literary Dracula far more menacing than the Dracula of the screen, who possesses a determinate shape and attacks individuals as an individual. Stoker's Dracula can be everywhere and nowhere, and the illusion that he "really" is an Eastern European aristocrat makes the menace he incarnates only greater. The literary Dracula is a singularly virulent vampire.

Stoker's Dracula came from a combination of fact and fiction. The author chose a historical figure, the Romanian prince Vlad Tepes (1431–76), to provide the name and basic character traits for his creation. Tepes was known as "Dracula" in his lifetime; in early-modern Europe, this name signified two very different perceptions of its bearer. On the one hand, "Dracula" is the diminutive form of the Latin *draco,* "serpent" or "dragon," and it indicates that Tepes was a member of the Order of the Dragon, a league that combated the influence of heretics and Turks in his native country. But on the other hand, in medieval Christian iconography, the dragon symbolizes the Devil (e.g., in the legend of Saint George); thus, Tepes's other appellation marked him as an evildoer to many contemporaries, particularly those adversely affected by his politics.[5] Centuries before Stoker's literary necromancy resurrected Dracula as a vampire, the name signified power, uncertainty, and fear.

Curiously, the original Dracula story proves as elusive as Stoker's shape-shifting Count. Horror literature about Vlad Tepes flourished in the German-speaking world after the ruler's death. Dieter Harmening has collected and produced a modern edition of texts that tell of the historical Dracula's cruelty and blood thirst.[6] These short works, which, on the whole, are rather unliterary (a treatment by Michael Beheim [1416–ca. 1472], who enjoyed the patronage of Holy Roman Emperor Frederick III, provides an exception), inventory an impressive array of atrocities: impaling enemies, boiling and roasting people alive, and forcing parents to eat their offspring. Harmening surmises that they all go back to a lost broadsheet published in 1462 or 1463, shortly after the Hungarian capture of Tepes.

Fifteenth-century "Dracula" narratives served as political propaganda against a despot hated by the German population of Wallachia. In the sixteenth century, printed accounts of Tepes's crimes presented him alongside Herod, Nero, and Diocletian as an incarnation of tyranny. The recently invented printing press made the multiplication of these narratives possible, and their principal site of reproduction was Nuremberg, the center of the German publishing world at the time. The historical figure who provided the name and inspiration for Stoker's Count was a media phenomenon even in his own day, and the German tradition was not the only one. There are also Russian and Romanian legends. In the former, "Dracula" represents the epitome of the "cruel but just" ruler, and in the latter, he is in fact a national hero: an anti-German and anti-Turkish patriot, as well as the eradicator of lawless elements of society. Radu Florescu and Raymond McNally, the biographers of Vlad Tepes, aptly title their book "The Prince of Many Faces."

Stoker spent years researching legends and folklore while writing his vampire novel. The author's study of polyphonous historical sources expresses itself in the way that his Dracula unifies contradiction in his ghostly person. Indeed, the fabric of Stoker's novel displays the same traits as the monster that lends the work its name: the diary entries, letters, and newspaper clippings that comprise the text are rich in ambivalence and equivocation. The power of *Dracula* lies in the fact that the novel sums up, within the space of a few hundred pages, diffuse fears and tensions in the society for which it was written, and gives them a single moniker.

Jonathan Harker, the valiant English foil to the diabolical Transylvanian Count, describes the events he witnesses as "nineteenth century up-to-date with a vengeance" (67). Following this interpretive lead provided by the novel, recent criticism has fleshed out the historical backdrop for *Dracula* and shown how it reflects the emergence of consumerist mass culture, the rise of an English professional class, and the broad-scale mobilization of electrically driven forms of communication.[7] Stoker's work remains timely more than one hundred years after its initial publication because its eponymous antihero draws his substance and strength as a monster from anxieties and uncertainties produced by transformations in the conditions of everyday life. Simply replace colonialism with globalization, ministries with multinationals, and telegraphy with the Internet: the Count continues to offer an allegory for economic, bureaucratic, and technological changes in the world.

This chapter explains the fascination exercised by Dracula as the effect of a narrative design that exploits uncertainty in order to make the vampire's element extend from a domestic milieu to strange, faraway lands. The worst an average Englishman can imagine, *Dracula* intimates, is quite possibly true.

Dracula begins with an office worker's wanderings outside the cozy island world he so gladly inhabits. Jonathan Harker, rejoicing that he is "now a full-blown solicitor" (45), makes his way to Transylvania on his first business trip, which will turn out to be a disastrous transaction.

Guilelessly savoring the local cuisine, Harker makes an entry in his diary: "I had for dinner, or rather supper, a chicken done up some way with red pepper, which was very good" (31). Eating habits and writing habits overlap for the Englishman representing his country and its interests abroad. This convergence reveals the main purpose that keeping a journal serves for Harker. Just as bland appreciation represents the outer limit of Harker's gastronomy, his writing serves no further purpose than to pacify his organism: "I turn to my diary for repose. The habit of entering accurately must help to soothe me" (68). Harker's journal puts his mind at rest in the same way that food satisfies his stomach. The diary performs a quasi-organic function in organizing its writer's prosaic sensibilities, and Harker uses it to calm and balance his system.

Unfortunately, Harker cannot maintain a comfortable equilibrium once he has set foot in a foreign environment — especially one like Transylvania — and the journal that he uses as an intellectual and existential pacifier begins to malfunction. His "habit of entering accurately" leads him to record data that he cannot process, and, as a result, his own writing begins to appear in a disturbing new light. Imprisoned in Castle Dracula, Harker observes that "this diary seems horribly like the beginning of the 'Arabian Nights,' for everything has to break off at cock-crow — or like the ghost of Hamlet's father" (61). The Englishman reaches for literary analogies in a dim intuition that the same journal that is intended for "repose" in fact harbors a nightmare.

The comparisons that Harker makes between life and literature enable him to reflect with some degree of success on his predicament: after all, in the fiction he really does stand before a supernatural state of affairs. However, the literary references he calls up from his school-days and fireside readings mark the limit of what he can process and understand. Harker, who employs his diary only in order to nourish his simple ways — taking its contents as a sign that reality has already been fully inventoried — cannot discern the ominous implications of what he himself has written.

Because the mysterious laws governing life (and death) in Transylvania denature the clerical supports of Harker's sense of self, his grip on reality weakens. The widening gap between what his hand has written and what his mind can process prompts the Englishman to call his sanity into question: "There is but one thing to hope for: that I may not go mad, if . . . I be not mad already" (67). Dutiful and habitual journal keeping does not "soothe" Harker, as he means for it to do. Instead, it opens the floodgates of horror. Harker experiences his most troubling vision — a visitation from the Brides of Dracula — precisely when he passes out "at a little oak table where in old times possibly some fair lady sat to pen, with much thought and many blushes, her ill-spelt love-letter" (67). The diary intended to produce peace and quiet reactivates an archaic inscription of unfulfilled desire; by writing in his journal, Harker unwittingly sets the stage for vampiric incubation.

As he lies there in a half swoon, the Englishman confronts visions that threaten him far more than anything he has yet encountered.

> I was not alone. [. . .] In the moonlight opposite me were three young women, ladies by their dress and manner. [. . .] All three had brilliant white teeth, that shone like pearls against the ruby of their voluptuous lips. There was something about them that made me uneasy, some longing and at the same time some deadly fear. I felt in my heart a wicked, burning desire that they would kiss me with those red lips. (68–69)

As critics have observed, Harker's terror rests on the forbidden yearning for unmanly passivity — "a wicked, burning desire" to be penetrated.[8] "Voluptuous lips" that beckon Harker to join a soft and fluid feminine ocean of sensuousness reveal "brilliant white teeth" that will invade his body and undermine its masculine stability. "I could feel the soft, shivering touch of the lips on the supersensitive skin of my throat, and the hard dents of two . . . teeth. . . . I closed my eyes in a languorous ecstasy" (70). The "white sharp teeth" (70) that Harker sees, like the "ill-spelt love-letter" that he imagines, express the rise of primordial forces that he cannot master — forces that will sweep him away and destroy him.

Why, the reader wonders, are there suddenly multiple vampires? Until now, the Count has stood alone. Why are these undead creatures female? In effect, Dracula's Brides (two of whom share his features) are extensions of him, and the impurity of their embrace stems at least in part from its latent homosexual charge. Harker's entries in his journal provide a breeding ground for undead perversion, a medium in which the vampire can mutate and take on unprecedented forms of terror.

To find out who — or what — Dracula "really is," Harker would need to turn away from his own diary and read in the Count's library. Harker does have one correct hunch: Dracula "would have made a wonderful solicitor" (63). The library in Castle Dracula consists solely of "such books of reference as the London Directory, the 'Red' and 'Blue' books, Whitaker's Almanack, the Army and Navy Lists, and . . . the Law List" (50); moreover, the Count takes a keen interest in learning all about the practical aspects of business that Harker shares with him. Dracula's fascination with the workings of commerce points toward his intimate connection to the written word. He calls the volumes comprising his utilitarian library "good friends" (50) and credits them with teaching him English ("I know your tongue through books"; 51). The business books and reference works have taught the vampire not only a foreign language, but also a way to worm his way into "mighty London" in order to "share its life, . . . its death, and all that makes it what it is" (51).

Dracula has used his book-friends to devise a plan that the guile-less British agent — whom he also calls "my friend" (51) — translates into action. Through Harker, Dracula sets up an array of property deeds and bank accounts that will allow him to move about on English soil undercover. These written documents provide the material basis for the spread of vampirism abroad. Moreover, they furnish the key to under-standing Dracula's protean nature. With Harker's unwitting assistance, Dracula forges an identity that, as Gary Day puts it, "is . . . a function of . . . documentation rather [than] an expression of individual essence."[9] This shadowy, purely formal identity, existing only on paper, stands at the center of who and what Dracula is. Stoker's novel later reveals that the Count can transform himself into various animals in order to escape notice, but through these documents he passes unseen in a more subtle way — by deploying a panoply of surrogate selves in writing.

Count Dracula has no true home. Perhaps on the model of Alexan-dre Dumas's *Thousand and One Ghosts* (1849) — which, as we saw in chapter 2, associated vampires and the Carpathian wilderness — Stoker makes Dracula's "native" ground Transylvania.[10] At any rate, Transyl-vania, which was annexed by the House of Habsburg in 1711, is prime vampire country. Like the border territories settled by the Serbian peas-ant-soldiers among whom the first vampire epidemics were recorded (see chapter 1), it forms a liminal space where East and West, Asia and Europe, converge and coexist uneasily — "ground fought over for cen-turies by the Wallachian, the Saxon, and the Turk" (52), as Dracula tells his English guest.

Dracula's obscure lineage resembles that of his equally infamous liter-ary counterpart Svengali, in George du Maurier's *Trilby* (1894). Svenga-li's haunt is Paris, not London, but he shares the vampire's predilection for English women, and, also like Dracula, he wields powers of hypnosis that transform them into his playthings[11] (more on this in a moment). Du Maurier's villain embodies all that is foreign, vile, and un-Western in his person. Displaying an alternately cunning and bullying character, Svengali is referred to, without clear distinctions being made between dif-ferent aspects of his background, as German, Polish, and, most impor-tantly, Jewish — that slippery category of identity which, once it has been uprooted from the ghetto or the shtetl, so often transforms into a corrosive nonidentity in nineteenth-century fictions.[12] The deep affin-ity between Dracula and Svengali is underscored by the fact that when, decades later, they appeared on screen in the same year (1931), the same cinematic vocabulary illustrated their demonic nature: close-up shots of a piercing gaze that transfixed female victims as if by a stake (or whatever else psychoanalytic theory might suggest).

Alternately, Joseph Valente has suggested that Transylvania, where ethnic categories and political orders are confused, be read as a code word for Ireland, and he observes that "the name *Dracula* puns on the Gaelic phrase *droch fhola,* meaning 'bad blood.'"[13] If Transylvania is "The Land beyond the Forest" with regard to metropolitan Vienna, Ireland occupies a "position . . . beyond the frontier"[14] vis-à-vis London, the capital of the English empire. Thus, Valente argues, Dracula is really Irish — like Stoker — and the combination of sympathy and disgust with which the vampire is portrayed in the novel reflects the author's conflicted position as an Irishman who wedded his personal and professional fortunes to England.[15] Stoker's vampire, in this reading, represents the author's ill will toward his adoptive country, sublimated into a literary fantasy of revenge. If so, Dracula's peers are not just the undead, but also political radicals. As the Fenian conspirator who sometimes goes by the name "Zero" in Robert Louis Stevenson's *The Dynamiter* (1885) darkly intones, "Mine is an anonymous, infernal glory." Speaking to a clueless young man (who, like Harker, has stumbled into danger of proportions he had never suspected), the terrorist continues:

> By any [name] you may address me, . . . for all I have at some time borne. Yet that which I most prize, that which is most feared, hated, and obeyed, is not a name to be found in your directories; it is not a name current in post-offices or banks. . . . [16]

These words could have come from Dracula's mouth.

According to Valente, Dracula seals his doom by stumbling into an alliance, not with blue-blooded England, but with a half-breed. The Count thirsts for the blood of Harker's fiancée (and later, wife), a "sweet-faced, dainty-looking girl" (257), whose maiden name is Mina Murray. As Valente observes,

> [Mina's] . . . Irish birth name filiates her with native Celts of the name O'Muireadhaigh, which was anglicized to Murray sometime during the colonial occupation, and with Protestant Scotch-Irish planters, the Murrays, who were part of that anglicizing occupation.[17]

Dracula, then, does not get what he wants when he preys upon Mina, who is crypto-Irish like himself. Valente's reading of *Dracula* in terms of the author's "avowed, though unorthodox, Irish nationalism" uncovers "something like a *coherent indeterminacy*" that moves between "racial . . . and political logics."[18] This feature of the novel accounts for the vampire's ambivalent status as a foreigner who, ultimately, is not a complete stranger, but rather a kind of "secret sharer."[19] The blood of Mina, the model representative of womanhood upon whom England's future symbolically depends, is as impure as Dracula's own.

Placed in the broader perspective of vampires' predilection for imposture and their constitutive inauthenticity, which the preceding chapters have explored in detail, another interpretation suggests itself: Dracula has no blood at all. The Count is a fearsome paper tiger, and he ghostwrites himself into existence. This is why Stoker's vampire can, depending on the reader's sensibilities, represent a host of ethnic "others" ranging from Slavic to Irish to Jewish to Turkish.[20] To pave the way for his campaign of terror, the Count simply posts a letter to "Hawkins and Harker" (191) and the junior partner of the firm comes running to him as a convenient snack. Once the latter is in Transylvania, Dracula needs only to do a little more paperwork in order to make his move to England, where he can harvest the unsuspecting citizenry. When he has received most of what he needs from Harker and can foresee the Englishman's imminent obsolescence, Dracula demotes the overproud pen pusher, who arrived in Transylvania exultant that he was no longer a mere "solicitor's clerk" (45), back to a subordinate position. "Last night," Harker records in his diary,

> the Count asked me in the suavest tones to write three letters, one saying that my work here was nearly done, and that I should start for home within a few days, another that I was starting on the next morning from the time of the letter, and the third that I had left the castle. (73)

Reading between the lines of his own writing, Harker realizes that he has just issued his own death notice. "I know now the span of my life" (73). In a perversion of his professional identity, he has written a carte blanche for the vampire who intends to kill him — or worse.

The writing-based imposture that enables vampirism in *Dracula* troubles not just notions of ethnic and political stability, but also gender roles. Mina, her protests notwithstanding, comes to play the part of the late-Victorian "New Woman" (123) as the novel progresses.[21] At the beginning of the story, she inhabits a neat and tidy world. An "assistant schoolmistress" (86), Mina exercises a traditional, womanly function in society. Her epistolary communication with her best friend, Lucy Westenra, defines her place in the social order. This exchange forms a more or less closed system, and it therefore reinforces each party's femininity: in their correspondence, the young women discuss marriage plans, clothes, social visits, etc. Mina also keeps a diary in which she cultivates a modest private sphere and anchors her identity — "a sort of journal . . . I can write in whenever I feel inclined" (86). Her every thought concerns how she can "be useful to Jonathan" (86) — a perfect wife to the man she will marry.

At the same time, however, the young woman pursues activities that predispose her to deviate from her place in the house and schoolroom:

> I have been practicing shorthand very assiduously. [. . .] And if I can stenograph well enough I can . . . write it out . . . on the typewriter, at which also I am practising very hard. [. . .] I shall try to

do what I see lady journalists do: interviewing and writing descriptions and trying to remember conversations. I am told that, with a little patience, one can remember all that goes on or that one hears said during a day (86).

Mina means only to assist Harker, but her stenography and typewriting deform her. To the extent that she devotes herself to clerical work, Mina invades Harker's space, even if she does not mean to do so.[22] Her side interests go hand in hand with a hunger for information in all its forms (when other characters marvel at her memory for the details of public transportation schedules, she replies, "You forget — or perhaps you do not know . . . — that I am the train fiend"; 379). As a result of an "unnatural" level of nosiness not restricted to the womanly sphere of gossip and intrigue, she peeks into Harker's "foreign journal" (216) without his permission. What Mina finds shocks her and, in imitation of the "lady journalists," she resolves to "get [her] typewriter this very hour and begin transcribing" (216). She thereby not only discovers that her husband has encountered a vampire, but practically becomes one herself.

On the one hand, Mina's data compilation is what enables the vampire hunters to track down Dracula and destroy him. On the other hand, this activity places Mina in a dangerous proximity to the monster. According to the plot of Stoker's novel, Mina receives a visit from Dracula in which he sucks her blood and infuses her with the demon seed (322) — indeed, this is the most intimate encounter she has had with anyone since her marriage to the convalescent Harker in a Central European hospital.[23] However, "the Vampire's baptism of blood" (362) is not the main reason why Mina takes on undead traits and, in exchange, develops powers of clairvoyance. Mina's second sight and partial metamorphosis stem from her move into the Count's sphere of influence when she begins transcribing. Parallel to the text that passes through her hands, animal magnetism courses through her body and soul; supernatural connections double material ones.[24] Even the somewhat obtuse Harker realizes as much when he witnesses his wife speaking in a mesmerized state: "I have heard her use the same tone when reading her shorthand notes" (353).

The transformation into a vampire of Mina's friend, Lucy Westenra, is also linked to perverse writing, which correlates with the all-pervasive anxiety in *Dracula* concerning the stability of traditional roles defining identity in the modern world. The epistolary form provides a lengthy tradition of novels reaching back at least to Samuel Richardson with a means of exploring sentiment and psychology.[25] In *Dracula,* however, it functions to develop the related phenomenon of self-alienation. We have already remarked how Harker encounters the Brides of Dracula where once a "fair lady" composed her love letters. Lucy's letters to Mina reveal why she is Dracula's first victim on English soil and the first full-blooded vampire outside of Transylvania.

"Do you ever try to read your own face in the glass? *I do*" (88), Miss Westenra writes. Lucy is definitely the more self-indulgent of the two women, and her narcissism manifests itself as wanton writing. Separated from Mina, Lucy tells her friend in an intimate epistle: "I wish I were with you, dear, sitting by the fire undressing, as we used to sit" (88).

This desire seems natural enough, given that, as Mina says, Lucy and she are "like sisters" (268), but it also contains sinister undertones insofar as it hints at Lucy's inability to tolerate the distance necessary to maintain a well-defined sense of self. Lucy loves to lose herself in others. At the beginning of *Dracula,* all the single men are courting her, and she would just as soon not commit to any one of them. She has promised herself to Arthur Holmwood, yet she writes to her friend: "Why can't they let a girl marry three men, or as many as want her, and save all this trouble?" (91). Even when Lucy focuses her sexual energy on her fiancé, she cannot restrain her effusions: "oh, Mina, I love him; I love him; I love him! [. . .] I do not know how I am writing this even to you. I am afraid to stop . . . and I don't want to stop" (88).

The unlucky girl's expansive heart and her free and loose correspondence suggest sexual promiscuity. Lucy eventually curbs her love for love and commits herself to Holmwood, but Dracula has already detected her availability and paid her a visit. After the vampire's embrace, Lucy languishes and dies, then rises from the tomb to prey upon unattended children. This vampiric resurrection inverts the role of nurturing mother that awaited her — had she been but more continent in her desires — and leads to one of the most grotesque scenes in the novel, when her betrothed goes to her tomb to destroy the woman he had meant to marry. This episode culminates in a spectacle of incredible perversion:

> Arthur took the stake and the hammer. . . . [He] placed the point over the Heart. . . . Then he struck with all his might.
> The Thing in the coffin writhed; and a hideous, blood-curdling screech came from the opened red lips. The body shook and quivered and twisted in wild contortions; the sharp white teeth champed together till the lips were cut, and the mouth was smeared with blood. But Arthur never faltered. He looked like the figure of Thor as his untrembling arm rose and fell, driving deeper and deeper the mercy-bearing stake. (254)

Lucy's bloody lips and wildly contorted body under Holmwood's vigorous thrusts form a terrible parody of a wedding night. Lucy, in her written outpourings of sentiment, unwittingly steps out into a shadowy world of illicit desire that she shares with Victorian adventuresses such as Lydia Gwilt, the red-haired "protovamp" (who, incidentally, is an adept forger) in Wilkie Collin's *Armadale* (1866). In the process, she signs a warrant for her own death.

Abnormal graphic practices also characterize affairs at the private nerve clinic run by Dr. John Seward, one of Lucy's other suitors. When Seward is introduced early in the novel, he confronts a case that baffles him. His patient Renfield has an unconventional diet — insects and arachnids — and he exhibits an unusual interest in tables and charts. As the doctor notes, "Spiders are at present his hobby, and [his] notebook is filling up with small figures" (136). Indeed, Renfield writes even when deprived of pen and paper; Seward observes him "catching flies and eating them, and . . . keeping note of his capture by making nail-marks on the edge of the door" (151). The madman's strange appetites, which evoke Dracula's unusual source of sustenance, gesture toward the Count's imminent arrival on English soil, even though Seward cannot see the writing on the wall (and in Renfield's notebook, and on the door jamb . . .). Renfield's ravings, writings, and appetite for vermin point, in a broader cultural context, toward the new value of madness as a touchstone for truth in late-nineteenth-century psychiatric theory and practice. As Carlo Ginzburg has observed, Freud's psychoanalytic investigation of patterns of behavior that make no sense on the surface but provide insight into the unconscious mind — a technique he developed at the same time that Stoker was writing *Dracula* — is related to the rise of the detective both in real-life police work and in narrative fiction.[26] (Ginzburg also draws attention to the method for dating works of art developed by Giovanni Morelli a few decades earlier; curiously, when Morelli published his theory between 1874 and 1876, he staged a game with his authorial persona that mirrors the confusion of identities in *Dracula* by inventing a Russian alter ego [Ivan Lermolieff] and a German one [Johannes Schwarze] to play the parts of "author" and "translator."[27])

Although *Dracula* begins and ends in Transylvania, the work revolves largely around domestic worries in England. Summarily stated, these are: the impersonality of modern business practices (Harker); the appetites awakened in women by social changes (Lucy); the potentially emasculating effects of the latter (Mina); and the relationship between madness and sanity in a world where every new day upsets tradition and received ideas (Renfield). As if in denial of the fact that it is England "herself" that has created these problems, the novel ascribes them to a foreign agent. However, Dracula, especially as a crypto-Irish, is an "invader" with a much closer point of origin than distant Transylvania. The fact that his campaign of terror unfolds in the realm of graphic reproduction — the text of *Dracula* is comprised entirely of collated documents — makes it very difficult to authenticate the real cause of the vampire epidemic.

* * *

As we have seen throughout this study, vampirism, in any and all of its many settings, only *appears* to come from without. Without exception, the vampire reflects its victims' failure to realize that they in some measure bear responsibility for their condition. If vampires can so readily penetrate the private sphere, this is the case because they are already there. No one in England has any idea that a vampire circulates among them. Because the monster's mode of being derives its power from victims' incomplete knowledge and (self-)misrecognition, an outsider's perspective is required.

Conveniently — that is, without much more explanation than Dracula's existence receives — the Dutch polymath Dr. Abraham Van Helsing shows up to rally the forces of the beleaguered and bewildered English just as vampirism reaches the point of paroxysm. Seward, his former student, describes Van Helsing as "one of the most advanced scientists of his day" (147). "[A] philosopher and a metaphysician," Van Helsing also "knows as much about obscure diseases as any one in the world" (147). Indeed, Van Helsing has so many degrees ("M.D., D.PH., D.LIT. ETC., ETC."; 148) and areas of expertise that even his pupil cannot keep track. When Seward fears that Van Helsing, because he comes from abroad, "might not be quite aware of English legal requirements," the Dutchman reminds him of the reach of his knowledge: "You forget that I am a lawyer as well as a doctor" (200).

Van Helsing is a figure as overdetermined and undefined as the vampire he hunts. He shares a Christian name with the novel's author, which suggests that Stoker, who may well have seen himself in Dracula, also conceived of the Count's nemesis as an alter ego.[28] Van Helsing's surname and interests also link him with Sheridan Le Fanu's Martin Hesselius, the fictitious German physician whose papers include the story of the Styrian vampire "Carmilla" (1872). A reader familiar with the works of Jules Verne might think of the latter's *Le château des Carpathes* (1892), in which the inventions of a mad scientist help a Transylvanian nobleman keep a village in the grip of superstitious terror (including the fear of vampires).[29] Finally, as we have seen, the phenomenon of vampirism has, since its inception in the early eighteenth century, challenged the expertise of men of science, especially medical doctors. Van Helsing's broad learning, Germanic accent, wandering ways, and unorthodox approach to the science of healing call to mind the legendary, early-modern Swiss polymath and medical reformer Paracelsus, whose adherents we encountered among the earliest examples of Continental vampirology.[30] His name also sounds quite a bit like that of Joan (alternately, Jan or Johannes) Baptista van Helmont (1579–1644), the seventeenth-century Paracelsian iatrochemist.[31]

Van Helsing alone shows no sign of suffering a pernicious influence when Dracula is in England. This is the case because Van Helsing is a double of Dracula and effectively a vampire himself. Dracula offers the mirror image of Van Helsing on every significant score. In his non-English English, Van Helsing reveals the Transylvanian's intellectual powers:

> [Dracula] was in life a most wonderful man. Soldier, statesman, and alchemist — which latter was the highest development of the science-knowledge of his time. He had a mighty brain, a learning beyond compare. . . . There was no branch of knowledge of his time that he did not essay (343).

Both Dracula and Van Helsing are foreigners on English soil, old men, mesmerists in touch with the supernatural world, and "mighty brains with learning beyond compare."

These similarities between the two enemies correspond to a deeper connection that is not readily apparent, but for this same reason even more profound. *Dracula* does not show its eponymous villain in action nearly as much as one might expect (or as one seems to recall after reading the novel). The Count is a shape-shifting creature who materializes only when closing in for the kill; his potential for destruction is based on his ability to conceal his whereabouts and activities until it is time to strike. And as we have seen, the concealing powers of ghostwritten, pseudonymous, and anonymous writing form the basis of Dracula's protean nature and shadowy moves. Here, too, Van Helsing resembles the Count. Van Helsing can say, do, and command what he wants: his many degrees lend his wishes and whims logical substance and force in the eyes of the English.

Van Helsing does not step onto the stage of the novel in person; instead, he makes his first appearance in *Dracula* through a cryptic missive:

> My good Friend, —
>
> When I have received your letter I am already coming to you. By good fortune I can leave just at once, without wrong to any of those who have trusted me. [. . .] Tell your friend that when that time you suck from my wound so swiftly the poison from that knife that our other friend, too nervous, let slip, you did more for him when he wants my aids and you call for them than all his great fortune could do. But it is pleasure added to do for him, your friend; it is to you that I come. [. . .] Till then goodbye, my friend John. VAN HELSING. (148)

This letter opens a series of questions that will remain unanswered, but which conjure up the (unreproduced) correspondence that Dracula used to initiate contact with the English. What "wrong" could Van Helsing, simply by leaving when he does, inflict upon "those who have trusted" him? What undisclosed power does he wield? Like Dracula (who calls Harker his "friend" back in Transylvania), Van Helsing seems unduly concerned with underlining the amicable relations between himself and others (especially "friend John"); such emphasis casts doubt on whether they really should get along or not. Finally, even if Van Helsing writes English so poorly that the precise details are hopelessly obscure, his intimate relationship to Seward goes back to a mysterious incident that looks like a quasi-vampiric encounter ("that time you suck from my wound . . ."). Indeed, the younger man refers to the foreigner as his "master" (154) — precisely the term that Renfield employs when speaking of the Count (e.g., 193).

Like Dracula, Van Helsing avoids leaving traces of his activities behind. Even though the Dutch doctor hardly quits the scene after his introduction one-third of the way through the book, he shares the Count's ghostly aspect. Van Helsing makes epistolary contact under the sign of bloodsucking, but then for the most part does not take up a pen; in the rest of the novel, his discourse is mainly reported in *other* characters' writings. Significantly, Van Helsing's graphic abstention goes along with an increase of influence. The Dutchman's sway over others only gets larger as the amount of written signs he leaves diminishes. The exceptions to this rule confirm the Dutchman's spectral qualities, most strikingly when Van Helsing parasitically claims Seward's phonographic journal for himself. Speaking into the electric diary, Dracula's supposed adversary barks a directive with vampiric echoes: "This to Jonathan Harker" (355). Because Van Helsing does not communicate his wishes to Harker in person, but instead has a machine do the talking for him (and someone else's machine, at that), because his English is full of barbarisms, and because his words are a command, the Dutch vampire hunter's speech evokes the Transylvanian Count's dictation to the unfortunate clerk earlier in the novel.

The English characters do occasionally remark something disturbing about their foreign companion. However, because the threat posed by Dracula and the tide of disorienting, undead data have unsettled all the habits and conventions that previously provided them with a clear sense of right and wrong, they can at most express discomfort and unease when Van Helsing seems to go too far. "Professor, are you in earnest; or is it some monstrous joke?" (243), Holmwood asks at one point. Even though the doctor protests, "I never jest! There is grim purpose in all I do" (166), his ascendancy in the latter half of the novel makes much of what happens seem like a sick joke (as when Holmwood defiles the corpse of his [un]dead fiancée at Van Helsing's behest).

On the surface, the battle between Dracula and the vampire hunters seems to present the victory of Good over Evil. On a deeper level, however, the moral and metaphysical trappings of Stoker's novel are irrelevant. As Friedrich Kittler observes, the side with the fastest data-relay system wins.[32] An impersonal, instrumental intelligence reestablishes Order under Heaven. This power does not belong to a benevolent and omniscient "Recording Angel" (367) above, as the none-too-bright Harker assumes. Instead, it belongs to an old man down on earth who commands the pious fingers of a young lady and the vigorous limbs of dutiful and compliant young men.

As the tables turn, the vampire trying to make it big in London shows himself to be out of touch with life in the metropolis, the pace of modernity, and the means of ensuring survival under these conditions. He uses the ridiculously *parvenu*-sounding name "Count de Ville" (312) as an alias and walks the streets wearing a straw hat — an accessory which, in the words of his nemesis, Van Helsing, "suit not him or the time" (357). More importantly, Dracula employs superannuated communications technology. Geoffrey Winthrop-Young observes that Dracula's foray into the foreign meat-market "resembles that of an early-modern merchant directly involved in all purchasing ventures."[33] The Count "does not advance beyond handwritten letters"[34] and personal interaction when he goes about his infernal business. These old-fashioned methods bring him a certain measure of success. After all, he lures Harker to Transylvania and then uses the clerk's contacts to set up a series of documentary covers for himself. Throughout the novel, the Count controls the mails.[35] But though Dracula wins a few initial skirmishes, he simply does not operate quickly enough in the epoch of typewriters and telegrams, nor can his "snail mail" compete with the data-processing network that Mina administrates and Van Helsing oversees. Dracula is stuck in the past; or, as Van Helsing contemptuously puts it, "in some faculties of the mind he . . . is . . . only a child" (343).

In contrast, the vampire hunters employ ultramodern and fast technologies. And since they operate with reproduced documents, not originals, Dracula does not stand a chance. The vampire tries to disrupt their system of information management, but Mina types out all the data she can gather into easily legible, standardized print and uses "manifold" — that is, carbon paper (262). When Dracula attempts to foil his enemies by breaking into their base of operations and making "rare hay" (325) of Mina's master text, the vampire hunters emerge unscathed because they can still avail themselves of another copy they have kept in a safe. Finally, Mina's transcript changes hands freely, and the information about vampiric activities that it contains is therefore the equal possession of all.

Dracula is a vampire, and he makes Lucy a vampire. Mina develops vampiric traits independent of Dracula, which the Count's visitation only reinforces. Van Helsing — the other creepy foreigner, who appears on the scene too suddenly and behaves too suspiciously to be fully trusted — also acts like a vampire. Finally, Holmwood, when he destroys his undead bride, also extinguishes Lucy's family line and inherits her money and a title, becoming "Lord Godalming" (204). Holmwood, too, thereby comes to resemble the predatory parasites multiplying around him — an echo of the "unjust Stewards and the dry Nurses of Great Estates" that, as we saw in chapter 2, were among the first vampires in England.

Who, one wonders, is not a vampire, at least potentially? One character we have passed over until now shows just how pervasive the scourge
is. The cohort of vampire hunters contains, besides Van Helsing, a second
foreign body. Introduced as one of Lucy's suitors early on, the American
Quincey Morris, like the best of his countrymen, is a free spirit and very
much his own person. When it becomes clear that he will not have Lucy's
hand, he is also a gracious loser. The English characters praise him as a
remarkably "nice fellow" (90), and they find his American idiom and the
colorful tales he tells charming. Yet what brings Morris to England? No
one in *Dracula* asks this question, but perhaps they should.

Franco Moretti has argued that Morris is another vampire. Like
Dracula, Morris is a foreigner who represents an economic system inimical to the English social order and his hosts' traditional way of life.
Breakneck American capitalism and atavistic Transylvanian feudalism
pose equal threats to the stability and well-being of Great Britain. As
Moretti observes, the word "vampire" appears in *Dracula* for the first
time when Morris tells his companions about an adventure in South
America: "one of those big bats that they call vampires" (188) drained
his horse of its blood in the Pampas. Furthermore, Morris acts in a sus-
picious manner at key moments in the vampire hunt. During a session to
plan the course of action against the Count, he takes leave of the others
in order to shoot at a big bat hanging outside the window and spying
on the proceedings. The American misses, Moretti suggests, because he
does not intend to kill Dracula at all; instead, he merely wants to provide
a smokescreen for himself. And when the vampire hunters find Dracula
physically assaulting Mina, Morris inexplicably runs off and hides "in
the shadow of a great yew tree" (323) before returning to tell the others
that the Count has escaped.

Like a true vampire, the American is fundamentally duplicitous.
"So long as things go well for Dracula, Morris acts like an accomplice.
As soon as there is a reversal of fortunes, he turns into his staunchest
enemy."[36] Morris eagerly participates in the hunt for the Count in Transylvania — that is, once the English have gained the upper hand and are
on the verge of destroying their adversary. Yet for no apparent reason,
the American suffers a mortal blow at the hands of the Count's Gypsy
allies[37] just as the vampire hunters catch up with their prey. It is only logical, Moretti argues, that Morris die when Dracula does. The American's
sudden and apparently unmotivated death at the last minute "fits perfectly into [the] sociological design"[38] of Stoker's novel, which presents
the exorcism of forces that are pernicious and destabilizing to the English
social body.

However, the final document included in *Dracula* suggests that a
complete purification does not occur. A note from Jonathan Harker's
hand concludes the novel:

Seven years ago we all went through the flames; and the happiness
of some of us is, we think, well worth the pain endured. It is an
added joy to Mina and me that our boy's birthday is the same day
as that on which Quincey Morris died. His mother holds, I know,
the secret belief that some of our brave friend's spirit has passed into
him. [. . .] We call him Quincey (419).

On the one hand, the way that things have worked out seems to fall in
line with the triumph of life. Seven years after the terror, Dracula has not
returned, and the Harkers have added a young member to their family.
Their son represents the renewal of full-blooded English stock in years to
come. But on the other hand, the new generation also provides a bridge
to the troubling past. The young Harker's birth coincides not only with
Morris's death, but also with Dracula's. As we have seen throughout this
study, vampires disappear only to reappear later in another form. In the
cyclical time of the calendar, the child's entry into the world overlaps with
the vampire's vanishing from it. This convergence points toward the possibility that the monster has wormed its way into another body and lies
dormant, waiting to strike when least expected. In addition, we have seen
in some detail how, in *Dracula,* the undead work under textual and ono-
mastic cover. The child's name is ominous. If in fact "some . . . spirit has
passed into" the young Harker, then a horror lies in store. Mina, of all
people, should know what it means for a "spirit" to pass from one being
to another.

In this light, we can understand why Dracula does not put up much
of a fight when his pursuers finally catch up with him and why, "in [the]
moment of final dissolution, . . . a look of peace" (418) appears on his
face. The vampire goes to rest secure that he will soon be reborn in a new,
and better, disguise. Dracula's many reincarnations since the publication
of the novel prove his confidence justified. The Transylvanian monster
has become, quite possibly, the most famous monster in history. Stoker's
work has gone through too many editions and adaptations to list. Dracula
has appeared in print, on stage, on the radio, on film, and in televised
programming. Diffused in the media, the vampire lurks in every home,
where each new generation receives him through the bloodstream of mass
culture like mother's milk. As we will see in the next chapter, which discusses a work by someone who most assuredly did not read *Dracula,* the
vampire's fame has become pandemic in modern times because undead
impostors are not entirely a figment of the imagination.

Notes

[1] Bram Stoker, *Famous Impostors* (London: Sidgwick & London, 1910), v.

[2] Stoker, v.

[3] Stoker, v.

[4] Page references to the novel follow Bram Stoker, *Dracula,* ed. Glennis Byron (Ontario: Broadview, 1998).

[5] See Radu R. Florescu and Raymond T. McNally, *Dracula: Prince of Many Faces* (Boston: Little, Brown and Company, 1989), 34–42.

[6] Dieter Harmening, *Der Anfang von Dracula: Zur Geschichte von Geschichten* (Würzburg: Königshausen + Neumann, 1983).

[7] Three essays that represent these trends in scholarship are: Jennifer Wicke, "Vampiric Typewriting," *ELH* 59 (Summer 1992), 467–93; Gary Day, "The State of *Dracula*: Bureaucracy and the Vampire," in *Rereading Victorian Fiction,* ed. Alice Jenkins and Juliet John (New York: St. Martin's Press, 2000), 81–95; and Geoffrey Winthrop-Young, "Undead Networks: Information Processing and Media Boundary Conflicts in *Dracula,*" in *Literature and Science,* ed. Donald Bruce and Anthony Purdy (Atlanta: Rodopi, 1994), 107–29.

[8] On this particular point, see Christopher Craft, "'Kiss Me with Those Red Lips': Gender and Inversion in Bram Stoker's *Dracula,*" *Representations* 8 (1984), 107–33; and Phyllis A. Roth, "Suddenly Sexual Women in Bram Stoker's *Dracula,*" *Literature and Psychology* 27.3 (1977), 113–21. Other worthwhile studies of sexuality and sexual anxiety in *Dracula* include Christopher F. Bentley, "The Monster in the Bedroom," *Literature and Psychology* 22 (1972), 27–34; Gail Griffin, "'Your Girls That You All Love Are Mine': *Dracula* and the Victorian Male Sexual Imagination," *International Journal of Women's Studies* 3 (1980), 454–65; and John Allen Stevenson, "A Vampire in the Mirror: The Sexuality of *Dracula,*" *PMLA* 103.2 (1988), 139–49.

[9] Day, 87.

[10] For a discussion of Stoker's sources of information on Transylvania and literary representations of this territory as they relate to the twentieth-century political history of Romania, see Ken Gelder, *Reading the Vampire* (London: Routledge, 1994), 2–8.

[11] Nina Auerbach, *Woman and the Demon: The Life of a Victorian Myth* (Cambridge: Harvard UP, 1984), 7–34.

[12] Daniel Pick, *Svengali's Web: The Alien Enchanter in Modern Culture* (New Haven: Yale UP, 2000), inventories the Semitic qualities ascribed to Svengali and draws parallels to Dracula; Anna Krugovoy Silver, *Victorian Literature and the Anorexic Body* (Cambridge: Cambridge UP, 2002), 116–35, explores the affinity further. Du Maurier's subsequent novel, *The Martian* (1897) takes the conceit of alien influence in the direction of science fiction (see conclusion).

[13] Joseph Valente, *Dracula's Crypt: Bram Stoker, Irishness, and the Question of Blood* (Urbana: U of Illinois P, 2001), 61.

[14] Valente, 52.

[15] See also David Glover, *Vampires, Mummies, and Liberals: Bram Stoker and the Politics of Popular Fiction* (Durham: Duke UP, 1996), 12–14, 25–31, and passim.

[16] Robert Louis Stevenson, *The Dynamiter* (London: Collins, [no date]), 180–81.

[17] Valente, 66.

[18] Valente, 2, 4, 4; stress in original.

[19] Joseph Conrad, from whom this phrase is borrowed, explored related themes in a more secular context. Like Stoker, Conrad was keenly aware of his own position between cultures. For an integrative approach to the latter's life and work, see Edward Said, *Joseph Conrad and the Fiction of Autobiography* (Cambridge: Harvard UP, 1966).

[20] The "real" Dracula, Vlad Tepes, was a Turkish hostage for some six years, making him a "Western" relay for supposed "Eastern" cruelty. Jimmie E. Cain, Jr., *Bram Stoker and Russophobia* (London: McFarland, 2006) analyzes the connection between the Crimean War and the monsters in Stoker's *Dracula* and *The Lady of the Shroud* (1909).

[21] See the documents collected in Carolyn Christensen Nelson, ed., *A New Woman Reader: Fiction, Articles, and Drama of the 1890s* (Ontario: Broadview, 2000).

[22] Indeed, according to the fiction of *Dracula*, Mina is the work's author. See Alison Case, "Tasting the Original Apple: Gender and the Struggle for Narrative Authority in *Dracula*," *Narrative* I.3 (1993), 223–43; and Marjorie Howes, "The Mediation of the Feminine: Bisexuality, Homoerotic Desire, and Self-Expression in Bram Stoker's *Dracula*," *Texas Studies in Language and Literature* 30.1 (1988), 104–19.

[23] *Dracula: Pages from a Virgin's Diary* (2002), by Canadian director Guy Maddin, emphasizes this aspect of the novel to comic effect; see also the conclusion of this book.

[24] See Alison Winters, *Mesmerized: Powers of Mind in Victorian England* (Chicago: U of Chicago P, 1998) for relevant cultural contexts. Significantly for our discussion of uncanny foreigners, the originator of these ideas of supernatural influence was a Viennese adventurer. A foundational study exploring the political dimensions of animal magnetism — which contested established orders of knowledge and power — is Robert Darnton, *Mesmerism and the End of Enlightenment in France* (Cambridge: Harvard UP, 1968). Maria Tatar, *Spellbound: Studies on Mesmerism and Literature* (Princeton: Princeton UP, 1978), examines the theme with a focus on German-language works.

[25] Bernhard Siegert, *Relays: Literature as an Epoch of the Postal System*, trans. Kevin Repp (Stanford: Stanford UP, 1999) explores how conventions of letter-writing informed the development of notions of interiority in early-modern and modern Europe.

[26] Carlo Ginzburg, "Clues: Roots of an Evidential Paradigm," *Clues, Myths, and the Historical Method*, trans. John and Anne C. Tedeschi (Baltimore: Johns Hopkins UP, 1989), 96–125.

[27] Commenting on "the twin masks," Ginzburg observes that "Morelli [is] a surname for which Schwarze is the equivalent [that is, a translation] and Lermolieff very nearly [an] anagram" (96).

[28] For a discussion of possible points of identification for the author — both in his fiction and his life — see Barbara Belford, *Bram Stoker and the Man Who Was*

Dracula (New York: Da Capo, 2002); the title refers to Stoker's employer, the great actor Henry Irving (1838–1905).

[29] Jules Verne, *Le château des Carpathes* (Paris: Livre de Poche, 1994), 87.

[30] See chapter 1.

[31] Walter Pagel, *Joan Baptista Van Helmont: Reformer of Science and Medicine* (Cambridge: Cambridge UP, 2002).

[32] Friedrich Kittler, "Dracula's Legacy," *Stanford Humanities Review* I (1989), 143–73.

[33] Winthrop-Young, 116.

[34] Winthrop-Young, 115.

[35] The evidence abounds; e.g., Harker's statement upon finding Dracula's correspondence: "It gave me almost a turn to see again one of the letters which I had seen on the Count's table before I knew of his diabolical plans. Everything had been carefully thought out, and done systematically and with precision" (265).

[36] Franco Moretti, *Signs Taken for Wonders: Essays in the Sociology of Literary Forms*, trans. Susan Fischer, David Forgacs, and David Miller (London: Verso, 1983), 95.

[37] On the one hand, Dracula's association with Gypsies is a continuation of the general racism pervading the novel; on the other, their itinerant status as people who move between borders calls to mind the unsettled position of Serbian *hajduks* (see chapter 1). The Roma — *Gypsies* is an exonym derived from the Greek word for "Egypt," from where they were long thought (erroneously) to originate — are another example of the "internal outsiders" connected with vampires; see Angus Bancroft, *Roma and Gypsy-Travellers in Europe: Race, Space and Exclusion* (Aldershot: Ashgate, 2005), 1–19.

[38] Moretti, 95.

Part III: Germany

5: Vampirism, the Writing Cure, and *Realpolitik:* Daniel Paul Schreber's *Memoirs of My Nervous Illness*

A T THE BEGINNING OF THE NINETEENTH CENTURY, the English poet John Stagg (1770–1823) set the stage for a Romantic ballad with the following historical reminder:

> The story of the *Vampyre* is founded on an opinion or report which prevailed in Hungary, and several parts of Germany, towards the beginning of the last century: — It was then asserted, that, in several places, dead persons had been known to leave their graves, and, by night, to revisit the habitations of their friends. . . . [1]

Decades later, Charlotte Brontë had not forgotten, either. In *Jane Eyre* (1847), when the heroine discovers Bertha Mason — the famous "madwoman in the attic"[2] — she struggles in vain to describe the "fearful and ghastly" apparition. Finally, as if she has been trying to avoid speaking the unspeakable, Jane breaks down: "Shall I tell you of what it reminded me? [. . .] Of the foul German spectre — the Vampyre."[3] At the end of the century, Bram Stoker's *Dracula* associated vampires with "Germany" both geographically and linguistically. Tellingly, Jonathan Harker's travel companion takes leave of him as the undead Count arrives by whispering words from Gottfried August Bürger's eighteenth-century ballad "Lenore": "die Todten reiten schnell" (the dead travel fast).[4]

The preceding chapters have returned again and again to an imaginary Germany, for the most part coextensive with the Austrian Empire in decline, teeming with the restless undead. At the turn of the twentieth century, the vague notion of haunted Germany corresponded to a real sense of uncertainty in territories where the dream of *Großdeutschland* still circulated about exactly how to define the borders of ethnicity, nation, and identity. This chapter examines a work whose composition was contemporary with Stoker's *Dracula:* the jurist Daniel Paul Schreber's *Denkwürdigkeiten eines Nervenkranken* (*Memoirs of My Nervous Illness,* 1903), an autobiographical description of vampirism.[5]

Schreber's *Memoirs* tell a story reminiscent of many of the narratives we have examined in the preceding pages. Significantly, the book presents what elsewhere is cloaked in fiction as unequivocally true to life.

Schreber is our real-world Renfield (see the previous chapter), who, in an actual asylum, drew the signs of an identity crisis induced by otherworldly attacks from undead entities.

In late 1893, nine years after a bout of severe hypochondria requiring professional help, Schreber, president of the Senate of the Superior Appeals Court in Dresden, sought medical treatment again. For half a year at the university *Nervenklinik* (psychiatric clinic) in Leipzig, his condition showed no signs of improving; indeed, it worsened. Entries from the clinic records of this period (1893–94) indicate the severity of Schreber's nervous collapse:

> *March 1.* [Patient] believes he is a young girl, fears indecent assaults.
> *March 15.* Promises attendant 500 marks for digging a grave.
> [. . .]
> *May 5.* [. . .] The doctor should immediately go to the hospital and report that there is a patient stricken with plague. He asks whether he has been dead for a long time.
> [. . .]
> *June 5.* Visit of wife. Later asks the attendant whether this was his wife in the flesh, believes she arose from the grave.[6]

Then, after two weeks at the Lindenhof, a private asylum in Coswig, Schreber began his stay at the Sonnenstein State Hospital in Dresden. While there, he wrote a book. In 1902, Schreber presented it to the courts as evidence of his capacity to reason, and on this basis he was released from the asylum. The following year, Oswald Mutze, a Leipzig editor specializing in occult literature, published the work. Schreber experienced a third, decisive crisis in 1907. He died in the Leipzig-Dösen Asylum four years later.[7]

If the existential malady of the seventeenth century went by the name "melancholy" — a preponderance of a morbid humor discoloring the soul — and its equivalent in the eighteenth century was thought to originate with insufficient use of the sanitary faculty of reason, the nineteenth century recognized as its own the condition of neurosis, whose history extends well into the twentieth.[8] Above all through the writings of Freud, the term "neurosis" has come to refer to a general psychological disease, the sense of personal ill-fittedness to the demands of life in civilization. Talk of nerves and nervousness — synonyms of "neurosis" before the meaning of the term became fixed — was in the air when Freud undertook his studies. Although Schreber's self-diagnosis of nervous illness does not mesh with Freud's theories, it draws on the same currents of European culture that gave the founder of psychoanalysis his inspiration and his vocabulary. The *Memoirs* represent a delirious attempt to deal with the diffuse pressures and anxieties that Freud addressed in another, more generally intelligible way.

The Revolution in France and Napoleonic Wars of some hundred years earlier, the liberal reforms in German-speaking Central Europe after 1848, the rise of Prussia to a position of unprecedented power thereafter, as well as the industrialization and social reorganization that fueled it — in a word, the process of modernization — led to spiritual unease in addition to material progress. The mixing of ethnicities and races in the whirling chaos of the modern metropolis produced, in the eyes of critical observers, an enervated and weak populace. The rise of workers' movements and socialism undermined the "organic" state that Romantics had envisioned. Women demanded suffrage, and Slavic peoples to the east were becoming restive. Jewish assimilation provoked anxiety about the potential corruption of the nation. In response to these threats to tradition, the reaction raised a battle cry, seeking to re-enchant the world, even if it meant cultural atavism.[9] As we have seen, the vampire stories analyzed until this point display a crypto-millenarian spirit that, while largely avoiding religious eschatology, nevertheless suggests impending doom. Schreber's *Memoirs* make explicit what is implied elsewhere. In a sense, then, the crazy *Memoirs* are one of the most matter-of-fact works treated in the study at hand.

Everything that Schreber wrote followed from his concern to establish a semblance of psychic equilibrium. In order to do so, he had to construct a unified representation of his experience. The elaborate nerve-metaphysics in the *Memoirs* stem from Schreber's attempt to produce a viable explanation of his condition for himself. Equally, his discourse about nerves and their properties is a performance intended for the medical community that sanctioned his long-term institutionalization. In the "Offener Brief an Herrn Geh. Rath Prof. Dr. Flechsig" (Open Letter to Herr Geheimer Rat Professor Dr. Flechsig) that serves as a preface to the *Memoirs,* Schreber effectively speaks to the medical profession as a whole. An appendix to the *Memoirs,* entitled "Unter welchen Voraussetzungen darf eine für geisteskrank erachtete Person gegen ihren erklärten Willen in einer Heilanstalt festgehalten werden?" (In what circumstances can a person considered insane be detained in an asylum against his declared will?), addresses a different audience. Through this letter/essay, Schreber means to reestablish the contact with his legal colleagues that he lost when he was hospitalized. Finally, Schreber presents the *Memoirs* as a work intended for humanity in general. He declares that he wishes to help parties interested in spiritual truths "zur Gewinnung richtiger Anschauungen über das Verhältniß zwischen Gott und Welt" (to correct views about the relationship between God and the world; 230–1/240). Schreber needs readers to acknowledge and share his concerns. He earmarks his text with indications that its contents, though difficult to believe, involve issues of broad, and even universal, interest. The prospect of recognition by others adds substance to claims that, were they to remain entirely private, would perhaps be unconvincing even to their author.

Denkwürdigkeiten (literally, "things worthy of consideration") is a common title for autobiographies by prominent figures in the nineteenth century. Schreber declares himself qualified to offer his judgments because he is a visionary whose ultimate fame is guaranteed. As he tells readers, "Nervenanhang" (nerve-contact; 14/48) has joined him with God and allowed him to discern affairs on earth hidden to others. Yet his status as a seer is characterized by discomfort and fear. Nerve-contact entails a "heillose[r] Wirrwarr" (unholy turmoil; 40/72) of visual and aural images. Schreber sees "flüchtig hingemachte Männer" (fleeting-improvised-men) teeming on, around, and in his body. He hears "Nervenstrahlen" (nerve-rays) chattering without interruption "in einer entsetzlich eintönigen Wiederholung derselben immer wiederkehrenden . . . Phrasen" (in a terrible, monotonous repetition of ever-recurring phrases; 40/72).[10]

Denied "das natürliche Recht des Menschen, seinen Verstandesnerven . . . die erforderliche Ruhe zu gönnen" (man's natural right to give the nerves of his mind their necessary rest; 38/70), Schreber confronts an invasion of his senses exceeding what the human organism can possibly process. In the tide of disjointed impressions, he sees the faces of Jews, Catholics, Slavs, and his first doctor, Professor Paul Emil Flechsig, trying to bring about his personal ruin. The confused parts that add up only to a spectral whole point toward a vast conspiracy in Heaven and on Earth to disintegrate his nerves, the common denominator of his body and soul.

Friedrich Kittler and Eric Santner have studied the ways that Schreber's delusions reflect the process of modernization. Kittler observes that Professor Flechsig was one of his generation's foremost advocates of materialist theories of the mind. In publications such as *Gehirn und Seele* (Brain and Soul, 1896), this positivist researcher argued that traditional notions of the psyche were outmoded, and that the human soul was nothing more than a constellation of nerve endings firing, as it were, in a spiritual vacuum.[11] Flechsig's theories form part of a historical picture that includes the broad-scale deployment of new electric technologies; these innovations provide the model for his theories of the human mental apparatus.

Significantly, new media also offer Schreber a means of representing his ideas about the brain and the soul. Describing the aural component of nerve-contact, Schreber writes:

> Es liegt vermuthlich eine ähnliche Erscheinung vor wie beim Telephonieren, d.h. die nach meinem Kopfe ausgesponnenen Strahlenfäden wirken ähnlich wie die Telephondrähte, sodaß die . . . Klangwirkung . . . *nur von mir* empfunden werden kann, wie nur der telephonisch angeschlossene Adressat, nicht aber beliebige dritte Personen . . . das mittelst Telephons Gesprochene zu hören vermögen.

[It is presumably a phenomenon like telephoning: the filaments of rays spun out towards my head act like telephone wires; the sound . . . is received *only by me* in the same way as telephonic communication can be heard only by a person who is on the telephone, but not by a third person who is somewhere between the giving and the receiving end.] (217/229)

In addition to the telephone, Schreber mentions artificial light, railways, and telegraphy in an effort to explain his experience. Thus, Kittler argues, Schreber is his physician Flechsig's negative image. Where the scientist sees progress toward a new, secular understanding of nature, the madman sees the intrusion of supernatural phenomena upsetting the balance of the world.

Santner situates the *Memoirs* in the aftermath of Bismarck's *Kulturkampf* of the 1870s, the theories of cultural degeneration that gained broad currency in the last third of the century, and the patient's difficult private life. He reads Schreber's breakdown as the result of a "symbolic investiture crisis."[12] In 1884, Schreber experienced his first nervous collapse after running unsuccessfully for office in the Reichstag on the ticket of the National Liberal Party, with the support of the Conservative Party; a socialist candidate defeated him. In 1893, Schreber was appointed to the post of *Senatspräsident* in the Supreme Court of Appeals; although this position represented a true professional success, he suffered his second breakdown soon thereafter. Schreber was relatively young to hold this office. He had suffered personal disappointment when his wife Sabine experienced a series of miscarriages in the period between her husband's bouts of illness. Moreover, Schreber's family, headed by the famous educator Daniel Gottlob Moritz Schreber,[13] viewed his marriage with a woman of lower social standing (Sabine had been an actress) with disapproval. Santner argues that career setbacks, the stress of new professional duties, and family trouble, amplified by a larger sense that the world of German *Kultur* was disintegrating, triggered Schreber's nervous breakdown. Schreber unconsciously disavowed personal responsibility for difficulties in his life when he fell ill, and he imagined that "others" had plotted his undoing. These parties came above all from ethnic groups whose perceived social ascendancy had corroded the integrity of the German state and undone stalwart German men like him.

Schreber, an extremely well-read man, refers throughout the *Memoirs* to contemporary works to add weight to his claims and bolster his arguments.[14] He knew all about the resonances that his experience held with the broader cultural anxieties to which Kittler and Santner draw our attention. Indeed, what distinguishes his authorial presence is the deployment of language and figures likely to enjoy broad currency among his potential readers.[15] By this means, Schreber gives symbolic form to his experience that others might understand and without which he would have failed to explain his condition even to himself.

The part of Schreber's discourse that has attracted the most attention he cryptically calls *Seelenmord* (soul murder).[16] Schreber presents himself as the victim of a crime, making the "Annahme, daß irgend einmal. . . . ein als Seelenmord zu bezeichnender Vorgang . . . stattgefunden habe" (assumption that at one time something called soul murder happened; 22/55). He refers to Goethe's *Faust,* Byron's *Manfred,* and Weber's *Freischütz* as literary representations of this act (21/55). None of these texts employs the term "soul murder," but as Zvi Lothane has observed, the phrase already "[had] been used in . . . European languages for . . . centuries."[17] Lothane cites a papal bull from Innocent IV in 1282, where the phrase "murderers of souls" refers to parties in league with the Devil. More generally, Lothane remarks, "soul murder" and similar formulations occur in works by authors from Shakespeare to Ibsen, where the words refer to dispiriting another person to the point that she or he gives up on life. We might add that Anselm Ritter von Feuerbach, the great jurist renowned for his reform of criminal law in Germany (and father of five accomplished sons, including the philosopher Ludwig), wrote of "soul murder" in his discussion of the famous early-nineteenth-century case of the foundling Kaspar Hauser.[18]

Schreber explains that the crime of soul murder occurs when the Devil "sich die Seele eines Menschen mittelst eines Tröpfchens Blut verschreiben läßt" (has the soul of a human being signed over to him by means of a drop of blood; 21/55). Schreber considers literary works that represent soul murder to belong to the "Reich der Fabel" (realm of fable; 21/56) because they contain depictions of the Devil, and he does not believe that the Devil exists. However, the principle of a fatal contract with a supernatural being — in his case, with God — still holds.

In *L'impuro folle,* a novelistic treatment of the Schreber case, Roberto Calasso refers to "vampirism of the divine substance."[19] This literary metaphor can be made to perform real theoretical work. Perhaps not coincidentally, the authors who composed *Faust* and *Manfred* also wrote poems about vampires.[20] Schreber reports that "dem ersten Seelenmorde . . . [sind] noch weitere Seelenmorde an den Seelen anderer Menschen gefolgt" (after the first, more soul murders were committed on the souls of other people; 22/55). His idiosyncratic quotation of Rabelais in this context — "L'appetit [*sic*] vient en mangeant" (appetite comes with eating; 22/55) — underscores the image of the ravenous undead expanding their reach indefinitely. A very short discussion by Merl Jackel adds evidence in support of the "vampiric" line of interpretation. Jackel, who does not explore the consequences in his two-page article, draws attention to the fact that the clinicians who observed Schreber during his confinement reported that the patient believed that "vampires and demons made game of him."[21]

In addition to his concern about nervous influences, Schreber also feared that he had been contaminated with syphilis — a condition often euphemistically referred to as "bad blood" in his day.[22] Finally, although it is unlikely that Schreber had read this work in particular, *Die christliche Mystik* (1836–42) by Joseph Görres (1776–1848) explains vampirism in terms that sound a great deal like the condition Schreber describes. Görres, a great champion of Catholicism in nineteenth-century Germany, accounts for vampiric influence as "eine nervöse Wirkung in die Ferne, die das Band zwischen dem Vampyre unter der Erde . . . und [dem] von ihm Heimgesuchten über der Erde knüpft" (a nervous operation through space, connected by the bond between the vampire under the earth . . . and the individual persecuted by the vampire above the earth).[23] Replace "earth" with "heaven," and "vampire" with "God," and one has Schreber's vision.

"Vieles [bleibt] dunkel" (much remains mysterious; 22/55) about soul murder, Schreber admits. However, the crime clearly entails the disruption of the border between the living and the dead. Soul murder undoes the rhythm and balance of the universe. Before the crime, "die Weltordnung" (order of the world; 14/15) was intact:

> Ein regelmäßiger Verkehr Gottes mit Menschenseelen fand . . . erst nach dem Tode statt. Den *Leichen* [näherte] sich Gott . . . um ihre Nerven, in denen das Selbstbewußtsein . . . ruhte, vermittelst der Strahlenkraft aus dem Körper heraus- und zu sich heraufzuziehen und sie damit zu neuem himmlischen Leben zu erwecken. . . . Das neue jenseitige Leben ist die *Seligkeit*.

> [Orderly interaction between God and human souls occurred only after death. God [approached] *corpses* in order to draw their nerves, in which self-awareness was . . . quiescent, out of their bodies and up to Himself by the power of the rays, thereby awakening them to new heavenly life. . . . The new life beyond is the *state of Blessedness*.]
> (14–15/48–49)

God's true office is Lord of the Dead, and "Blessedness" for mortals means that they are really dead. Ever since the soul murder, however, Heaven and Earth overlap in a chaotic fashion, for God feels inexorably drawn toward the "Nerven *lebender* Menschen" (nerves of *living* human beings; 14/48) — especially Schreber's.

> Das . . . ununterbrochen fortdauernde Zuströmen von Gottesnerven in meinen Körper [hat] den Verlust der ganzen . . . angesammelten Seligkeit und die vorläufige Unmöglichkeit der Neubegründung von Seligkeit zur Folge gehabt, sodaß die Seligkeit sozusagen suspendirt ist.

[The uninterrupted influx of God's nerves into my body has led to the total loss of all the states of Blessedness which had accumulated . . . and made it impossible for the time being to renew them; the state of Blessedness is so to speak suspended.] (17/60)

The fleeting-improvised-men and nerve-rays are parasitic offshoots from God that worm their way from the open crypt of Heaven into humanity through Schreber's person.

Earlier chapters have revealed that vampirism always poses questions of epistemology and causality. Where do vampires come from? Academics in the early eighteenth century sought to answer the question in religious and natural-scientific terms. Enlightenment wits responded with economic theories. Literary writers, who exploited the monster for entertainment, nevertheless pointed toward concrete historical processes; the vampire's preferred hunting ground, as we have seen, connects with fears that gave rise to the "original" vampires in Serbia.

Schreber, too, is divided on the matter of explaining the vampirism he experiences. In addition to his theocentric theory, he offers somewhat more "down-to-earth" speculations involving two clans, the Schrebers and the Flechsigs. Both families, Schreber writes, belong to "dem höchsten himmlischen Adel" (the highest nobility of Heaven; 22/55); his own ancestors have long been known as the "Markgrafen von Tuscien [*sic*] und Tasmanien" (Margraves of Tuscany and Tasmania; 22/55).[24] Schreber does not state unequivocally who perpetrated soul murder upon whom by signing the fatal contract. The guilty party could potentially come from either group, as could the victim; indeed, Schreber reports that he himself has been suspected of the crime (22/55). The ambiguous account does not reflect confusion, however. By cultivating an aura of mystery around his person and his family history, Schreber promotes himself and takes distance from the incoherent world surrounding him. The narrative of soul murder permits him to recover from the debilitating shock of nervous collapse and to become, if only hypothetically, the author of his own destiny. In the story Schreber tells, God's vampiric penetration of the human realm originates in an act that he himself could have performed, even if he did not.

As Kittler observes, Flechsig really was a kind of "soul murderer." In his influential writings (which Schreber had read), the neurophysiologist sought to boil the immortal spirit down to an array of physical processes. Moreover, Flechsig based his research on the postmortem examination of patients. The allegation of the Flechsig family's involvement in soul murder reflects Schreber's contemptuous attitude toward the doctor and his methods. Schreber does not name any of his own ancestors who might be involved in the crime. Instead, he dwells on the other side:

Aus beiden Familien kommen verschiedene Namen in Betracht, aus der Familie Flechsig insbesondere außer dem Professor Paul Theodor Flechsig auch ein Abraham Fürchtegott Flechsig und ein Daniel Fürchtegott Flechsig.

[Several names of both families are concerned: of the Flechsigs, besides Professor Paul Theodor Flechsig, particularly an Abraham Fürchtegott Flechsig and a Daniel Fürchtegott Flechsig.] (22/55–56)

Schreber's feelings about his former physician notwithstanding, the historical fiction that he creates serves as more than a means of assigning blame. Schreber contravenes soul murder and its effect, nerve-contact, when he writes about the ancient blood feud. Soul murder and nerve-contact produce confusion; Schreber's theory proposes clarity.

The patient's father and grandfather were named Daniel *Gottlob* Moritz Schreber and Johann *Gotthilf* Daniel Schreber. Schreber calls his physician Paul *Theodor* Flechsig instead of Paul *Emil* Flechsig, his real name, and he refers to the doctor's forebears as Abraham *Fürchtegott* Flechsig and Daniel *Fürchtegott* Flechsig.[25] As William Niederland observes, Daniel Paul Schreber is the only name in this constellation without the Greek or German word for "God" in it.[26] Schreber knows full well his doctor's real name, and he admits that he is not certain "ob unter den Vorfahren des jetzigen Professors Flechsig sich wirklich ein Daniel Fürchtegott Flechsig und ein Abraham Fürchtegott Flechsig befunden hat" (whether there actually had been a Daniel Fürchtegott Flechsig and an Abraham Fürchtegott Flechsig among the forebears of the present Professor Flechsig; 22/56). But mere facts do not matter, for Schreber wants to illustrate a higher truth. Through the genealogical name game, he asserts that everyone in the two families has a predetermined connection to God, *except for him*.

Just as the idea of soul murder permits Schreber to trace nerve-contact back to the contract drafted by an unspecified ancestor or member of the Flechsig family, his notion of the "Aufschreibesystem" (writing-down-system; 90/118) allows him to localize the source of his troubles in writings of some sort — a text he can counter with his own work. The two fantasies serve the same purpose: to provide the patient with a mirror in which he can make sense of his alienation and mark his independence from God, thereby causing the vampiric interpenetration of nerves to cease.

The writing-down-system keeps track of every aspect of Schreber's life:

Man unterhält *Bücher oder sonstige Aufzeichnungen,* in denen nun schon seit Jahren alle meine Gedanken, alle meine Redewendungen, alle meine Gebrauchsgegenstände, alle sonst in meinem Besitze oder meiner Nähe befindlichen Sachen, alle Personen, mit denen ich verkehre usw. *aufgeschrieben* werden.

[*Books or other notes* are kept in which for years have been *written down* all my thoughts, all my phrases, all my necessaries, all the articles in my possession, all persons with whom I come into contact, etc.] (90/119)

Schreber theorizes that a caste of idiot angel-scribes administrates the writing down:

[ich] vermuthe . . . , daß das Aufschreiben von Wesen besorgt wird, denen auf entfernten Weltkörpern sitzend nach Art der flüchtig hingemachten Männer menschliche Gestalt gegeben ist, die aber . . . des Geistes völlig entbehren und denen . . . die Feder zu dem ganz mechanisch von ihnen besorgten Geschäfte des Aufschreibens sozusagen in die Hand gedrückt wird.

[I presume that the writing down is done by creatures given human shape on distant celestial bodies in the manner of the fleeting-improvised-men lacking all intelligence; their hands are led automatically, as it were, . . . for the purpose of making them write down.] (90/119)

The writing-down-system functions like a feedback loop animating the "unholy turmoil" engulfing the unlucky man.[27] Nerve-contact, we have noted, makes it impossible for Schreber to "give the nerves of his mind their necessary rest." Schreber finds himself in a perpetual state of excitement and agitation because incomplete thoughts and fragmentary phrases constantly present themselves to him. Thus, although Schreber does not explicitly say so, the writing-down-system presents an alternate vision of the process at work when nerve-rays storm his senses. More importantly, by copying the writing-down-system in his own writing, Schreber invests himself with power. He discerns the way that nervous energy circulates in the universe, and having identified the "Technik" (technique; 25/58) at work, he knows how to counteract the disruption of his body and mind by intruding rays.

Ich vermag von allen Erinnerungen aus meinem Leben . . . durch lebhafte Vorstellung derselben Bilder zu schaffen mit der Wirkung, daß dieselben . . . sowohl für meine eigenen Nerven, als für die mit denselben in Verbindung stehenden Strahlen da, wo ich die betreffenden Dinge wahrgenommen wissen will, sichtbar werden. [. . .] Gerade so wie durch Strahlen . . . gewisse Bilder, die man zu sehen wünscht, auf mein Nervensystem geworfen werden, bin ich umgekehrt in der Lage, den Strahlen meinerseits Bilder vorzuführen, deren Eindruck ich diesen zu verschaffen beabsichtige.

[By vivid imagination I can produce pictures of all recollections from my life. . . . so that these images become visible . . . where I want

them to be seen by my own nerves and by the rays that are connected to them. [. . .] In the same way as rays throw on to my
nerves pictures they would like to see . . . I too can in turn produce
pictures for the rays which I want them to see.] (159–60/180–81)

Schreber calls this process "Zeichnen" — a term that the translation
somewhat misleadingly renders as "picturing" (159/180). On the one
hand, "Zeichnen" involves a mental operation that seems no different
from "imagination" in the conventional sense of the word. On the other
hand, however, Schreber considers the images he produces to be real,
physical things with real, physical effects.[28]

"Zeichnen" literally means "drawing," and Schreber clearly believes
that he is operating on his upset being when he "produce[s] pictures for
the rays." The original German stresses the quasi-magical effectiveness of
the activity. "Das 'Zeichnen' . . . glaube ich . . . mit Recht . . . ein umge-
kehrtes Wundern nennen zu dürfen" ("drawing" . . . may rightly . . . be
called a reversed miracle; 160/181). The operation is a miracle not just
because it renews the self-determination and autonomy that the patient
lost when he fell ill, but also because it turns back the flow of nerve-
rays in the cosmos. Schreber's main concern is to counteract the vampiric
invasion of his person. Through "drawing," the patient seeks to uphold
the integrity of his being in the face of nervous dissolution.

This is the proper context for Schreber's much-discussed assertion
that he has been transformed into a woman in order to salvage the vanished Order of the World. Freud, in his influential reading of the *Memoirs,*
argues that a homosexual fantasy underlies the patient's feminization.[29]
Schreber's statement that he experiences "Seelenwollust" (soul-volup-
tuousness; 68/98) seems to support this claim. Ida Macalpine and Richard A. Hunter, who translated *Denkwürdigkeiten* into English, argue that
"Schreber fell ill when a wish-fantasy that he could, would, or should
have children became pathogenic."[30] This interpretation also appears
plausible in light of the fact that the patient was in a childless marriage
before falling ill; indeed, Schreber declares at one point in his autobiography that his transformation into a woman will bring forth "neue Menschen aus Schreber'schem Geiste" (new human beings out of Schreber's
spirit; 82/112). Freud, Macalpine, and Hunter's claims may be too literal
minded, however. Schreber chides those who would take what he says
in a vulgar sense: "honny [*sic*] soit qui mal y pense" (shame upon him
who thinks evil of it; 160/181). His voluptuousness concerns his *soul.*
Likewise, he intends to bring forth new humans out of his *spirit.* Even
if "soul" and "spirit" mean "nerves" for Schreber, he does not harbor a
commonplace kind of wish. His primary objective concerns the creation
of distance between himself and a phenomenal world in which it is impossible for him to retain an integral identity of any sort.

Jacques Lacan, who devoted his third seminar to the *Memoirs,* provides the tools necessary to understand the mechanics of Schreber's sex change.[31] According to Lacan, the mutability of everything that Schreber sees and hears through the nerve-rays exemplifies the psychotic condition. Psychotics are excluded from the Symbolic, the sum total of potential signifying operations that enable communication within a social group and assure psychic stability for its individual members. Psychotics have no access to the Symbolic because they are not "castrated." Lacan's dramatic formulation refers to the fact that the subject, in order to enjoy a reasonably healthy psychic life, must forego certain roles in order to perform others. Exemplarily, this occurs when the polymorphously perverse infant, an entity that does not distinguish between itself and the world around it, is assigned points of identification ("boy" or "girl") structuring its subsequent development and socialization.[32] Castration enables individuals to display symptoms, that is, to bring invisible tensions and unresolved conflicts in their lives into focus. From a Lacanian perspective, Schreber at his most acute levels of nervous illness cannot discern the semiotic structures that nonpsychotic persons employ to navigate the world. The distinctions between "above" and "below," "living" and "dead," "man" and "woman" have vanished for him. Schreber floats in a nonspace — like the half-dreaming, half-waking state of Dracula's victims Harker, Mina, and Lucy — unsure both about his gender and general place in the world.

The psychotic condition, of which Lacan makes Schreber the exemplar, was not permanent for the patient. Schreber managed to lay hold of a defined place within a set of symbolic coordinates by fashioning himself as a woman. In other words, he castrated himself. This operation did not only work negatively; indeed, Schreber describes it in positive terms:

> Ich kann . . . mir selbst und den Strahlen den Eindruck verschaffen, daß mein Körper mit weiblichen Brüsten und weiblichem Geschlechtsteil ausgestattet sei. Das Zeichnen eines weiblichen Hinteren an meinen Körper . . . ist mir so zur Gewohnheit geworden, daß ich dies beim Bücken jedesmal fast unwillkürlich thue.

> [I can give myself and the rays the impression that my body has female breasts and a female sexual organ. . . . The picturing of female buttocks on my body . . . has become such a habit that I do it almost automatically whenever I bend down.] (160/181)

When he relates how he "draws" himself with feminine features, Schreber counteracts the denaturing forces that have upset his being. Since these are the same forces that have imperiled the Order of the World, his feminization opens the way for the return of balance to the cosmos as a whole. This is why Schreber pursues his transformation with such ardor.

Ich habe . . . die Pflege der Weiblichkeit mit vollem Bewußtsein auf meine Fahne geschrieben und werde dies . . . auch fernerhin thun, mögen andere Menschen, denen die übersinnlichen Gründe verborgen sind, von mir denken, was sie wollen.

[I have wholeheartedly inscribed the cultivation of femininity on my banner, and I will continue to do so . . . whatever other people who are ignorant of the supernatural reasons may think of me.] (124/149)

The "supernatural reasons" to which Schreber refers concern God. "Zeichnen" holds back the infiltration from above and keeps the vampiric denaturing of the mortal realm in check. Schreber engineers a divide between Heaven and Earth and rebuilds, at least in part, the "wundervoller Aufbau" (miraculous structure; 20/54) of the universe that went missing with soul murder.[33]

To the extent that Schreber managed, by picturing ("Zeichnen"), to assert control over the portion of life still remaining to him, the shadowy fleeting-improvised-men revealed themselves as insubstantial apparitions of no real danger, the curse of soul murder weakened its grip, and the vampiric aspects of the Almighty started to fade.

This space that the patient thereby marked out also allows us to make sense of what Santner has called "Schreber's Jewish question."[34] This issue pertains to Schreber's acute sense of personal dislocation, which he portrays as a matter of "living death" or, if one prefers, "death in life."

As we noted earlier, Schreber describes vast conspiracies of internal and external agitators intent on taking over Germany and his own person — the Fatherland and its citizen-son. At the same time, the patient at points calls *himself* "der ewige Jude" (the Eternal Jew; 41/73), the German name for a figure known in English literature as "the Wandering Jew." Santner argues that Schreber writes "from the perspective of those figures in whom modern European society 'secreted' its disavowed knowledge of chronic structural crisis."[35] He cites Sander Gilman's discussion of the relationship between Schreber's *Memoirs* and late-nineteenth-century stereotypes about Jews in Germany.[36] As Gilman observes, in Schreber's day a wide array of racist medical and biological discourses represented Jews as possessing physical structures different from those of Aryans. These discourses, which would gain in currency until the atrocities perpetrated by the National Socialists in the twentieth century, centered on what Gilman calls the "diseased Jew." Their rhetoric portrayed members of the Semitic race as enervated, degenerate beings. Schreber, Gilman notes, applies the same vocabulary to himself. Santner gives Schreber ideological credit for this appropriation and argues that he "managed to avoid . . . the totalitarian temptation"[37] because he identified with the ethnic group that, years later, Hitler would attempt to destroy.

Santner is too generous. The resonances in the *Memoirs* that Gilman identifies with contemporary scientific ideas are substantial, but Schreber's assumption of traits coded as Jewish does not mean that he sympathizes with real Jews. Numerous authors who would have been known to Schreber (and any other educated German) used the figure of the Eternal Jew in their literary creations.[38]

The myth of the Eternal Jew originated in monastic chronicles of the thirteenth century that told of a man who mocked Jesus on his way to Golgotha. Christ, according to the tale, pronounced a curse damning the man to wander the earth until the end of time. The story entered into broad circulation through sixteenth-century chapbooks; for the next two hundred years, its many retellings stressed the repentance of the sinner who had come to see the truth after much suffering. In the eighteenth century, in keeping with the encyclopedic and secularized spirit of the times, the Eternal Jew represented the wisdom of the ages: he had traveled through time and space for millennia and witnessed the greater part of human history. In the nineteenth century, when the Romantics and their heirs made the myth the subject of their writings, the Eternal Jew became a much more complex and contradictory creature. Shelley, for example, endowed the Eternal Jew with Promethean characteristics, and later writers followed his lead by representing this figure as a defiant spirit who existed in opposition to divine authority.

Many literary incarnations of the Eternal Jew valorized the figure's quest for human freedom, but others lent him diabolical traits and made him responsible for historical catastrophes. Which of the literary treatments Schreber knew does not matter. The composite image that emerges from them is that of an individual leading a timeless, undead existence; the Eternal Jew can show kindness or cruelty towards his human associates, and he can adopt a contrite or a rebellious attitude toward God, but he is always alone. The figure's unique mode of being — his "vampirized" condition — is why Schreber presents himself as the Eternal Jew.

Schreber's "core identification with the . . . body of the Jew"[39] is entirely self-centered, for he readily abandons the alterity that being Jewish signifies.

> Wenn ich mir vergegenwärtige, welche Opfer . . . mir auferlegt worden sind, so ergiebt sich für mich das Bild eines Martyriums, das ich in seiner Gesammtheit nur mit dem Kreuzestod Jesu Christi vergleichen kann.

> [When I think of my sacrifices . . . the picture emerges of a martyrdom which all in all I can only compare with the crucifixion of Jesus Christ.] (201/214)

At another point, Schreber presents himself as a German "Nationalheiliger" (National Saint; 82/112) destined to redeem his country. He clearly considers his metamorphosis a means to an end. Schreber gives up being the Eternal Jew in order to be the King of the Jews. His further representation of himself as a German Joan of Arc negates his real openness to otherness and situates him in a decidedly conservative political camp.[40]

The mythology that Schreber wrote welcomed Jewishness because it signified personal difference, not ethnic difference. He was not a more tolerant person when he composed his *Memoirs* than he had been before his nervous illness. Clinic records reveal that Schreber saw himself as a diseased, feminized being even when first hospitalized in Flechsig's clinic. This perception was a source of terror for the patient before he realized that he could transform fear into strength. By embracing what God logically could not be (a being of the "weaker" sex and an outcast of an "inferior" race), Schreber redrew the dividing line between Heaven and Earth. As we have seen, the patient devised an elaborate set of instances regulating his connection to the world with which he lost touch at the outset of his nervous illness: his ideas of a "soul murder" based on a contract, the "writing-down-system," and "picturing" all provided the means by which he could posit a divide between his person and the rest of the universe in order to claim a particularized site of subjectivity for himself. Schreber repeatedly forged distance between himself and God when he offered his theories of how "nerve-contact" works. In the process, he constructed a framework in which he occupied a conflicted but relatively fixed place as an undead, androgynous Jew-for-Germany. Schreber thereby transformed his abjection into a sign of greatness.

* * *

The process of infiltration and the state of terror described in the *Memoirs* mirror vampire fictions, which, as previous chapters have shown, are characterized by haunting encounters with doubles, twilight states of consciousness, and the occult transfer of mind and matter. In these works, depictions of channels of communication between the natural and supernatural worlds transpose, into an imaginary dimension, the opening of boundaries that occurred in reality through imperial expansion, the entry of women into the workplace, the implementation of new technologies speeding exchanges between distant parties, as well as other cultural transformations.

Nineteenth-century literature recorded anxieties surrounding struggles for dominance by competing groups within the always combative "family of man." "Don Juan von Kolomea" (Don Juan of Kolomea, 1866), the first literary success of Leopold von Sacher-Masoch (1836–95) — another writer whose name has become synonymous with pathology — offers a prime example.[41] The tale, set in lands immediately adjacent to Schreber's Germany, contains a description that reads almost like the patient's conflicted self-image. In the following excerpt, the narrator relates how a Jewish woman gazes upon the hero of the story:

> Sie war schön, als [ihr Mann] sie heimführte. . . . Jetzt ist alles so befremdend scharf in ihrem Gesichte. Schmerzen, Schande, Fußtritte, Peitschenhiebe haben lange in dem Antlitz ihres Volkes gewühlt, bis es diesen glühend welken, wehmütig höhnischen, demütig rache-lustigen Ausdruck bekam. Sie krümmte ihren hohen Rücken, ihre feinen, durchsichtigen Hände spielten mit dem Branntweinmaß, ihre Augen hefteten sich auf den Fremden. Eine glühende, verlangende Seele stieg aus diesen großen schwarzen wollüstigen Augen, ein Vampir aus dem Grabe einer verfaulten Menschennatur, und saugte sich in das schöne Antlitz des Fremden.

> [She was beautiful when [her husband] first led her home. . . . Now, everything is strangely harsh in her face. Injuries, shame, kicks, whip-pings have raked across her people's countenance for so long that it has acquired this glowing but limp, wistfully contemptuous, humble yet vengeful expression. She bent her high back. Her delicate, trans-parent hands played with the pitcher of brandy. Her eyes fixed them-selves on the stranger. A glowing, yearning soul emerged from those big, black, lustful eyes — a vampire from the grave of a human nature that had grown rotten — and sucked upon his handsome visage.][42]

Like Sacher-Masoch's other works, "Don Juan" evokes the heavy burden of the past in the multiethnic Galician territories of the Habsburgs.[43] On the one hand, the author advocates ethnic and religious toleration, but on the other the unremitting war of the sexes he portrays belies the fantasy of peace; the vampiric quality of the Jewish woman at the inn stems from disappointed desire and humiliation that are not hers alone, but also belong to her people.

The period also abounds in less sympathetic portrayals of the vampiric state and desire for revenge. Thus, Arthur Conan Doyle's "The Parasite" (1894) tells how an old, West Indian woman uses her powers as a medium to threaten the career and marriage of a young university professor, thereby threatening both the reproduction of knowledge and the preservation of the Victorian family. Guy de Maupassant's "The Horla" (1887) is narrated by a man who suspects that he has fallen victim to the influence of a "new being"[44] originating in Brazil; this creature, which cannot be seen by the naked eye, threatens to replace humankind as the next step of evolution.

Such fantastic stories flourished during what historians sometimes call "the long nineteenth century," a period bookended by two cultural cataclysms, the French Revolution and the First World War. The era is distinguished by industrialization, the professionalization of medicine and science, the institution of the modern police and penal systems, as well as the birth of mass politics. The *Memoirs,* like their more purely literary counterparts, explore the effects of modernization on a morbidly sensitive individual consciousness. However, the undeniable seriousness of Schreber's nervous collapse does not preclude the possibility that he also possessed a certain wry perspective on his situation, which he knew confounded just about every bit of received wisdom.[45] Schreber's *Memoirs* do not present only the story of a passive victim suffering unjust torment. They also describe how the author came to embrace his condition.

The quasi-holy delirium of the exceptional individual is a Romantic topos that grants writers the means to claim special vision and an exalted position from which they can indict the ways of other men. Among many literary examples one might cite, the enigmatic *Nachtwachen* (*Night Watches,* 1804) of the pseudonymous "Bonaventura" offers the best point of reference. This satirical work, in its condemnation of human hypocrisy, also speaks of soul murders (indeed, it employs the very phrase), madness, vampires, and the Wandering Jew. The first-person narrative unfolds as a loose series of episodes centering on an author who is a mystery to others, himself, and God:

> Ich bin schon oft darangegangen, vor dem Spiegel meiner Einbildungskraft sitzend, mich selbst leidlich zu porträtieren. . . . Da bin ich denn über mich verrückt geworden, und habe als den letzten Grund meines Daseins hypothetisch angenommen, daß eben der Teufel selbst, um dem Himmel einen Possen zu spielen, . . . mich gleichsam als eine lex cruciata für unseren Herrgott niedergeschrieben habe, bei der er sich am Weltgerichtstage den Kopf zerbrechen solle.

> [I've already often made a start, sitting before the mirror of my imagination, at passably portraying myself. . . . I then became bewildered over myself and assumed hypothetically as the final ground of my existence that the very Devil himself, in order to play a trick on heaven, . . . inscribed me . . . as it were as a *lex cruciata* for our Lord God, over which He should break His head on Judgment Day.][46]

"Bonaventura" makes declarations that could stem from Schreber's pen:

> Dieser verdammte Widerspruch in mir geht so weit, daß z.B. der Papst selbst beim Beten nicht andächtiger sein kann, als ich beim Blasphemieren. . . . Wenn andere verständige und gefühlsvolle Leute in die Natur hinauswandern um sich dort poetische Stifts- und Taborshütten zu errichten, so trage ich vielmehr dauerhafte und auserlesene Baumaterialien zu einem allgemeinen Narrenhause zusammen. . . .

[This cursed contradiction in me goes so far that, for example, the pope himself cannot be more devout in praying than I am in blaspheming. . . . If other sensible and feeling people wander out into nature in order to erect poetic tabernacles and shrines there for themselves, I prefer to gather together lasting and choice building materials for a general fools-house. . . .][47]

Schreber's *Memoirs*, like the *Night Watches*, make the world appear as a single asylum, and the narrator/author its unacknowledged ruler.

Needless to say, the *Memoirs* are extraordinarily difficult to read, and the patient realizes as much. Near the end of his work, Schreber appeals for more thorough and careful physical inspection than he has received until now:

mir [bleibt] nichts weiter übrig, *als meine Person der fachmännischen Beurtheilung als ein wissenschaftliches Beobachtungsobjekt anzubieten.* Hierzu einzuladen ist der *Hauptzweck, den ich mit der Veröffentlichung meiner Arbeit verfolge.*

[I can do no more than *offer my person as object of scientific observation for the judgment of experts.* My *main motive in publishing this book* is to invite this.] (243/251)

Schreber believes that, were qualified individuals only to look at him in the proper manner, they would see tangible evidence supporting his claims. However, he is not particularly optimistic about receiving the attention anytime soon.

Aeußerstenfalls muß ich hoffen, daß dermaleinst durch *Sektion meiner Leiche* beweiskräftige Besonderheiten meines Nervensystems werden konstatirt werden können.

[Short of this I can only hope that at some future time peculiarities of my nervous system will be discovered by *dissection of my body,* which will provide stringent proof.] (243/251)

The patient expects vindication only in death. As Kittler observes, Schreber presents his *Memoirs* as the "transposition of a body into a corpus."[48] The data contained in the wires of his nerves mirrors the information that his book contains. The final gesture that the patient makes in his autobiography underscores the central paradox of his vampiric state. He views himself as neither entirely dead nor alive and "exists" as a cadaver-in-the-making.

The *Memoirs* secured Schreber's release from Sonnenstein. Although the court judged the manuscript "the product of a morbid imagination,"[49] it determined that the author possessed a remarkable intellect and was capable of managing his own affairs. Indeed, released from the asylum, Schreber subsequently led a quiet life as a private citizen for four years, doing legal work and even adopting a daughter with his wife.[50] In 1907, his mother died in May and his wife suffered a stroke in November.[51] These events overtaxed Schreber's system, and he experienced a nervous crisis on November 27, which led him to be institutionalized for the third time. Schreber died in the asylum in 1911. Although clinic records from the final period of illness are few, one of the last entries available (April, 1910) underscores the therapeutic value the patient attached to writing until the end: "At times writes something on his note pad, but the writing is far removed from anything resembling written characters."[52] The glyphs that Schreber took down were charged with nervous energy in excess of what his system could support. They signified that the "miraculous structure" of the universe was soon to be restored, when God welcomed a compliant corpse to Heaven.

While Schreber lay dead, perhaps dreaming in blessed sleep of the cosmic order he had held in balance during his hellish incarceration, the world returned to its former state. Eleven years after the publication of the *Memoirs,* the European body politic yielded to the very conflict that Schreber had sought to combat with his writing campaign. The war of 1914–18, which mobilized nationalist sentiment, cults of manhood, myths of ethnic identity, and hypermodern technologies of impersonal killing, disarticulated the bodies and destroyed the souls of the human cogs in its machinery. It is rightly called the First *World* War.

The supposed catharsis of universalized combat seemed welcome to the generation that stepped onto the stage of history just as Schreber made his exit. Even artists and writers — among others, Otto Dix, Max Ernst, Oskar Kokoschka, Alfred Döblin, Georg Trakl, and Richard Dehmel (at the age of fifty-one, no less) — volunteered for military service. Thomas Mann, one of the leading lights of the intelligentsia, exclaimed: "die Herzen der Dichter [standen] sogleich in Flammen . . . , als jetzt Krieg wurde!" (the hearts of the poets were immediately aflame . . . , now that war erupted!).[53] Before long, however, the soldiers who emerged from the open grave of the trenches — where corpses had stared them in the eye and poisoned life with death — brought a psychic contagion home to infect the small part of the civilian populace that had not already succumbed to the modern miasma. Austria was transformed from a great empire to a rump state. Germany was stripped of Alsace-Lorraine, its colonies, and its army. The Slavs grew more powerful than ever before, especially after the October Revolution in Russia. Jews and Socialists entered the new, republican government in Weimar. The reparations imposed on the losing German side threatened to leech off the last reserves of lands already deprived of a substantial part of their manpower. This enervated state, which reproduced for millions the situation Schreber had confronted some twenty years earlier, led to the vampires of interwar Germany, which the next chapter explores.

Notes

[1] John Stagg, *The Minstrel of the North; or, Cumbrian Legends. Being a Poetical Miscellany of Legendary, Gothic, and Romantic Tales* (Manchester: Mark Wardle, 1816), 228.

[2] See the highly influential feminist study by Sandra M. Gilbert and Susan Gubar, *The Madwoman in the Attic: The Woman Writer and the Nineteenth-Century Literary Imagination* (New Haven: Yale UP, 2000); this book first appeared in 1979.

[3] Charlotte Brontë, *Jane Eyre*, in *The Brontës: Three Great Novels* (London: JG Press, 1995), 222.

[4] Bram Stoker, *Dracula*, ed. Glennis Byron (Ontario: Broadview, 1998), 41.

[5] References will be given parenthetically and follow the text printed in Daniel Paul Schreber, *Denkwürdigkeiten eines Nervenkranken* (Wiesbaden: Focus, 1973); the second number indicates corresponding pages in the English translation — Daniel Paul Schreber, *Memoirs of My Nervous Illness*, trans. Ida Macalpine and Richard A. Hunter (Cambridge: Harvard UP, 1988). Unless otherwise noted, emphases occur in the original; occasionally, the translation has been slightly modified.

[6] Quoted in Zvi Lothane, *In Defense of Schreber: Soul Murder and Psychiatry* (Hillsdale: The Analytic Press, 1992), 471–72.

[7] For the most complete biography of Schreber to date, see Lothane.

[8] The term, coined in 1769 by the Scottish doctor William Cullen, originally described a disordered sensorium; see W.F. Bynum, *Science and the Practice of Medicine in the Nineteenth Century* (Cambridge: Cambridge UP, 1994), 15–16.

[9] For a discussion of this topic as it relates to the emergence of National Socialism, see Peter Viereck, *Metapolitics: The Roots of the Nazi Mind* (New York: Capricorn, 1965); and George L. Mosse, *The Crisis of German Ideology: Intellectual Origins of the Third Reich* (New York: Howard Fertig, 1999).

[10] Alex Proyas's *Dark City* (1998), a futuristic film noir in the vein of Ridley Scott's *Bladerunner* (1982), features a mad visionary (Kiefer Sutherland) named Daniel Paul Schreber; the film's debt to the *Memoirs* comes out especially in the host of chattering, spectral beings clearly inspired by the patient's "fleeting-improvised-men." Improbably, then, Schreber has found an advocate in popular culture.

[11] Friedrich Kittler, *Discourse Networks, 1800/1900*, trans. Michael Metteer with Chris Cullens (Stanford: Stanford UP, 1990), 293–98.

[12] Eric Santner, *My Own Private Germany: Daniel Paul Schreber's Secret History of Modernity* (Princeton: Princeton UP, 1996), 26.

[13] Lothane, 106–98, provides the biography of Schreber *père*.

[14] Elisabeth Schreiber, *Schreber und der Zeitgeist* (Berlin: R. Matzker, 1987), charts and discusses the various forms of discourse that echo in the *Memoirs*.

[15] In his introduction to the *Memoirs*, Schreber writes: "Um einigermaßen verständlich zu werden, werde ich viel in Bildern und Gleichnissen reden müssen" (To make myself at least somewhat comprehensible I shall have to speak much in images and similes; 8/41).

[16] See especially Morton Schatzman, *Soul Murder: Persecution in the Family* (New York: Signet, 1974).

[17] Lothane, 416.

[18] See Martin Kitchen, *Kaspar Hauser: Europe's Child* (New York: Palgrave, 2001), 66–80.

[19] Roberto Calasso, *L'impuro folle* (Milan: Adelphi, 1974), 33.

[20] See James B. Twitchell, *The Living Dead: A Study of the Vampire in Romantic Literature* (Durham: Duke UP, 1985), 76–79, for a discussion of *Manfred* as a vampire story.

[21] Merl M. Jackel, "A Note on Soul Murder: Vampire Fantasies," printed in appendix to Niederland, *The Schreber Case: Psychoanalytic Profile of a Paranoid Personality* (Hillsdale: The Analytic Press, 1984), 164. See Philip D. Jaffe and Frank Dicataldo, "Clinical Vampirism: Blending Myth and Reality," in *The Vampire: A Casebook*, ed. Alan Dundes (Madison: U of Wisconsin P, 1998), 143–58, for a survey and discussion of the term's use in twentieth-century psychiatric discourse.

[22] Here, one may find further connections with *Dracula*, which is obsessed with tainted bodies; the novel's author is sometimes alleged to have died from the illness. See Barbara Belford, *Bram Stoker and the Man Who Was Dracula* (New York: Da Capo, 2002), 122, 320–21.

[23] Joseph von Görres, *Die christliche Mystik*, 5 vols. (Graz: Akademische Druck- u. Verlagsanstalt, 1960), III, 287. Should Schreber have read certain essays of August Strindberg (or, for that matter, the latter's friend Stanislaw Przybyszewski, among others), he would have encountered similar notions of nervous transfer explicitly described as "vampirism." For example, Strindberg's *A Blue Book* (1907–1912), though published after Schreber's *Memoirs*, has an entry entitled "The Vampire," as well as many discussions of telepathy, the properties of nerves, and magnetic influence; these topics recur throughout many of Strindberg's other works. Przybyszewski (1868–1927) shares this fascination with the occult; his essay on the paintings of Edvard Munch gave one of the latter's untitled pictures the title "Vampire," by which it has come conventionally to be known (Stanislaw Przybyszewski, "Ohne Titel ["Das Werk des Edvard Munch"], *Kritische und essayistische Schriften*, ed. Michael M. Schardt (Paderborn: Igel, 1992), 151–59).

[24] Niederland, 85–91, discusses the titles Schreber gives his clan. Tasmania, Niederland observes, was a British penal colony; the opulent and bloody history of Florence, he argues, signified sin and crime to Schreber.

[25] For biographical information on Flechsig and an account of his views on his most famous patient, see Lothane, 199–259.

[26] Niederland, 46–48.

[27] Niederland argues that the writing-down-system represents a paranoid version of the blackboard that Schreber's father used to record the improper behavior of

his son (80). He also suggests that the idiot angels and fleeting-improvised-men that Schreber mentions are a hallucinatory reminder of the drawings of exercises in the callisthenic manuals his father wrote (Niederland, 45–46, 80, 94–95). Martin Stingelin, in contrast, has linked the patient's obsession with recording angels and spectral watchers to the clinical practices of observation in the asylum where he was interned. Martin Stingelin, "Die Seele als Funktion des Körpers: Zur Seelenpolitik der Leipziger Universitätspsychiatrie unter Paul Emil Flechsig," in *Diskursanalysen 2: Institution Universität*, ed. Friedrich A. Kittler, Manfred Schneider, and Samuel Weber (Opladen: Westdeutscher Verlag, 1989).

[28] "Das 'Zeichnen' [hat] . . . für mich . . . eine . . . wesentliche Bedeutung. Das Sehen von Bildern wirkt . . . reinigend auf die Strahlen, sie gehen dann ohne die ihnen sonst anhaftende zerstörende Schärfe bei mir ein" ("Picturing" holds a deep significance for me. Seeing pictures purifies rays . . . ; they then enter into me without their usual destructive force; 161–62/182).

[29] See Sigmund Freud, "Psychoanalytic Notes on an Autobiographical Account of a Case of Paranoia (Dementia Paranoides)," in *Three Case Histories*, ed. Philip Rieff (New York: Collier, 1963).

[30] Ida Macalpine and Richard A. Hunter, "Translators' Analysis of the Case," in Schreber, *Memoirs*, 385.

[31] Jacques Lacan, *The Seminar, Book III: The Psychoses*, trans. Russell Grigg (New York: W. W. Norton, 1993); see also Lacan's essay on Schreber, "On a question preliminary to any possible treatment of psychosis," in *Écrits: A Selection*, trans. Alan Sheridan (New York: W. W. Norton, 1977), 179–225.

[32] See Lacan's essay, "The Mirror Stage as Formative of the Function of the I as Revealed in Psychoanalytic Experience," in *Écrits*, 1–7.

[33] Schreber has derived his conception of the universe's structure from his readings in contemporary natural science and philosophy; see Schreiber, 32–57.

[34] Santner, 103.

[35] Santner, 144.

[36] Sander L. Gilman, *Freud, Race, and Gender* (Princeton: Princeton UP, 1993), 152–54; see Gilman's excellent and wide-ranging study, *The Jew's Body* (New York: Routledge, 1991), for a fuller picture.

[37] Santner, xi.

[38] George K. Anderson, in *The Legend of the Wandering Jew* (Hanover: Brown UP, 1991), thoroughly documents and discusses the many articulations of the story, including Central European and Scandinavian variants.

[39] Santner, 111.

[40] See the concluding portion of Elias Canetti, *Crowds and Power*, trans. Carol Stewart (New York: Farrar, Straus, and Giroux, 1984), which argues that Schreber's paranoia anticipates Hitler's megalomania; Santner essentially makes the reverse case.

[41] For a discussion of the connections between the author's biography, fictions, and the clinical discourse surrounding them, see Barbara Hyams, "Causal Connections: The Case of Sacher-Masoch," in *One Hundred Years of*

Masochism: Literary Texts, Social and Cultural Contexts, ed. Michael C. Finke and Carl Niekerk (Amsterdam: Rodopi, 2000), 139–54. Gilles Deleuze, in *Masochism: Coldness and Cruelty,* trans. Jean McNeil (Cambridge: Zone Books, 1991), offers a comparative analysis of Sacher-Masoch and Sade, as well as a philosophical discussion of differences between masochism and sadism.

[42] Leopold von Sacher-Masoch, *Mondnacht: Erzählungen aus Galizien,* ed. Karl Emmerich (Berlin: Rütten & Loening, 1991), 28.

[43] Karl Emmerich, "Nachwort," in Sacher-Masoch, 441–53.

[44] Guy de Maupassant, "The Horla," *Demons of the Night: Tales of the Fantastic, Madness, and the Supernatural from Nineteenth-Century France,* ed. Joan Kessler (Chicago: U of Chicago P, 1995), 303.

[45] See in this regard Lacan, *The Seminar, Book III,* 75–79.

[46] Ernst August Friedrich Klingemann (Bonaventura), *Die Nachtwachen des Bonaventura,* ed. and trans. Gerald Gillespie (Austin: U of Texas P, 1971), 110–11. Text and translation are taken from this bilingual edition.

[47] Klingemann, 110–11.

[48] Kittler, *Discourse Networks,* 293.

[49] Quoted in Samuel M. Weber, "Introduction to the 1988 Edition," in Schreber, *Memoirs,* xxv. This text was originally published in German as the introduction to Daniel Paul Schreber, *Denkwürdigkeiten eines Nervenkranken* (Berlin: Ullstein, 1973).

[50] See Lothane, 84–88.

[51] Lothane, 93.

[52] Lothane, 482.

[53] Quoted in Thomas Anz, "Vitalismus und Kriegsdichtung," *Kultur und Krieg: Die Rolle der Intellektuellen, Künstler und Schriftsteller im Ersten Weltkrieg,* ed. Wolfgang J. Mommsen (Munich: Oldenbourg, 1996), 235.

6: Vampires in Weimar: Shades of History

THERE IS GOOD REASON, Siegfried Kracauer argued in his classic study *From Caligari to Hitler* (1947), why Weimar Germany provided the crucible for horror cinema. The social, historical, and political conditions of the country between the First and Second World Wars created a style in the new mass medium that exalted elemental passions and turbulent states of mind.[1] Lotte Eisner, another authority on the period, entitled her influential book *L'écran démoniaque* (*The Haunted Screen*, 1952). The visual language of Weimar cinema, Eisner observes, is characterized by a stunning use of light and darkness. The signature chiaroscuro of these films gives shape to themes of doubles, fantasies of revenge, and passion.[2] Eisner's formal analysis complements Kracauer's psycho-historical approach by articulating the imagery of socially and politically determined unease in post-Armistice and pre-rearmament Germany.

When Germany surrendered in 1918, the country had not yet been defeated militarily. For the brief life span of the Weimar Republic, the right wing felt grave resentment that the newly established government had agreed to what it called the *Schandfrieden* (shameful peace) at Versailles. At the same time, the far left viewed the political moderates who now headed the state with contempt for retaining the superannuated bureaucratic and institutional structures of the collapsed empire. The loss of territory, the burden of reparations, and the lingering sting of war formed an unhappy constellation: Weimar Germany faced almost as many enemies within as the imperial state had faced from without. The climate of mistrust, fear, and bitterness created the conditions necessary for the emergence of a uniquely dynamic — because uniquely conflicted — period of artistic creation.[3] Weimar film, both in style and substance, reflects the energies loosed by historic cataclysm. As this chapter will show, the vampire embodies the political tensions of the short-lived Weimar Republic, as well as longer-standing troubles that contributed both to its creation and its destruction.

If photography, the technological forerunner and basis of moving pictures, is, as its etymology indicates, "writing in light," cinema mobilizes darkness. The workings of the medium entail a certain arrangement of the human sensorium. As Paul Virilio has observed, the "logistics of perception" for the camera operator are like those of the marksman: to delimit the field of vision and zero in on a target.[4] The editing process, moreover, offers parallels to a military campaign inasmuch as both activities stake out and schematize a terrain, transforming it into a set of tactical coordinates. Friedrich Kittler draws attention to a further connection between the film camera (a means of creation) and the machine gun (an instrument of destruction).[5] The movie camera and the Gatling gun were invented at the same time and have the same essential feature of design: a magazine mechanically connected with a shutter and a barrel. The one device stops what lies in the objective by capturing its image on a light-sensitive surface; the other freezes targets by analogous, if reversed, means: instead of recording its operations on a glass plate, sheet of paper, or celluloid strip, it makes its mark on the object itself, which its projections (that is, bullets) leave unmoving and perforated with black holes. To adopt a phrase from William Blake, who viewed the technological innovations of his own age with horror, camera and gun present a "fearful symmetry."[6] The machine gun transports what it shoots into one kind of afterlife, and the movie camera translates its target into eternity of another sort.

Virilio's and Kittler's observations about the proximity between the technologies and organizational structures of war and art, while generally applicable to cultural modernism throughout Europe, further illuminate Kracauer's and Eisner's theories of Weimar film.[7] Kracauer remarks that the escapist tendency of early German cinema, which favors an archaizing, mythical setting, symptomizes both the inability to confront political events directly and the disavowed desire to do so. Eisner, in turn, traces how the stylistic lineaments of Weimar fantasy cloak ugly realities in the Republic. The paradox of an apolitical cinema suffused with politics, which appears in the ambiguities, contradictions, and metamorphoses of personages, events, and worlds on screen, stands on the bodies of the dead left by the march of history — dead who haunt the dreams of the living and prey on them during the technologically induced sleep of reason.

Robert Wiene's *The Cabinet of Dr. Caligari* (1920) has come to signify metonymically Weimar cinema as a whole. Its visuals offer the fullest realization, in film, of the Expressionist aesthetic, the signature style of the period.[8] Equally, *Caligari* presents the narrative structures, themes, and general atmosphere of dread evident in countless other works of the day. Caligari's name, which is the present passive infinitive of the Latin *caligare*, "to make dark," is synonymous with the spread of night and terror. The elaborate set of the film presents the small German town of Holstenwall as a mysterious place. Streets are jagged and narrow, houses lean on each other precariously, and space is cramped and claustrophobic; the juxtaposition of angles presents an array of contradictory perspectives that constrict the field of vision instead of liberating it. *Caligari* tells the story of a string of murders; the film's hero, a young man named Franzis, must discover the party responsible before disaster befalls him and those close to him. Instead of employing a straightforward mode of exposition, *Caligari* places events in a framing narrative that calls into question the hero's sanity: Franzis, it turns out, is an inmate in an asylum run by the man he alleges is responsible for the killings, Caligari.

Critics tend to follow Kracauer's assessment that the narrative frame disqualifies the criticism implied by Franzis's story. According to this interpretation, the framing narrative, which puts the young man in the asylum, transforms the film from a statement of protest into an affirmation of the status quo.[9] However, since by far the greatest part of the film is shot in a manner that reinforces Franzis's perspective, and since the central narrative shapes the audience's perception of the asylum director (Werner Krauss plays both the alienist and Caligari), this reading is questionable. The film itself does not come down on one side (Franzis right, and Caligari a murderer) or the other (Franzis is crazy and himself a danger; "Caligari" is harmless — benign, even); rather, it encodes undecidability into the story itself.

Other aspects of the film reinforce the ambiguity generated by the opposition between framed and framing narratives. *Caligari* does not specify a time when the story takes place. The small town, the traveling mountebank, and the costumes evoke a temporally remote setting, but at the same time, the film presents a highly stylized, modernist vocabulary of images. *Caligari*'s setting in an indeterminate, "other" time transforms events into a second screen upon which the unresolved tensions of the present appear in an uncanny light, as foreign yet familiar phenomena. Equally remarkably, the names of the characters in this German film — Franzis, Jane, Alan, Caligari, and Cesare — are decidedly non-German, even though the town (which has a decidedly Teutonic name) and its people retain a distinctly German appearance. *Caligari* condenses the confusion of nations and identities and displaces this chaos from an international stage to a claustrophobic local setting. Distance alternates with uncomfortable closeness.

An analogous movement between open-ended possibilities is at work in the characterization of Caligari. The villain, with his black cloak, cane, and generally theatrical bearing, looks every bit the conjurer and practitioner of the dark arts. The story line makes the sinister screen presence he incarnates split up and bleed over into other beings. Caligari, especially when he dons a pair of glasses that intensify his mesmeric gaze, calls to mind the well-known fiend Coppelius/Coppola from E. T. A. Hoffmann's "The Sandman."[10] Caligari's name and manner also evoke the (in)famous traveling eighteenth-century charlatan Cagliostro.[11] Near the end, the film shows a musty old tome that contains a narrative of how, in the 1700s, there existed an itinerant magician also named Caligari, who used his charismatic powers to illicit ends. The scene in which the doctor staggers outside the asylum and the phrase "Du mußt Caligari werden" (You must become Caligari) fills the screen in varying sizes and shapes rounds out the picture of a supernatural antagonist with a diffuse being who can transfer his spirit from one age to another and from one body to another. Caligari, it seems, can even inhabit more than one form at once: Cesare, the sleepwalker who carries out the doctor's directives without thinking, possesses no will of his own and can thus be considered Caligari's murderous hand.

The systemic vagueness of reference that finds its most condensed expression in the double — indeed, multiple — aspects of Caligari invites viewers to provide a personalized framework in order to make sense of on-screen events. Kracauer sees in the doctor a figure of tyranny and a foreshadowing of Hitler.[12] This reading is hardly wrong, but *Caligari* is no more a record of clairvoyance than any other work of art. Rather, the shadows that the villain alternately embodies and commands come from the past.

Besides the ethnically coded unease about alterity evoked by his Italian-sounding name, Caligari stands for a form of strangeness internal to German culture. In the frame narrative, he is an alienist. By the beginning of the Weimar era, the basic ideas of psychoanalysis, which taught that the human soul consisted of a seething cauldron of unconscious drives and repressed conflicts, were common currency. Of course, the subtleties of Freud's thought were less well appreciated, but precisely for this reason — and because a vulgar conception of psychoanalysis resembled equally fashionable forms of spiritualism — *Caligari* captures popular ambivalence about the new breed of *Seelenforscher* (psychologist; literally, "researcher into the soul") professing privileged knowledge about human nature, mental life, and what constitutes normality and pathology. In this context, the words spoken by the doctor at the very end of the film ("I know exactly how to cure him") reveal a particularly ominous quality.

The mindless automatism of Cesare, the somnambulist who follows instead of leading — in parody of his imperial name — evokes the paradoxically passive actions of combatants in modern warfare, which is characterized by the impersonality of mass mobilization and the monotonous horror of the trenches.[13] Equally, the sleepwalker's complete lack of an individual, waking life — Cesare lies in a coffin-like box until Caligari, the modern necromancer, raises him to do his bidding — calls to mind the legions of physically wounded and psychically scarred ex-soldiers who filled Germany after the First World War. Cesare's personal consciousness has been all but extinguished. The mute human remainder appears briefly when Caligari reanimates him and the camera shows a close-up of his fluttering eyes; Cesare seems to be plagued by the same fear that he inspires in others.

Cesare's automatism, which culminates in the abduction and attempted murder of Franzis's beloved, Jane, also calls to mind the host of serial killers that filled the German imagination in the years between the wars. Georg Grosz, Oskar Kokoschka, Alfred Döblin, and Robert Musil — to mention only some of the more prominent artists and writers — all treated the theme. The same period witnessed the famous cases of the serial killers Fritz Haarmann in Hanover and Peter Kürten, nicknamed the "Vampire of Düsseldorf."[14] Maria Tatar has argued that the popularity of *Lustmord* (sexual murder) in works of Weimar art stems from the psychological, political, and sometimes literal emasculation that occurred as a result of the First World War: the sex-murderer's killing of women represents a displaced fantasy of revenge against the nations that had severed vital parts from the empire and dissolved it into a demilitarized and powerless rump state.[15] Were Cesare able to speak, his words might resemble those of Peter Beckert, the child-killer of Fritz Lang's *M* (1931): "Ich — kann ich denn anders? Hab' ich nicht dieses Verfluchte in mir — das Feuer, die Stimme, die Qual?!" (I — can I do anything else? Don't I have this accursed thing in me — the fire, the voice, the torture?!).[16]

In whichever way one chooses to take the film, *Caligari*'s core equivocation on the levels of narrative and character generates the film's themes and orients its visual imagery. The resulting constellation forms a web that, while delicate in structure, holds fast the general anxiety in the air of Weimar Germany. "Caligari," the predator who moves nimbly on nearly invisible strands, seems to possess supernatural power over the unfortunate souls who get trapped. This fatal tissue, however, hangs suspended on a material and real frame: the political and cultural order left in pieces by historical upheaval.

Friedrich Wilhelm Murnau's *Nosferatu* (1922), perhaps the greatest vampire film of all time, pours the dark matter of *Caligari* into a form that is less equivocal. *Nosferatu* does not possess the narrative perspectivism — and hence the structural complexity — of *Caligari*. Like a production of the Grand Guignol adapted for the screen, it features a grotesque villain, the rat-like vampire Count Orlok,[17] who invades a peaceful town and assaults the virtue of a blameless young woman. The film ends when she sacrifices herself by yielding to him at daybreak, knowing that the rays of the morning sun will destroy him, even as he destroys her. However, though *Nosferatu* leaves little room for ambiguity in terms of the narrative, the characterization of the vampire oozes out into other figures and points toward historical scars that are imperfectly healed.

Nosferatu purports to be "A Chronicle of the Great Death in Wisborg in 1838." This fictional conceit establishes a distant framework for events that conceals their actual proximity. *Nosferatu*, like all other artistic creations, exists first and foremost in relation to the world contemporary with its production, and the setting in an earlier historical period serves to place pressing concerns at a safe remove. The nineteenth-century town that the vampire attacks, with its Hanseatic architecture and general air of long-standing propriety, provides the idealized picture of a simpler time and place. Similarly, the main non-vampiric characters, Hutter and his wife, Ellen, connote a purer form of "Germanness" than the kind found in the world in which the film was made. Whenever he is on screen, Hutter gambols about like a puppy, lavishing affection on his wife and laughing gaily at everything. Ellen incarnates the ideals of constancy and piety. A scene early in the film shows her playing gently with a kitten, and she even reprimands her husband for cutting — and thereby killing — the flowers he brings her. Given that Ellen is able to offer herself as a pure victim at the film's end, it would appear that the couple has not consummated their union and that husband and wife live in childlike innocence.

Nosferatu, like *Dracula*,[18] is composed of two parts: a first half set in the East and a second half set in the West. Hutter travels as the representative of a real-estate firm to meet a client, Count Orlok, who is interested in acquiring some property in Germany. Along the way, he stops in the vicinity of the Count's castle to rest for the night. The inn is full of good-natured country folk who react in horror when the traveler mentions his destination. The woman who prepares his room hands Hutter a book, *Of Vampires, Terrible Ghosts, Magic, and the Seven Deadly Sins.* With characteristically imbecilic cheer, he casts it aside after only cursory examination. The film thereby sets up a parallel between the native haunts of the vampire and the German town he invades. One picture of "natural society" mirrors the other. This symmetry does not mean identity, but rather separation and discrete wholeness governed by tradition. The villagers of Eastern Europe know the value of pious fear; on this count, they have much to teach their metropolitan counterparts. Behind *Nosferatu*, and logically anterior to the crisis it stages, there is a desire for a segregated, static world that is vertically integrated into estates — the peasants of the East on the bottom, and the burghers of the West above them, each group happy in its own sphere.

Nosferatu, like the rustics and like Ellen, represents a principle. His name, which means "plague bearer" (*nosos*, "plague" and *pherein*, "to carry," in Greek) signifies impurity, and his movement from an Eastern realm to a Western one entails the contamination of one world by the other. Nosferatu incarnates the breakdown of health and identity, and he distinguishes himself among screen vampires by the metamorphoses he undergoes throughout the film. When the monster first appears, he presents a picture that is unsettling, yet still human. Orlok is tall and gaunt, and makeup accentuates his angular features to make them appear exaggeratedly sharp; in particular, his eyes have been outlined and his nose and fingers elongated to reach beyond natural proportions. He wears a long black coat and a hat vaguely resembling a turban. His dress evokes indeterminate foreignness that does not fit clearly into an established type — one that is equally European and "Oriental."

Toward the end, in contrast, the film shows Orlok as a spreading shadow. His silhouette still bears the traces of a man, but his hands have become extended talons, and his hooked nose is more animal than human; instead of evoking darkness, he now *is* darkness. In between, *Nosferatu* shows the vampire shedding the aristocratic demeanor he still possessed in Transylvania and transforming into a creature with visible, projecting fangs. This change occurs in keeping with his journey westward, to a German port. The closer the vampire comes to his target, the more diffuse and impalpable he becomes physically. As he undergoes this process of volatilization, the threat he poses becomes more manifest. Nosferatu is virulent, changing, and, through the metamorphoses that compound his foreign nature, always increasingly "other."

At the same time, the opposition the film establishes between good and evil, domestic and foreign, and separate estates reveals fissures. Hutter's employer, the real-estate agent Knock, in fact belongs to two worlds. On the one hand, he operates a business in Germany — a perfectly legitimate enterprise. On the other hand, because this venture necessarily involves the impersonality that comes with market transactions, Knock is associated with the unknown. Knock's person receives an occult coloration when the film shows him poring over letters from Orlok that resemble nothing so much as pages from a sorcerer's spell book. Knock's appearance, moreover, connects him with the vampire on a physical level: with his bald pate and sly, lateral glances, he is an endomorphic version of the Transylvanian. Indeed, the sinister aspect of the businessman predominates, inasmuch as the vampire's move westward could not occur without an "inside man" in Germany. Thus, despite its idealization of a stratified and segregated world order, *Nosferatu* implies, on an "unconscious" or "textual" level, a criticism of the organization of German society. Without commerce — an institution the film does not explicitly call into question — there could be no vampire and no plague.

The other figure whose presence breaks down the binary framework of the story is Bulwer, the film's counterpart to Van Helsing in Stoker's *Dracula*.[19] Bulwer, a follower of Paracelsus,[20] spreads as much darkness as light. He draws the parallel between the horrors afoot in Wisborg and vampirism, true, but his pronouncements are just as mystical as they are scientific. The doctor first appears speaking to students about "the mysterious ways of nature." "In horror," the students look upon a Venus flytrap consuming an insect. "Isn't it — like a vampire!" their teacher exclaims. In the next exhibit, "a polyp with tentacles" (as the intertitles tell viewers, "almost a phantom") is devouring another microscopic creature. The figure of Bulwer, a man of science, also suggests an additional level of meaning for the name "Knock": in nineteenth-century Scotland, the surgeon and anatomist Robert Knox (1791–1862) became infamously associated with the "resurrectionists" William Burke and William Hare, who procured "subjects" (as cadavers were called in the trade) not just by grave robbing, but also by murder.[21] Knox, too, welcomed death as a key to understanding life.

The scene featuring Bulwer appears to represent a secular and rational explanation of the supernatural, inasmuch as it describes the monstrous as part of the natural cycle of life and death. However, the analogy it provides between the vampire and the invisible world of biological processes in fact heightens the menace the undead monster embodies. *Nosferatu,* by displaying an affinity with a further dimension of reality beyond the ken of all but the initiated, throws a long shadow. Bulwer's "scientific explanation" does not lead to a means of combating the vampire; a quasi-religious act of exorcism is still required. The doctor's presentation of vampirism as something that occurs everywhere and all the time in nature has the effect of generalizing the threat that Nosferatu poses to include every plane of existence.

Hutter also displays cracks in his wholesome façade. On the one hand, he is a dutiful husband and employee. On the other hand, his actions, which follow from his simple character, are the most concrete cause for the demise of his fellow citizens and, ultimately, his wife's death. Thomas Elsaesser draws attention to a key scene at Orlok's castle:

> As the Count is about to sign the papers, [Hutter] accidentally (?) displays/exhibits the medallion that bears the image of [Ellen]. Nosferatu grasps it, and . . . this image . . . is substituted for money that would otherwise seal the deal. [. . .] Nosferatu is [Hutter]'s double . . . in so far as [Ellen] acquires the lover that [Hutter] seems so reluctant to be.[22]

This second side of Hutter — the "good German" who brings about disaster — reflects, in displaced form, the contradictions of the society in which *Nosferatu* was produced and consumed.

The characterological perversion evident in *Nosferatu* symptomizes cultural conflict. As Peter Gay has observed, the Weimar Republic sought to unite "two Germanies."[23] After the First World War, the fledgling government tried to institute new policies in line with socialist and democratic principles of state organization. At the same time, it inherited the old bureaucracy of the imperial state. In a parallel development, the German citizenry divided, broadly speaking, into two camps: those who favored the idea of a new political system, and those who clung to old ways. The unprecedented scope of the First World War had shattered many people's faith in tradition, and this led to renewed militancy on both the right and the left before the dust had even settled; Germany's borders were redrawn, and the country lost its colonial holdings; most importantly, millions had died, and even more had been mutilated, disfigured, disabled, or rendered otherwise less than whole in body and spirit.

Hutter's fundamentally agreeable nature and simple-minded readiness to do as he is told scans as a reflection of the compliant Germans who, when deployed abroad, inadvertently brought back ruin to their homeland. Alternately, it evokes the dutiful civil servants of the imperial bureaucracy retained by the republic, who perpetuated the out-of-date practices of an ossified government apparatus with catastrophic results for the new democracy. In broader terms, a psychoanalytic interpretive framework also allows us to see images of sexual anxiety in *Nosferatu*.[24] When Orlok rises abruptly and mechanically from his coffin, he resembles a monstrous penis; his nocturnal passage through the arched gates of Wisborg conjures up the act of sexual penetration, and the film culminates in his invasion of a sleeping woman's bedroom. However, even here, the vampire refers back to Hutter and, through him, to German manhood in general: if Nosferatu incarnates a sexual disease, this disease is politically charged.[25]

The plague storyline in *Nosferatu* calls to mind the Black Death of the mid-fourteenth century. The nineteenth-century setting of the film threatens to slide backward into the Middle Ages. The evocation of a period popularly associated with darkness and death reveals the proximity of barbarism not just in the time when the fiction is supposed to occur, but in the twentieth century, as well.

As René Girard has observed, the plague is not just a biological event, but also a social one that entails the breakdown of the normal rules governing communal life.[26] Everyone in afflicted communities is equally at risk, and the unpredictable course of the plague means that it affects all sectors of society indiscriminately. Parallel to the invisible circulation of disease, which strikes seemingly at random, the habits and rhythms of day-to-day existence are thrown into chaos that seems universal in scope. Moreover, times of plague demand that order be reestablished through special laws of exception. The general upheaval entails drastic measures of repression.

Historically, the reintroduction of social stability has led to the persecution of persons and groups deemed responsible for the community's affliction. In premodern Europe, the "guilty" parties in times of plague were often thought to be the Jews.[27] The precise modalities of antisemitism in this period are too varied to be inventoried here, but the fundamental dynamic is simple enough. The Jewish people, who had rejected Christ's teachings and handed him over to the Romans for execution, still clung to their ancient ways and formed an outsider group within Christendom; their refusal to live by the laws of their fellow men marked them as potential troublemakers. To parties who had no interest in cultural pluralism and no understanding of the biological origins of disease, it was, unfortunately, only logical that this group, which did not obey the rules in other respects, had somehow, whether willfully or not, brought about the problems that now afflicted everyone. Because Jews already stood out in the social body as an unassimilated element, they provided a "natural" focus for persecution when affliction that no one understood beset a community.

Medieval antisemitism has no direct bearing on our discussion, but the imaginary retrojection that occurs in *Nosferatu,* like the displacements that occur in a dream, betokens a causality different from that of conventional, waking, rational thought. And this "other" logic, shaped by the seeming unreality of all that occurs on the silver screen, where desires and fears coalesce, connects with modern antisemitism.

Modern antisemitism, while undergirded by long-standing prejudices that can find expression in religious terms, employs, above all, the language and conceptual categories of science. Michel Foucault has called the modern discourse seeking first causes for the characteristics and behavior of individuals and groups in superpersonal, organic forces "bio-power."[28] The biologically focused mode of explaining the world has a political correlate. Sovereignty in premodern political systems, Foucault observes, derived from the right of rulers to deal death to unruly subjects. The sovereign of the ancien régime was not concerned with normative regulation of the lives of those he ruled. Infractions were treated harshly, but everyday existence was not the object of the ruler's supervision and discipline.[29] Beginning in the eighteenth century, however, political power increasingly manifested itself in efforts to analyze and control subjects' bodies and behavioral patterns. The nineteenth century, when industrialized centers hosted a concentration of people not governed by traditional social hierarchies and agrarian ways of life, witnessed a new concern for shaping the potentially volatile masses that comprised the citizenry. Revealing the seething cauldron of discontent and lawlessness that many now saw in the entrails of European civilization, thought about the dynamics of society, colored by evolutionary theory and framed by models of capitalist competition, concentrated on struggle. The focus on conflicts between different cultures and ethnicities corresponded to a conception of nature as a battleground in which different species of organism, and, within each species, different races, fought for dominance and survival.

The enfranchisement of the middle classes after 1848 and the subsequent extension of political rights to the lower classes created a new formation of the body politic. No longer a political structure integrated along a vertical axis, society revealed hands and feet that could potentially operate independently of directives received from above. The literature of the period thematized anxieties about cultural and class identity. Thus, as José Monleón observes,

> Eugène Sue opened his *Mystères de Paris* (1842–43) by calling the reader's attention to the fact that . . . the savages he would be introducing did not belong to remote countries but were to be found

"among ourselves." Reynold's *The Mysteries of London* (1845–48) . . . follow[ed] a similar pattern with a savage depiction of the English "low" life. [. . .] The new scenery in popular literature became, especially after 1848, the "unknown country" of the bas-fonds.[30]

Writers of fiction were, of course, not the only ones aware of the situation. In the latter half of the nineteenth century, criminology, race theory, and social Darwinism[31] sought to reestablish the clear differences between the members of society that a stratified and fixed system based on birthright had formerly assured. Cesare Lombroso, in *L'uomo delinquente* (1876) and a follow-up work, *La donna delinquente* (1893), built a complex system of physiological classification to identify the "barbarians" that lived among civilized men.[32] His influential contemporary Max Nordau likewise addressed the "degeneration" produced by the modern world, which he believed could only be remedied through racial separation and "hygiene."[33]

This change in the "world picture" illuminates the racialized fears that *Nosferatu* evokes. *Nosferatu* is not an antisemitic film.[34] However, it draws on cultural anxieties and uses strategies of representation that inform the worst forms of contemporary antisemitic rhetoric and art.[35] Therefore, it provides a ready allegory for the vampire as a Jew. The right-wing reaction in Germany after the First World War clung to the idea that Jews and Socialists had betrayed the Fatherland and were responsible for the ignominy of the Versailles Treaty (this is the so-called "Stab-in-the-back" legend). In *Mein Kampf* (1925), Hitler portrayed Jews as "blood-sucking" parasites — an image he derived from the antisemitic chorus given voice decades earlier by Viennese mayor Karl Lueger, who held office from 1897 to 1910.[36] *Blutsauger* (bloodsucker) as an abusive term for Jews occurs widely in literature set in the late nineteenth and early twentieth centuries (indeed, even the Nazi-fighter Winston Churchill employed the phrase).[37]

When Fritz Hippler's notorious *The Eternal Jew* (1940) paired pictures of Jews with images of teeming rats, the film employed a juxtaposition from *Nosferatu* equating an undesirable social element with vermin. Linda Schulte-Sasse, in her study of popular culture in the Third Reich, argues that Veit Harlan's equally ill-famed *Jud Süss* (made at the same time as Hippler's film) tells a story of vampiric invasion and corruption of the state:

> Like Dracula . . . Süss demonstrates a great mobility with respect to his physical appearance. [. . .] He becomes indistinguishable from nobility, indeed, surpasses in physical appeal the legitimate ruler of Württemberg. Süss also recalls Dracula's spatial mobility, his sexual threat to the male order, his predominant choice of female

victims, his contamination of these victims . . . , and, . . . his role as
an ambiguous figure located somewhere between the self and the
Other. Finally, the narratives of *Jew Süss* and Stoker's novel are strikingly similar in trajectory. Both revolve around the transgression of
oppositional spaces associated with an alien East . . . and a domesti-
cated West . . . with their concomitant cultural associations.[38]

From a distanced, critical perspective, it is evident that *Nosferatu* provided a model for later, tendentious works that simply substituted "Jew"
for "vampire." Because the fantastic film lends itself so easily to these
appropriations, it possesses a structure that, though not in itself prejudi-
cial, comes easily to possess an ideological charge.

One could adduce many contemporary texts to inscribe the fears thematized in *Nosferatu* into a web of broader cultural correspondences. One
of the most fitting, for reasons of the readership it enjoyed and the grand-
scale perspective and historical pathos it offered, is Oswald Spengler's *The
Decline of the West*. This work, which appeared in two volumes in 1918
and 1922, presents a view of history modeled on biological processes of
generation and decay. It reads as a summa of nineteenth and early-twenti-
eth-century philosophy and science. Instead of understanding the present
as the culmination of foregoing ages (as had Spengler's intellectual ancestor Hegel, for whom history represented the progressive, material realization of Spirit), Spengler posits that the modern age in Europe merely
rehearses the fate of other, earlier civilizations.

Ours, Spengler writes, is the "Faustian" epoch, in which Europe has
reached the overtaxed state previously achieved by the "Apollonian" and
"Magian" ages, which were centered in the ancient Greek and medieval
Arab worlds, respectively. These cultures, Spengler argues, once flourished to the extent that their inborn genius permitted, but then they fell
into periods of "modernism" and "decadence." Spengler holds an ambivalent view of his own society: on the one hand, its achievements are undeniable, but on the other hand, History — that is, the "Living Time"[39]
that sweeps away civilizations just as impersonal Nature exterminates
species — will surely bury it, and soon. The nervousness of cosmopolitan-
ism, the mixing of races and cultural traditions, and the dehumanizing
effects of technology herald the imminent end of the Occident.

Nosferatu presents a nightmare vision of the social body in the age of
bio-power, class struggle, social Darwinism, and the Faustian Zeitgeist. The
vampire obeys the law of self-preservation by eliminating competing organ-
isms. By the end of the film, Orlok has transformed into purely destructive
vital dynamism and come to represent the "degree zero" of nature: the
death-dealing drive of life that triumphs at the expense of individual beings
and even species. Even if one does not read Nosferatu as Jewish or even
Eastern, the vampire still struggles for supremacy. Portraying a fiction of

past horror, the film indicts its own day and, in its antimodern modernism, implies nostalgia for still-earlier, presumably less-conflicted times.[40]

The preceding chapters have shown how the vampire came to represent the fears associated with modernization — that is, new forms of technology and science, new pathways of mediated communication, new structures of government, new roles for men and women, the newfound political ascendancy of disadvantaged classes, and the increased presence of foreigners in traditionally homogeneous social bodies. *Nosferatu* weaves the web of its fiction out of the same anxieties that compose Stoker's *Dracula* and Schreber's *Memoirs*. In particular, the vampire reflects the biological theory that originated in the nineteenth century but gained even broader currency in the twentieth: the idea that individuals' racial makeup determines their character and actions.

Murnau's vampire story perverts and parodies the mystical value that blood held in premodern societies. Formerly associated with divinity and the God-given hierarchy that underwrote the power of nobility, blood, in the age of bio-power, becomes a new kind of social liability when it is impure. In Transylvania, Orlok retains his (admittedly strange-looking) human properties; in Germany, where he poses the threat of miscegenation, he gives them up entirely. This is also the reason why Ellen must sacrifice herself to free the land of the plague: once contaminated by the vampire, her blood is no longer a fitting medium for perpetuating the German race.[41]

Besides his animal-like claws and hooked nose, Nosferatu's piercing eyes are his outstanding feature. In his first screen appearance, Orlok keeps the lower half of his face covered and stares menacingly at Hutter. The oblique angle of his gaze suggests cunning and cruelty. As the film continues, it shows the vampire looking at the camera dead-on with increasing frequency. This progression culminates in Wisborg, where the vampire stands at the window and transfixes Ellen intently from across the street. Nosferatu remains outside the exchange of glances that communicate human warmth and community. The film does not integrate the vampire into scenes structured by the shot/countershot pattern that endows characters with interpersonal subjectivity. Framed by darkness and looking like nothing so much as a vicious animal in a cage, Nosferatu possesses a gaze that holds out no promise of reciprocity — a visual sign of his alien bloodline.

The points of contact with contemporary cultural tensions revealed by our analysis of *Nosferatu* find expression in numerous other films of the period, e.g., Murnau's version of *Faust* (1926), *Der Golem* (by Henrik Galeen and Paul Wegener, 1915; remade in 1920 by Wegener), and *Alraune* (Eugen Illés and Joseph Klein, 1918; remade by Henrik Galeen, 1928). *Faust*, like *Nosferatu*, foregrounds a plague narrative, while *Der Golem* and *Alraune* thematize the power of esoteric knowledge to create destructive forms of undead "life." A further example is Paul Leni's *Wachsfigurenkabinett* (1924), which is comprised of a series of framed narratives exploring

the fluid boundaries between the everyday, on the one hand, and uncan-
nily proximate eroticism and cruelty, on the other. The connections with
contemporary literature abound, as well. To cite just one example, the
novel *Vampir* (1920) by Hanns Heinz Ewers — a friend of English occultist Aleister Crowley, aficionado of Edgar Allan Poe, and screenplay writer
for *The Student of Prague* (a film about a young man's fateful encounter
with his double, 1913) — tells the disjointed story of German adventurer
Frank Braun in North and South America during the First World War. The
book's subtitle is "Ein verwilderter Roman in Fetzen und Farben" (An
Overgrown Novel in Ribbons and Colors), and the book's style reflects the
protagonist's confused and often drug-addled perceptions of events. *Vampir* presents the same nexus of fear and desire that we have been analyzing,
only here the gender roles are reversed: the vampire is one Lotte Lewi, who
haunts Braun both for reason of her erotic appeal and because she seeks the
mystical and political union of the Jewish and German peoples.[42]

* * *

Caligari and Nosferatu have become international icons of terror. Their
celebrity stems to a large extent from the fact that the films to which they
give their names take place in a removed setting that encourages viewers
to see them as timeless and universal. However, as the foregoing discussion has shown, the villains owe their substance to the anxieties engendered by modernization. Caligari is a doctor and therefore linked with
medical science and experimentation, and his automaton Cesare carries
out directives with the unthinking precision of soldiers mobilized for the
First World War. Nosferatu presents a menace corrupting the lifeblood of
a town that stands for an entire culture, and the film underwrites the reality of the threat through Bulwer's pronouncements, which echo contemporary race theory and philosophies of history. The spectral nature of the
antagonists in both films records the persistence of recent historical events
and shows how the present is tied to unresolved conflicts.

Dr. Mabuse, a relatively neglected villain of Weimar, is the final vampire
who commands our attention. Fritz Lang's *Dr. Mabuse, der Spieler* (Dr.
Mabuse, the Gambler, 1922) and *Das Testament des Dr. Mabuse* (The Testament of Dr. Mabuse, 1933) are up-to-date and take place in the bustling
big city. However — and especially when taken together — *Gambler* and
Testament present affinities with *Caligari* and *Nosferatu*. *Gambler* features
an antagonist who changes appearance at will, possesses mesmeric powers,
and presides over a network of agents who do his bidding as mindlessly as
Cesare executes Caligari's commands. In *Testament*, Mabuse dies, but, like
Nosferatu, he continues to terrorize society as an undead presence. The
1933 sequel unfolds as a resurrection of the terror supposedly vanquished
in the 1922 film, thereby engineering a traumatic temporality of belated

recurrence and involuntary repetition.[43] The Mabuse films "mythologize" their subject by presenting a villain who exists independently of a secure temporal and spatial framework; indeed, Mabuse has become a German icon, the subject of numerous lesser books and films.[44]

Norbert Jacques invented the mysterious doctor in a novel published in serialized form, *Dr. Mabuse, the Gambler* (1921/1922). In Jacques's original novel, the villain is in many respects little more than a glorified thug. The scope of the literary Mabuse's activities, though international, concentrates on a smuggling operation in the border regions of states centered on the Bodensee, and Mabuse drinks, swears, and carouses like any other gangster. Lang's reworking of the material in the 1922 film, on the one hand, transforms the relatively provincial criminal into a big-time operator based in an unspecified metropolis generally understood to be Berlin.

By means of swift cuts that show Mabuse changing roles as rapidly as the rise of inflation in Weimar Germany, the villain's character becomes energized by the circulation of money that Voltaire and Marx both associated with vampires.[45] Mabuse has no substance, but his style is razor sharp. In Lang's 1933 film, Mabuse's being is even more virtual, even as it remains strangely real. The doctor dies halfway through the movie, yet he gains in power via his last will and testament, a piece of writing that enables his resurrection as a vampiric power.

Each version of Mabuse highlights an otherworldly aura that the villain emanates. In a 1928 essay, Jacques wrote that he chose the name of his master criminal because it "is strangely at home between languages, sounds German, yet has in itself the ring of other, entirely foreign languages."[46] In the novel, Mabuse not only moves across European borders, he also operates on different continents. Mabuse has traveled to the tropics, where he tasted power and even owned slaves. Now the narrow predictability of life in Europe oppresses him; he longs to abandon it forever and — after overseeing a cataclysmic crime leaving the Old World bankrupt — to found "Eitopomar," a personal "Kaiserreich in den Urwäldern Brasiliens" (empire in the primeval forests of Brazil; 59).

Jacques's novel presents a villain full of blood and bile — a presence that drips overheated desire and rage. Jacques's Mabuse is also hot in a sexual sense. One of his female admirers describes him to a rapt interlocutor:

> Er ist doch eine Welt für sich. Er . . . ist ein Dschungel und ein Urwald. Mir ist, als habe er Tiger und Schlangen in sich. Alles, was stark ist in der Natur. Und ganze riesenhafte Bäume und weite undurchdringliche Schilfwälder! Weißt du, man kann sich in ihm verlieren! Kommt an kein Ende und ist doch in ihm!

> [He is a world unto himself. He . . . is a jungle and a primeval forest. He seems to have tigers and snakes in him. All that is strong in nature. And whole, giant trees and wide, impenetrable woods! You

know, you can get lost in him! You reach no end and are still within him!] (131)

Mabuse radiates the tempestuous vitality of new and uncharted lands. The combustion of large quantities of alcohol fuels his ambitions and operations (e.g., "er trank und feuerte seinen bösen, starken Geist an" [he drank and fired up his strong, evil spirit; 72]), and he makes his underworld associates participate in his excesses. Subordinates who burn out are conscripted into the foreign legion, where they wither and die under the scorching African sun. In Munich, Mabuse preys on his victims both as a crooked gambler and as a crooked doctor. His magnetic force hits them like a "Hitzstrahl" (heat-ray; 143).

Numerous characters liken the doctor to a lycanthrope, and Mabuse himself makes the equation in a way that evokes his future vampiric incarnation: "Ich bin ein Werwolf. Ich sauge Menschenblut in mich! Jeden Tag brennt der Haß alles Blut auf, das mir in den Adern läuft, und jede Nacht sauge ich sie mit einem neuen Menschenblut voll" (I am a werewolf. I suck up human blood! Every day, hatred burns off all the blood that runs in my veins, and every night I fill them with a new victim's blood; 183). His heat is contagious; the police describe him as a "Seuche[, die] die Stadt fiebern macht" (plague that makes the city feverish; 25). The Mabuse of the novel has no real appetite for plasma and never turns into an animal, but his proud declaration points toward the vampiric nature that his cinematic resurrections will display. Like many a vampire, Mabuse also possesses a terrifying gaze; "his great, gray eyes" — a phrase repeated throughout the book — intimidate all who catch sight of him.

Jacques's *Gambler* is character-based and character-driven. The fiery imagery makes Mabuse a determinate, marked presence in the book. The portrayal of Mabuse's nemesis, *Staatsanwalt* (State Attorney) von Wenk, is also strongly delineated and conventional: the officer of the law is a war hero, possesses unimpeachable professional integrity, and is single-minded in his prosecution of justice. The third personage who completes the central cast is also clearly drawn. Countess Told is so unfazed by events around her that she acts as a magnet for villain and hero alike. Wenk ultimately defeats Mabuse only because the phlegmatic aristocrat, nicknamed "die Unaktive" (The Idle Lady; 126), fascinates both men. Mabuse's passion makes him sloppy, and Wenk's infatuation with the statuesque beauty puts him in the right place at the right time. In Jacques's novel, the sluggish nobility lifts a finger, and the cat-and-mouse games promptly end.

The traditional form of the narrative corresponds to its ideological content inasmuch as it transmits conservative cultural values. Mabuse stands in opposition to law and order. Wenk, even though a civil servant (and therefore a potential object of mistrust for a public wary of governmental authority),[47] is noble in purpose and, as the preposition *von* before his name indicates, of high birth. Countess Told is a far more ambivalent figure, but she has class and a real pedigree going for her. Style and substance agree: the established way of doing things is best.

Lang's version of the material thoroughly embraces the modern, whereas Jacques's novel looks back to literary and cultural tradition. The silent film eliminates practically all discourse. Instead of words, it trades in images. As a result, a dizzying array of ever-changing appearances substitutes itself for the in-depth explorations of personality and motivation that comprise the novel. The intensive becomes extensive, and Mabuse turns into a more diffuse and more threatening villain with an even greater reach than before. At the same time, Wenk, Countess Told, and the other, lesser characters flatten out into thin stage masks. Since the impersonal and aggressively superficial new cinematic medium shows Mabuse's new features to be larger than life while it erases the traits that personalize his antagonists, the film transmits a highly equivocal moral message — to the extent that it passes any judgment at all on what it portrays.

Lang's cinematic treatment of the novel does away with the werewolf references, but Rudolf Klein-Rogge's sharp features and stagy dress evoke the dandy vampires of melodrama. This association between Mabuse and vampirism is underscored by the fact that, as Tom Gunning has noted, the villain operates like "a parasite dependent on the systematic nature of modernity."[48] Mabuse works with the structures and rhythms that already command everyday life and perverts them to his own ends. The first half of the film, subtitled "A Picture of the Times," concludes with an image of the doctor hovering over a female victim stretched out in a swoon on a couch, like the supine beauty in Henry Fuseli's painting *The Nightmare* (1781) and Ellen at the end of *Nosferatu*. Lang's *Gambler* shows how people play with their well-being in the hope of achieving a surge of energy — a nervous frisson from an accelerated lifestyle. Mabuse thrives in the flow of money and desire that others let loose when they gamble with their fortunes and fate, and he feeds off the energy that this exchange releases. When things are going his way, the doctor is a preternatural leech sucking from the social body and rerouting its vital substance according to his own plans.

Throughout *Gambler*, the camera focuses on the criminal mastermind's face again and again: superimposed on the plundered stock exchange, transfixing a gambling partner in a shady dive, lighting up at a mesmeric exhibition, etc. At no point in *Testament* does the villain possess a comparable screen presence. Mabuse appears for the first time on a slide projected in a university lecture hall. The black border around the image and the fact that he is shown in profile on a hospital bed reinforce his separation from the world. Mabuse sits in an asylum cell for half the movie then dies without any fanfare: an extremely brief sequence simply shows his foot being tagged for the mortuary. Significantly, the only scene in which a living Mabuse appears to throw a glamour like his old self occurs just before he dies; his beaked nose, wide brow, and clenched jaw fill the screen. An attendant comments: "Er . . . sitzt da wie ein lebendig Toter . . . — und die Augen, die Augen — die lähmen einen ja förmlich!" (He . . . sits there like a *living corpse* . . . — and his eyes, his eyes — they just paralyze you!).

Mabuse in *Testament* no longer needs to be alive at all in order to perpetrate crime; his wickedness is simultaneously so diffuse and so great that it exceeds the power of a single gaze. And just as Mabuse cannot be limited to one viewpoint, he also confounds another sense: hearing.[49] *Testament* plays with the difference between silence and sound, coding them at alternate moments both as carriers of information and as obstacles to communication. The film splits Mabuse into scattered visual and acoustic images that occasionally meet up but never produce a unified object of representation.

In the space of a few frames at the beginning, *Testament* sets up a discursive framework in which life and death, Heaven, Hell, and Earth provide the key terms. As the unprepossessing "hero" Inspector Lohmann[50] is on his way out the door to see a production of Wagner's *Walküre,* his secretary announces a call. Because he does not want to be kept from the opera, Lohmann tells his assistant: "Leider bin ich tot" (Unfortunately, I am dead). Eventually, however, Lohmann relents and greets the caller: "Scheren Sie sich zum Teufel!" (Go to Hell!). Wagner's opera concerns supernatural beings that take fallen warriors to the next world. Lohmann describes the Valkyries to his secretary: "Das sind die Mädels, die die toten Kriminalkommissare . . . direkt in den Himmel [bringen]" (Those are the girls who bring dead police commissioners . . . directly to Heaven). When the desperate caller implores the secretary to put him through, he states that "es geht um Tod und Leben" (it's a matter of life and death). Lohmann is on his way to Heaven, the informant is going to Hell, and something has unhinged the gateways separating the mortal and immortal realms.

The ending of *Testament* reinforces this metaphysical openness. A complex story line reveals that a certain Professor Baum, the doctor in charge of the asylum in which Mabuse has spent the last years of his life, has been following his patient's written directives and transmitting plans for the systematic terrorization of society to a network of agents. Baum winds up an inmate in his own madhouse, where the caller from the beginning of the film has been locked away — in the deceased Mabuse's cell, no less. The closing shot in the film shows the professor sitting on an asylum bed, like Mabuse, surrounded by scattered sheets of paper. "Hier hat ein kleiner Kriminalkommissar nichts mehr zu suchen" (A mere police commissioner has no business here anymore), Lohmann says. The door closes, and the film ends. Lohmann correctly senses that a full explanation of events goes beyond the secular scope of detective work.

No one else has any more insight into the vampiric state of affairs. A second subplot of the *Testament* follows the members of a versatile criminal association that robs banks, traffics in drugs, and manufactures bogus currency. Sections and commandos, none of which has any permanent or direct contact with any other, make up the operation. When their boss, who identifies himself as "Mabuse" — a factual impossibility that nevertheless is strangely real — issues his directives, he employs only telegrams and the telephone — forms of modern communication that allow him to call the shots entirely from behind the scenes. The closest the gangsters ever get to finding out their leader's identity occurs when he occasionally summons them in small groups to a nondescript room. But even under these circumstances, he does not show himself. The "Man Behind the Curtain" (as the criminals call him) sits behind a screen, visible only as a silhouette. On the one hand, Professor Baum is the "Man Behind the Curtain," and therefore responsible for the wave of corruption, drugs, and counterfeiting that plagues the city. On the other hand, he is a decoy that conceals a far more sinister evil. *Testament* equivocates about the precise degree of Baum's responsibility; he does not devise the plans whose execution he administrates, and it is not clear to what extent he is truly aware of his own role in the events that transpire.[51]

In contrast to the 1922 film, in which Mabuse repeatedly stages the spectacular demonstration of his powers, *Testament* shows a villain who makes his influence and control felt by covert means. Contamination takes the place of performance, and a text — the testament of the film's title — serves as the conduit for evil, à la Caligari. Baum is wholly replaceable and even disposable. Anyone else who occupied himself with the patient's writings could take the doctor's place and play his part. When the professor reads the testament, he becomes an automaton — a zombie taken over by the undead Mabuse and an unthinking puppet of evil like the countless agents whom he instructs to pursue pointless crimes. The document Mabuse has produced exhibits vampiric properties inasmuch as it controls the border between the living and the dead, and serves as a medium of contagion. Once it is up and running, the text forms a self-perpetuating machine that recreates its author in its reader. In principle, it will reproduce Mabuse's madness on an ever-larger scale until "Herrschaft des Verbrechens" (the rule of crime) commands the entire world. Paradoxically, Mabuse is more alive than ever once he dies, and the reach of lawlessness greater than ever.

The progressive disembodiment of Mabuse and Lang's increasing dissociation of the villain from a particular time and place, as well as the director's use of speech and sounds that connect to no apparent source, reveal a kinship with Carl Dreyer's enigmatic *Vampyr*, made the same year as *Testament*. David Rudkin, in a meticulous shot-by-shot analysis of Dreyer's film, has shown how a "systematic . . . dyscoherence [*sic*] and . . . dislocation"[52] of visual and aural images plunge characters and audience alike into a world without clear limits between dream and waking, self and other, and life and death. *Testament* employs the techniques of *Vampyr* to somewhat more conventional narrative ends, but it engineers unease and fear by much the same means.

Subsequent cinematic articulations of the Mabuse myth profited from the fact that almost anyone can play the doctor's part, and they tend to show a madman bent on creating an army of drones to execute his will. After buying the rights to Mabuse in 1953, Artur Brauner, Germany's biggest post-war producer, persuaded Lang to make one last film (*The Thousand Eyes of Dr. Mabuse*, 1960), then enlisted lesser talents to capitalize on the famous name of the master criminal.[53] These works are not nearly as interesting or sophisticated as Lang's. Conceived as mass entertainment, they have no room for the intricate and studied ambiguity that distinguishes the first Mabuse films.

However, the fall into formulaic seriality is a perverse triumph for Mabuse, just as it is for the vampire in general. The complexity of history vanishes and yields a myth — something far more powerful in its stark, enduring simplicity. By replicating himself in so many different films, Mabuse achieved immortality. In this timeless dimension, the doctor's infamy draws on the strength of other wicked luminaries. *In the Steel Net of Dr. Mabuse,* the first of the films not directed by Lang, features a portentous book on the many incarnations of the Devil. This work contains a chapter on Mabuse alongside chapters on werewolves and vampires. To those who have followed Mabuse's career from the beginning, the book is redundant. Jacques and Lang already indicated the evil doctor's association with lycanthropes and the undead. The parade of simulacra that trace Mabuse's shifting shape includes more and less "authentic" images, but none is absolutely reliable. Lang's 1933 film comes closest to showing the villain's "true" form because it erases the traits it draws as soon as it presents them. The final word on Mabuse is contained in a book through which the vampire constantly resurrects himself.

The "haunted screen" of German cinema "from Caligari to Hitler" retains its power to shock and disconcert more than eighty years after its genesis. Now, as then, the films' images, which divide into a host of shifting forms — each with an array of possible referents that are not concretely given — display an affinity with the changing face of the world and, in so doing, evoke the morbid exhilaration of regression into chaos. Their double structure, which confuses the modern and the atavistic and confounds the very history it calls forth, transforms the mind into a second, psychic screen where horror is endlessly renewed. The undead of Weimar represent evils to come, even as they disguise themselves as eruptions from an earlier age.

Notes

[1] Siegfried Kracauer, *From Caligari to Hitler: A Psychological History of the German Film*, ed. Leonardo Quaresima (Princeton: Princeton UP, 2004).

[2] Lotte Eisner, *The Haunted Screen: Expressionism in the German Cinema*, trans. Roger Greaves (Berkeley: U of California P, 1973).

[3] Peter Gay, *Weimar Culture: The Outsider as Insider* (New York: W. W. Norton, 2001).

[4] Paul Virilio, *War and Cinema: The Logistics of Perception*, trans. Patrick Camiller (London: Verso, 1989).

[5] Friedrich Kittler, *Gramophone, Film, Typewriter*, trans. Geoffrey Winthrop-Young and Michael Wutz (Stanford: Stanford UP, 1999).

[6] This phrase, from the poem "The Tyger," is also the title of the best work of scholarship on the poet: Northrop Frye, *Fearful Symmetry: A Study of William Blake* (Toronto: U of Toronto P, 2004).

[7] See Vincent B. Sherry, *The Great War and the Language of Modernism* (New York: Oxford UP, 2003), as well as Paul Fussell's classic study, *The Great War and Modern Memory* (New York: Oxford UP, 1975). Anton Kaes, in *M* (London: British Film Institute, 2000), 38–53, focuses on the Weimar context.

[8] Rudolf Kurtz's *Expressionismus und Film* (Berlin: Verlag der Lichtbildbühne, 1926), forms the basis for subsequent studies of the subject.

[9] For a summary of the controversial narrative design of *Caligari*, see David Robinson, *Das Cabinet des Dr. Caligari* (London: British Film Institute, 1997), 7–23. The claims at the center of the debate, made by Hans Janowitz, one of the film's two screenwriters, are reprinted in Mike Budd, ed., *The Cabinet of Dr. Caligari: Texts, Contexts, Histories* (New Brunswick: Rutgers UP, 1990), 221–39. The case has been revisited most recently by Dietrich Scheunemann, "The Double, the Décor, and the Framing Device: Once More on Robert Wiene's *The Cabinet of Dr. Caligari*," *Expressionist Film: New Perspectives*, ed. Dietrich Scheunemann (Rochester: Camden House, 2003), 125–56 (especially pp. 144–49).

[10] Freud uses this story to illustrate his argument about the uncanny in his famous essay of the same name (1919). Hoffmann's anthology of fantastic tales, *Die Serapionsbrüder* (*The Serapion Brethren*), includes a story about a case of possible vampirism. As in all his works, however, the emphasis falls on the unknowability of the truth; see Rüdiger Safranski, *E. T. A. Hoffmann: Das Leben eines skeptischen Phantasten* (Frankfurt am Main: Fischer, 2005).

[11] This fascinating figure's biography is told by Iain Mccalman, *The Last Alchemist: Count Cagliostro, Master of Magic in the Age of Reason* (New York: Harper, 2004).

[12] Kracauer, 77–87.

[13] On the relationship between mechanized combat and aesthetic production, see Modris Eksteins, *Rites of Spring: The Great War and the Birth of the Modern Age* (Boston: Mariner, 2000).

[14] See Maria Tatar, *Lustmord: Sexual Murder in Weimar Germany* (Princeton: Princeton UP, 1995) for an overview and discussion of real and imagined serial

killings in the interwar period; Elisabeth Lenk and Katharina Kaever, *Peter Kürten, genannt der Vampir von Düsseldorf* (Frankfurt am Main: Eichborn, 1997), collects contemporary documents from the press and police records.

[15] Tatar, 3–19.

[16] See Kaes, *M*, 26–38, for an excellent discussion ("Serial Murder, Serial Culture") that bears on other films discussed here.

[17] As if a testament to the vampire's power of resurrection and ability to assume new, unexpected forms, Wiene directed a film in 1924 called *Orlacs Hände* (The Hands of Orlac). A concert pianist (Conrad Veidt) whose hands have been mutilated in an accident receives a murderer's appendages in an experimental operation and soon finds himself compelled to carry out bloody acts. The story provided the basis for a number of subsequent films, most notably Expressionist cinematographer Karl Freund's American-made feature *Mad Love* (1935), starring Peter Lorre.

[18] Florence Stoker, the widow of the author of *Dracula*, sued for copyright infringement and was successful in obtaining a court order that *Nosferatu* be destroyed; thankfully, this did not occur. See David J. Skal, *Hollywood Gothic: The Tangled Web of Dracula from Novel to Stage to Screen* (New York: W. W. Norton, 1990), 56–63.

[19] This character, like Van Helsing, offers a darkly intimated parallel to the vampire not only for the reasons to follow in the main text, but also on account of his name. Edward Bulwer (1803–1873), who added his mother's surname upon inheriting her ancestral estate, belonged to the ranks of English Germanophile authors. It was he who authored the notorious opening line, "It was a dark and stormy night," which has become synonymous with bad writing. (Since 1982, the English Department at San Jose State University in California has awarded a Bulwer-Lytton prize for execrable prose.) Bulwer-Lytton began as an admirer of Byron, and his novels and plays explore the amoral egoism celebrated by his hero. The themes of the occult, opposition to the "herd mentality," and the quest for transcendence through personal rebellion struck a chord with nineteenth-century Germans. Among his many admirers was Richard Wagner, who drew inspiration from Bulwer-Lytton's novel *Rienzi* for his third opera. Thus, in *Nosferatu*, the very name "Bulwer" connotes magic and mystery with undertones that, in 1920s Germany, harken back to nineteenth-century fantasies of the will to power that were in the process of becoming politicized to disastrous effect. See Richard A. Zipser, *Edward Bulwer-Lytton and Germany* (Bern: Herbert Lang, 1974).

[20] See chapter 1 for the significance of this figure in the early stages of vampire history.

[21] According to documents collected and examined by Alanna Knight in *Burke and Hare: Crime Archive* (London: National Archives, 2007), they only obtained bodies through killing; whatever the truth may be, Burke and Hare, besides being unambiguously fiendish, have also gone down in history for defiling the resting place of the dead.

[22] Thomas Elsaesser, *Weimar Cinema and After: German's Historical Imaginary* (New York: Routledge, 2000), 239. I have substituted the proper names for the ones from *Dracula* that Elsaesser, in the confusion occasioned by vampirism, incorrectly (but also fittingly) uses.

[23] Gay, 1.

[24] Roger Dadoun, "Fetishism in the Horror Film," *Fantasy and the Cinema*, ed. James Donald (London: British Film Institute, 1989), 54–55.

[25] See Daniel Paul Schreber's obsession with disease, discussed in the previous chapter.

[26] René Girard, *The Scapegoat*, trans. Yvonne Freccero (Baltimore: Johns Hopkins UP, 1986), *passim*.

[27] Starting in the twelfth century, Jews provided a common target for this surgical social operation. In 1144, Jewish leaders in eastern England were executed after a monk who had converted from Judaism alleged that Jews had abducted a Christian child. According to the informant's account, the Jews had crucified the boy and drained his body of blood for occult purposes. Some 150 similar incidents occurred in England and on the Continent throughout the late-medieval and early-modern periods. The charge was also brought against Jews that they had stabbed or otherwise desecrated the host — that is, the body of Christ — in a diabolical parody of the crucifixion. These stories resurfaced in the late nineteenth and early twentieth centuries to add "historical proof" to new claims about the dangers posed by Jews. For a collection of documents from premodern Europe, see Jacob R. Marcus, ed., *The Jew in the Medieval World: A Source Book, 315–1791* (New York: Atheneum, 1969). Alan Dundes, ed. *The Blood Libel Legend: A Casebook in Anti-Semitic Folklore* (Madison: U of Wisconsin P, 1991), provides interpretation and analysis of the myth and its diffusion from the Middle Ages to the twentieth century. For an excellent treatment of cases in early-modern Germany, see R. Po-chia Hsia, *The Myth of Ritual Murder: Jews and Magic in Reformation Germany* (New Haven: Yale UP, 1988), discussed in chapter 1 of this study.

[28] Michel Foucault, *The History of Sexuality*, trans. Robert Hurley (New York: Pantheon, 1978), 140–41, 143–44.

[29] Michel Foucault, *Discipline and Punish: The Birth of the Prison*, trans. Alan Sheridan (New York: Vintage, 1995).

[30] José B. Monleón, *A Specter Is Haunting Europe: A Sociohistorical Approach to the Fantastic* (Princeton: Princeton UP, 1990), 63.

[31] For an excellent discussion of the latter point, see Mike Hawkins, *Social Darwinism in European and American Thought, 1860–1945: Nature as Model and Nature as Threat* (Cambridge: Cambridge UP, 1997).

[32] Daniel Pick, *Faces of Degeneration: A European Disorder, c. 1848–1918* (Cambridge: Cambridge UP, 1993), 109–54.

[33] For an examination of the phenomenon in comparative context and broad historical scope, see J. E. Chamberlin and Sander Gilman, eds., *Degeneration: The Dark Side of Progress* (New York: Columbia UP, 1985). Significantly, Nordau was also a founding figure of Zionism.

[34] Cf. Michel Bouvier and Jean-Louis Leutrat, *Nosferatu* (Paris: Cahiers du Cinéma/Gallimard, 1981), 26, who call Nosferatu "a Shylock from the Carpathians" (quoted in Skal, 52).

[35] Kaes, 71, discusses how "the nexus of sexual deviancy and criminality carried antisemitic undertones" in Weimar Germany.

[36] Linda Schulte-Sasse, *Entertaining the Third Reich: Illusions of Wholeness in Nazi Cinema* (Durham: Duke UP, 1996), 68–69.

[37] David Biale, *Blood and Belief: The Circulation of a Symbol between Jews and Christians* (Berkeley: U of California P, 2007), 123–61, discusses continuities and points of difference in the symbolic value attached to blood in medieval times and under National Socialism.

[38] Schulte-Sasse, 62–63.

[39] Oswald Spengler, *The Decline of the West*, vol. 1, trans. Charles Francis Atkinson (New York: Alfred A. Knopf, 1926), 392.

[40] Significantly, Murnau's first American film, *Sunrise: A Song of Two Humans* (1927), may be regarded as a kind of remake of *Nosferatu* inasmuch as it focuses on the threat posed by a sensuous woman who conspires to infect a young man with moral and physical contamination that almost makes him his wife's murderer. Early in the film, the evil "Woman from the City" is shown skulking about in a foggy marsh and lying in wait outside the couple's house. Throughout, she is clad entirely in black and radiates sexual independence and lust. At the end, after her enticements have proved unsuccessful, she is wheeled away, like a witch to the stake, in a wagon. *Sunrise* retains the structure of Murnau's vampire film while reversing the gender and origin of the being that menaces domestic bliss: Nosferatu comes from the country and is male and hideous; his female counterpart is urban(e) and beautiful. However, the focus of both films — endangered tradition — is identical. Eric Rentschler has compared Leni Riefenstahl's *The Blue Light* (1932) to *Nosferatu* and called this directorial debut by the maker of the infamous *Triumph of the Will* (1935) "a vampire film" (*The Ministry of Illusion: Nazi Cinema and Its Afterlife* [Cambridge: Harvard UP, 1996], 31–38).

[41] A similar fictional demand dictates the death by drowning of Dorothea, the young woman whom the Jewish "vampire" rapes in *Jud Süss* (see Schulte-Sasse, 85–89).

[42] Rather shockingly, then, Ewers later joined the Nazi Party and published *Horst Wessel: Ein deutsches Schicksal*. For a discussion of the author's "irresponsible" life, see Wilfried Kugel, *Der Unverantwortliche: Das Leben des Hanns Heinz Ewers* (Düsseldorf: Grupello, 1993).

[43] See Cathy Caruth, *Unclaimed Experience: Trauma, Narrative, and History* (Baltimore: The Johns Hopkins UP, 1996), for a discussion of how this Freudian concept relates to works of fiction.

[44] In a recent study, David Kalat cites a poll finding that 95 percent of German teenagers in the mid-1980s recognized the name Mabuse. David Kalat, *The Strange Case of Dr. Mabuse: A Study of the Twelve Films and Five Novels* (Jefferson, North Carolina: McFarland and Company, 2001), 282.

[45] Bernd Widdig, *Culture and Inflation in Weimar Germany* (Berkeley: U of California P, 2001).

[46] Norbert Jacques, "Dr. Mabuse," in Norbert Jacques, *Dr. Mabuse, der Spieler*, eds. Michael Farin and Günter Scholdt (Hamburg: Rogner & Bernhard, 1994), 264; hereafter cited parenthetically in the text.

[47] Gay discusses the popular "rejection of politics" (70) in Weimar, which reflected contempt for established institutions and procedure.

[48] Tom Gunning, *The Films of Fritz Lang: Allegories of Vision and Modernity* (London: British Film Institute, 2000), 98.

[49] Michel Chion, *The Voice in Cinema*, trans. Claudia Gorbman (New York: Columbia UP, 1999), 31–47, 66–69.

[50] This flatfooted character debuted in *M*, where he was somewhat more efficient.

[51] Gunning, 148–49.

[52] David Rudkin, *Vampyr* (London: British Film Institute, 2005), 75.

[53] In the early sixties, *In the Steel Net of Dr. Mabuse* (1961), *The Invisible Claws of Dr. Mabuse* (1962), a vastly different remake of *Testament* (1961), *Scotland Yard Hunts Dr. Mabuse* (1963), and *The Death-Rays of Dr. Mabuse* (1964) appeared under the banner of Brauner's CCC-Filmkunst. Variously, "Mabuse" possesses a mind-control drug, an apparatus that modifies the vibrations of matter to confer invisibility, an insanity-inducing contraption, a device that permits mind-control, and a "death star" satellite that can project a laser beam.

Conclusion: The Vampire in the Americas and Beyond

The vampire as we know it, its frequent allure of great antiquity and exotic provenance notwithstanding, is fundamentally a modern, European monster. Each of the vampire's many incarnations draws on the anxiety and desire loosed by accelerating social transformations since the 1700s. The first half of this study examined the monster in light of economic changes, political conflicts, and encounters between different ethnicities in the eighteenth and nineteenth centuries. The last three chapters have explored how the vampire subsequently mutated and thrived in the imaginary space shaped, at the turn of the twentieth century, by modern technologies — all the while retaining its connection to the open-ended categories of religion, race, and class inherited from earlier times. It would be remiss to close the book on the vampire without a few words on the forms the monster has assumed in the latter half of the twentieth and at the beginning of the twenty-first centuries. Equally, the task remains of exploring how the vampire left the Old World for the New and, in the process, rejuvenated itself.

The ministers, clerics, and men of finance referred to as "vampires" in rationalist polemics from the London *Craftsman* to Marx's *Capital* (see chapter 2) represent the barbarism that modern societies can displace and change in appearance, but which always remains one step ahead of projects of improvement — as if new agents of power enjoyed an inherited right. Polidori's vampiric impostor Ruthven (chapter 3) possesses the august dignity of a nobleman. Murnau's vampire (chapter 6) is named *Count* Orlok. Stoker's Dracula boasts an ancient bloodline (chapter 4), and Schreber claims that the "soul murder" underlying his vampiric condition goes back to a long-standing feud between august families (chapter 5). In each case, however, we saw that vampires incarnate unease contemporaneous with the works' production.

An imaginary tie to the past characterizes most of the vampires examined here, even though the monsters uniformly feed off the weak spots in modern culture. These vampires seem old and entitled, but it is never wholly clear what legitimates their claims on the living. Of late — that is, in the past fifty years or so — the temporal disjunction and difficulties of authentication that vampires have "traditionally" embodied have increasingly been oriented toward the future. In a supposedly postmodern age of instant messaging, high-speed data retrieval, and late capitalism, the monster has grown young.

The emergence of a new vampire breed has undermined the status of Dracula, the most iconic of vampires. Despite the fact that a work featuring the Count renews his lease on life every few years, Dracula has transformed into a somewhat pathetic figure. For example, Fred Saberhagen's 1975 novel, *The Dracula Tape* (which purports to be the transcript of a dictation made by Stoker's Count), offers a portrayal of the arch-vampire as a misunderstood person. "You will accuse me of the death of Lucy Westenra," the book begins. "Ah, I would swear my innocence. . . . I embraced the lovely Lucy, it is true. But never against her will. Not she [*sic*] nor any of the others did I ever force."[1] Saberhagen's Dracula pines away in doomed immortality for Mina Harker, whom he hopes somehow, someday, to make his own and grant "[a] life in which I trust she will find, despite its continuation of earthly sorrows, some great joys, too, unknown to those who merely breathe . . . !"[2] Francis Ford Coppola's cinematic version of the Dracula story (1992) offers another example of the maudlin vampire. The film's subtitle reads "True Love Never Dies," and the story features a Count whose sentiments are simply out of place in the modern world.

Painfully enough for Dracula's many acolytes, it seems that his slide into absurdity began largely in reaction to his former ability to inspire fear. Early cinematic successes played a key role in this process. The Count in Stoker's novel is protean and therefore terrifying (chapter 4), but Dracula's first screen appearances — most notably, Bela Lugosi's portrayal of the title role in Tod Browning's 1931 film — created a type that soon lent itself to caricature. Once Dracula's image was fixed and permanently associated with a particular actor and "look," the ever-changing world of cinematic images ensured that his style would fall behind the times. Ignominiously, Lugosi — although he continued to be cast in vampire parts — played Dracula himself only one more time, in the 1948 farce, *Abbott and Costello Meet Frankenstein*. In later decades, his image has lived on, in degraded form, in the math-hungry "Count" of the children's show *Sesame Street* and General Mills' "Count Chocula" breakfast cereal.

There are many examples of Dracula's awkward old age that one might cite: *Blacula* (1972), *Love at First Bite* (1979), and *Dracula: Dead and Loving It* (1995), to mention but a few. The best is perhaps the Andy Warhol-produced *Blood for Dracula* (1974), by Paul Morrissey. The film features a moribund Count (Udo Kier) desperate to find a bride who shares the old-fashioned values to which he still adheres.[3] Weakened to the point where he must be pushed around in a wheelchair, Dracula sets out for Italy in an attempt to find the virgin blood he needs. There, the moral decadence of his aristocratic hosts and the revolutionary militancy of their hunky Marxist handyman (played by Morrissey/Warhol regular

Joe Dallesandro) ensure his doom. Both Dracula and his employers represent a social order destined for destruction.

Blood for Dracula toys with the stereotyped representations of the Count inherited from Hollywood and late-night reruns of classic vampire movies. Kier's pale skin, his piercing eyes, and his accented speech possess a commanding quality that suits him well to the type established by Lugosi. However, at every turn the film undermines the actor's ability to incarnate the vampire role. While the credits are still rolling, the viewer sees Dracula before a mirror, applying hair dye and makeup in an effort to present a strong image — and even so, he fails to make a serious impression on those he meets. Morrissey's version of the Count, ridiculously enough, travels by automobile, with his coffin and wheelchair mounted awkwardly on the roof. The people who encounter him all think he is a vegetarian (!) because of his sickly appearance and lack of vigor.

The father of the family that welcomes the Count in Italy (played by neorealist director Vittorio de Sica) does not even recognize the venerable title of "Dracula." After repeating the name in the manner of an enologist tasting a wine — gargling the syllables and swishing them around in his mouth — the patriarch eventually detects the Count's pedigree and declares that he "should be kept preferably in the horizontal position, away from the light. . . . Yes, a gentleman, as you might say, aged in wood — of excellent stock." Dracula is a joke.[4] At the film's end, Dallesandro's character, the rebellious "servant" of the family, destroys the Count and defiantly announces: "The only future is in socialism!"

As we saw in chapter 2, irony suffuses many representations of the vampire. Once-imposing and earnest incarnations of the monster, having become well known, can assume an absurd quality unanticipated by their creators. Because vampires exhibit exaggerated traits of the people in the societies where they parasitically exist, their grotesque qualities easily spill over from horror into humor. The promiscuous proliferation of the undead engenders irreverence and scorn.

Parallel to Dracula's decline, a new breed of vampires began to emerge. These vampires are young and full of life — if anything, they are *too* full. Laurence Rickels associates this incarnation of the undead with what he calls the "Teen Age" — that is, the youth-obsessed culture of the entertainment industry.[5] The development has its origins in the early twentieth century. During and after the Great War, which taxed and depleted the manpower of nations, women entered the workforce in unprecedented numbers and came to occupy more visible positions in the public sphere.[6] The film industry both mirrored and participated in the general cultural shift, in the United States and abroad, which redefined the roles played by women not just on-screen, but also in real life. Actresses (like actors) became iconic figures instantly recognized by millions. The line separating celebrities' screen identities from their private selves was often indistinct, and media personae — images that imitated life in the space between fiction and reality — multiplied.[7] In this realm of "seeming" (that is, to follow the German distinction, the sphere of *Schein,* or appearance, as opposed to *Sein,* being), personal and cultural cynicism prevails.[8]

One of the earliest stars of the American movie industry was Theda Bara, born Theodosia Goodman in Cincinnati, 1890.[9] In *A Fool There Was* (1915) — a film based on Rudyard Kipling's poem, "The Vampire" — the raven-haired, dark-eyed beauty plays a gold digger who drives her beau to the grave. The final sequence shows the she-vampire commanding her dead suitor to kiss her while she scatters rose petals over his corpse. Publicity shots for Theda Bara featured the actress in exotic makeup, poised sphinx-like over a skeleton. Press releases claimed that she had been born in the Sahara, the child of a European father and an "Oriental" mother. Goodman's stage name, an anagram for "death" and "Arab," renewed the connection between the vampire and the menacingly foreign, Muslim world that colored the earliest form of our monster (chapter 1).

Theda Bara's briefly ascendant star established a new kind of character in the movies and brought a new word into cultural circulation. The term "vamp" came to designate any strong-willed, sexual female character, even when there was no hint of the supernatural. The studio fabrications about Bara's background exploited the ready-made mythology of the Romantic Fatal Woman, now updated and vulgarized for mass culture. The vamp represented a hyperbolic version of femininity that was self-confident and threatening to a male-dominated society.[10] Throughout the twentieth century — and now in the twenty-first — vixens, sirens, and vamps (it is not by chance that the names evoke the worlds of fairy tale and myth) have channeled fear of, and fascination with, the changes in women's place in society. Bara's disappearance from the screen opened the way for others. Consequently, nearly every self-possessed actress, from Marlene Dietrich to Sharon Stone, has at one point or another been honored by the title of "vamp."

However, the fortunes of the vamp, like those of all film stars, depend wholly on how much money can be made. Marx's economic vampirology (chapter 2) has lost none of its timeliness with the advent of what Max Horkheimer and Theodor Adorno called the "culture industry."[11] Although (to the best of my knowledge) the fact has passed unnoticed by critics, the word "vamp," while evidently derived from "vampire," has a homonym with a complementary set of significations in a related sphere of modern culture. In music, to *vamp* means "to improvise." If opportunistic, money-hungry women who make their way to ill-gotten gains by beguiling victims with off-the-cuff lines and a flashy wardrobe have become known as "vamps," the popularity of this name probably owes something to the Jazz Age, which Adorno, the conservative communist, despised.[12]

Vamps and vampiresses, while reflecting social changes, belong to the world of fictional image making; as such, the power they seem to possess is not really their own. The story of Hammer Studios in England illustrates the point.[13] After a profitable run of B-grade horror movies in the late 1950s, the firm began to lose money. The company sought to remedy its diminishing returns by making movies that added nudity and sex to the tales of terror that had, for decades, provided a mainstay of cinematic entertainment. The centerpiece of these productions, *The Vampire Lovers* (1970), features nubile beauties sought out by an equally attractive female vampire who initiates them into a supernaturally tinged world of eroticism. The film claims to be based on "Carmilla," a story written by the Irish author Sheridan Le Fanu (1872). However, the film has a wholly different orientation.

As Nina Auerbach has remarked, the vampirism in Le Fanu's story represents "an interchange, a sharing, an identification, that breaks down the boundaries of familial roles and the sanctioned hierarchy of marriage."[14] The literary Carmilla shows the feminine virtues of nurturing and personal involvement with others. The screen version, in contrast, offers little of the sort. At best, a tendentious interpretation might equate women's bodies on display with a form of "sexual liberation." In her Hammer incarnation — the cynic suspects — Carmilla's primary purpose is to provide titillation for a heterosexual male audience by initiating adolescent girls into forbidden sensuality. Following the conventions of narrative cinema analyzed by Laura Mulvey, the female vampire serves as a lens to focus the hungry masculine gaze.[15] Auerbach quotes fellow critic Andrea Weiss's "categorical but depressingly accurate diagnosis": "What has survived of 'Carmilla' from Victorian literature and worked its way into twentieth-century cinema is its muted expression of lesbianism, no longer sympathetically portrayed, but now reworked into a male pornographic fantasy."[16]

On the whole, female vampires have not been as numerous as their male counterparts in literature.[17] This is the case, I have argued, because the vampire's career has been fueled by new forms of social mobility. It was not until the late nineteenth century that women were "on the move" politically. Goethe's "Bride of Corinth" and Gautier's Clarimonde in "The Dead in Love" owe their undead existence to prohibitions that kept them cloistered, away from fulfilling their desires while alive (chapter 2). The same is still true of Dracula's women, locked away like chattel in a feudal castle in politically retrograde Eastern Europe (chapter 4).

Bram Dijkstra has noted the emergence, at the time of the "New Woman" — when social roles were transforming dramatically — of pictorial representations of female vampires; at the fin de siècle, he writes, they "were . . . everywhere"[18] in the arts. In contrast to the images of vulnerable women in stylized poses of sacrifice that enjoyed popularity earlier,[19] the end of the nineteenth century witnessed an outpouring of images of menacing women. Works of note include paintings by Edvard Munch and Philip Burne-Jones. The latter's "Vampire" (ca. 1897) looks like a reversal of Henry Fuseli's famous *Nightmare* from a century earlier — only, now, it is a woman perched upon an unconscious man, not an imp astride a swooning lady. Today, since the latter half of the twentieth century, the sisters of the Carmilla from *The Vampire Lovers* are legion. Exploitation filmmakers (such as Jess Franco, who directed the genre "classic" *Vampyros Lesbos* [1971]), as well as directors of greater artistic ambitions (e.g., the novelist and filmmaker Alain Robbe-Grillet[20]), have made vampire movies that parade flesh in the prime of unnatural life. A quick Internet search will reveal more recent examples. There is little in these works to challenge a masculinist view of the world.[21]

The new breed of vampire that wants to stay forever young also has male specimens. Thus, Joel Schumacher's film *The Lost Boys* (1987) features a group of vampiric teenagers-in-perpetuity who make an amusement park their haunt, hazing new members into their order in the manner of college fraternities. Although "homosocial" relations characterize the boys' interactions, this fact only reinforces heterosexual norms of gender,[22] with a girl — whose cipher-like name is simply "Star" (Jami Gertz) — providing the object of rivalry and exchange. The divorced mother of the two brothers who are the film's main characters winds up dating the owner of a local video store. The latter, it turns out, serves as a father figure to the vampire crowd the boys have fallen in with. *The Lost Boys,* a comedy-horror inversion of the 1970s *Brady Bunch,* registers as a conservative, Reagan-era complaint about the broken American family.

In the late sixties and early seventies, the daytime television serial *Dark Shadows* still featured a morose vampire (with the very unglamorous name of "Barnabas Collins") lurking about a New England town. This descendent of Dracula belonged to a dying breed. The show's 1990s primetime equivalent, *Buffy the Vampire Slayer,* is not set on the gloomy East Coast (with its echoes of Europe). Instead — and like *The Lost Boys* — *Buffy* takes place in California. In the all-American town of "Sunnydale," the spirited blonde heroine saves the world over and over by combating the forces of darkness that emerge in the halls of her high school and the nightspots where youth congregate. Buffy's boyfriend Angel — a vampire who has repudiated his bloodthirsty past — exemplifies the new kind: torn between antisocial impulses and the desire to live in a human community and do good, he is not so much a monster as misunderstood — like so many other young people.

In recent decades, then, the vampire has come to provide a privileged metaphor for representing the conflicts of adolescence. For young men, reformed monsters like Angel incarnate the tension between the self-serving impulse to gratify urges at the expense of others and the (often-belated) awareness of the social unacceptability of such behavior. For young women, the boyfriend-vampire combination crystallizes ambivalent feelings about the company they keep (and what they do with these companions). In affirmation of the standing patriarchal order — that is, to make sure that Buffy grows up properly — she has been appointed a benevolent "Watcher" as a substitute for her missing father.

An essential feature of the vampire in the latter half of the twentieth century is the creature's assumption of a group-defined identity. The vampiresses of Hammer films need sorority sisters for their slumber parties, and the lost boys form nothing so much as a teenage gang. Buffy the vampire hunter has a team, too; as her friend Willow puts it in an early episode, "You're the Slayer, and we're, like, the Slayerettes."

Anne Rice's *Interview with the Vampire* (1976), which inaugurated an enormously popular series of novels, presents a first-person exposition of what it means to be a vampire who is part of a family. The vampire Louis, haunted by the blood thirst of his kind, relates the moral troubles of his two-hundred-year life, which began when a senior vampire initiated his new existence in the eighteenth century. The narrative focuses on Louis's conflicted relationship with his father figure Lestat and, by extension, the norms and conventions of older generations of the undead, who are European in origin and sensibility. Besides the (probably fortuitous) association of Louis's "vampirization" with the age that witnessed the entry of the vampire onto the historical stage (chapter 1), it is worth remarking that Rice sets Louis's narrative in New Orleans, a city distinguished by the strong presence of different cultures (English, French, and African/Caribbean); this fact calls to mind the conflicted religious and ethnic diversity of the Central European lands where vampires were first recorded. On the one hand, colonial Louisiana is a site of hybridity; on the other, it preserves estate society.

Louis shares the elitist, aristocratic values of his elders, but he evinces a young person's — and, moreover, a young American's — standoffish attitude towards tradition. The novel, which purports to be the transcript of a tape recording, does not name Louis's interlocutor, but calls him simply "the boy." This figure, obviously entranced by the vampire's story, doubles, in an updated setting, the young Louis. *Interview* showcases the seductive appeal of vampirism for youth as a means of never aging and belonging to an in crowd whose popularity never fades. Tellingly, in the book's sequel, *The Vampire Lestat* (1985), the elder vampire gets over his old-world reserve and becomes a rock star. In real life, the author underwent a complementary conversion, albeit in the opposite direction. After spending most of her adulthood professing atheism, Rice returned to the Catholic faith in 1996; since then, she has written works of historical fiction about Jesus Christ.[23] There is no hierarchy like the one inherited from Rome, and no story of life after death as compelling as the one told in the Christian Bible.

A discussion of vampiric images, themes, and echoes in popular music — from the defiant posturing of heavy metal to "Goth" subcultures that claim to embrace transgression and evil — would require another book entirely.[24] Here, too, the vampire has achieved the boundless morbidity/vitality of a disease in its terminal stages. The sickness is sexy — and catching. Even as one generation wastes away, its place is taken by another host for the vampire to prey upon.[25]

Youth's openness to futurity and ignorance of the past have facilitated a merger, in a market economy that always looks forward, between the vampire and another creature of fantasy fiction, the cyborg. Rob Latham has surveyed cultural productions ranging from "cyberpunk" novels to MTV and Hollywood films, and he has shown the ubiquity in contemporary culture of figures that transcend the borders between the organic and the inorganic, the living and the dead.

> These figures metaphorically embody the libidinal-political dynamics of the consumerist ethos to which young people have been systematically habituated. . . . The vampire is literally an insatiable consumer driven by a hunger for perpetual youth, while the cyborg has incorporated the machineries of consumption into its juvenescent flesh. [. . .] The conspicuous unnaturalness of both figures, their frankly mutant character, serves to point up how deeply youth has come to be defined by its ensnarement in the norms and ideologies of consumption, rather than by more conventional measures of identity rooted in the structures of family life.[26]

The hybrid fictional formations that Latham examines refract a social reality increasingly shaped by new media and markets that deterritorialize (to use Gilles Deleuze and Félix Guattari's term[27]) established definitions of subjectivity and boundaries of self. Youth, ever a site of confrontational energies, feeds off the rapid social transformations wrought by the expansion of networks of communication, new machinic interfaces, and high-speed connections that shape culture at the turn of the millennium; at the same time, youth is embodied in forms given definition by these same forces. Because the turbulence inherent in youth meets up, now more than ever, with the accelerated pace of cultural change, the vampire-cyborg — a creature that defies tradition and received conceptions of life — represents the spirit of the new age of technological reproduction.[28]

If vampires and cyborgs have fused, that is because science fiction in the twentieth century took up where nineteenth-century literature of the fantastic left off. The themes are the same; only the referential framework has changed. Inner space has become outer space, and technology has taken the place of magic. A point of transition may be found in Auguste

Villiers de l'Isle-Adam's *L'Ève future* (Tomorrow's Eve, 1886), which tells how a fictional Thomas Edison creates an artificial woman; tellingly, the novel likens the android to a vampire.[29] Andreas Huyssen has perceptively argued that the female robot in Fritz Lang's *Metropolis* (1927) — a film offering both criticism and a celebration of modernity — displays the seductiveness of the vamp in her incitement of workers to revolt.[30]

The twentieth- and twenty-first-century monsters that come from the stars give shape to fears that originate down on earth, just as the otherworldly ghosts of yesteryear appeared between the shadows of everyday affairs. Not surprisingly, then, the space alien has also assumed many traits of the vampire, and vice versa. The common denominator is that while appearing to be wholly *other,* monsters — a word etymologically related to the Latin vocabulary of wonder — are in fact unsettlingly familiar.

Popular representations of extraterrestrial menace feature enlarged versions of beings that do in fact exist, but which are hidden from the naked eye: multi-limbed, vaguely insectoid creatures (like the microorganisms the Paracelsian scientist Bulwer shows his students in *Nosferatu* [chapter 6]). A key point of reference for this mutated image is the alien in Ridley Scott's film of the same name (1979), which incubates parasitically in a human body before destroying its host. More recent examples include films such as *Species* (1995) and *Starship Troopers* (1997). The unearthly monsters featured in these works, like Maupassant's Horla (chapter 5), crystallize fears engendered by modern science and technology — that "man" is but another rung in a chain of being that has not been designed by God, but instead follows the purposeless whims of a Nature indifferent to humankind.

The most elaborate presentation of this form of "cosmic terror"[31] can be found in the works of H. P. Lovecraft (1890–1937), who dealt with the vampire theme in a short story, "The Shunned House" (1924). In this tale, the narrator/protagonist sets out to solve the mystery of numerous deaths at a particular New England residence, which superstitious minds have attributed to vampires. "There are horrors beyond horrors, . . . nuclei of all dreamable hideousness which the cosmos saves to blast . . . an unhappy few,"[32] Lovecraft's hero earnestly remarks. The reason behind such terrors lies in the realm of positive fact, even if we do not have the means of apprehending it:

> In this case an overwhelming preponderance of evidence from numerous authentic sources pointed to the tenacious existence of certain forces of great power and, so far as the human point of view is concerned, exceptional malignancy. To say that we actually believed in vampires . . . would be a carelessly inclusive statement. Rather must it be said that we were not prepared to deny the possibility of certain unfamiliar and unclassified modifications of vital force and

attenuated matter; existing very infrequently in three-dimensional space because of its more intimate connexion with other special units, yet close enough to the boundary of our own to furnish us occasional manifestations.[33]

"The Shunned House," notwithstanding its Gothic title, is science fiction, and the putative vampire a fungal, alien life form that obeys laws as yet unknown to human science. Here as elsewhere, the vampire inhabits a border zone. Only, now, the frontier does not lie so much between states and segments of society as between the earth and the planets of other solar systems.[34]

Lovecraft's obsession with hostile forms of brute materiality[35] goes well beyond most others' images of life from beyond. To return to more conventional schemes of representation, the obverse of the insect-like space alien that multiplies at the expense of human life is the hairless, featureless, sexless alien in films such as Steven Spielberg's *Close Encounters of the Third Kind* (1977). The American author Whitley Strieber acquired a literary reputation with the vampire novel *The Hunger* (1981); *Communion* (1987), a book purporting to recount actual events, describes encounters with "gray" aliens (also simply called "visitors") with the same lack of distinguishing characteristics as the beings in Spielberg's film. These figures, upon closer reflection, possess a deep affinity with their more obviously monstrous kin. Devoid of particularizing traits, they, too, efface the differences that determine individual identity. Their large eyes on an oversized head and their undersized bodies make them resemble, more than anything else, a human infant. While it is generally disallowed to equate babies with monsters, young children are parasitic beings whose unrealized potential and unformed appearance provoke unease even in those who love them.[36] The vaguely anthropomorphic space alien, like the infant, represents a "degree zero" of ontology that holds open the border between humanity and the processes of growth and decline that command life.[37]

There is neither world enough nor time for a full discussion, but a brief mention of the figure of the zombie also belongs here. Like the vampire and the space alien, the zombie represents a principle of uncanny energy that defies conventional understandings of life, nature, and society. In Marxian terms, zombies are the *Lumpenproletariat* of monsters — an inarticulate, if not wholly voiceless, segment of the population, yet they do, all the same, belong to "the population," for they are unmistakably human in origin, even if their shuffling, undead state of being seems to contradict this assessment.[38]

The word first appeared in English in Robert Southey's *History of Brazil* (1819), where the ruler of a polity of runaway slaves in the 1690s is reported to have borne the title "Zombi."[39] Markman Ellis has pointed out the "semiotically confusing" nature of the term, which evoked for white colonialists "a black republic led by a devil-king."[40] The major articulations of the zombie are tied to the fortunes and misfortunes of the island of Haiti. The first black-ruled nation on the globe, Haiti acquired its freedom in an eighteenth-century slave rebellion before it was conquered again, in 1915, by the United States.[41] As Ellis observes, Victor Halperin's *White Zombie* (1932), the film that brought the zombie into mass circulation, "[represents] the American occupation as a new imperialism and a renewed slavery."[42] In the fiction, the diabolical "Murder" Legendre presides over automatons mindlessly carrying out factory work in a manner that is modeled on the working conditions of laborers in the real-life Haitian-American Sugar Company (HASCO).[43] Although the film's storyline focuses on an innocent white woman deprived of her will — thereby evoking a standard racist fear of potential miscegenation — this has occurred through the workings of Legendre, and at the behest of another white man; thus, the movie implicitly condemns the dehumanizing effects of colonial capitalism.

More recent zombie films have largely abandoned a Caribbean setting, but the radical alienation of the creature, which results from market forces, is still strong. So is the subtext of racial conflict. There is no glamorous specimen of the zombie, which represents, at the height of its glory, a brain-dead consumer.[44] George Romero's classic *Night of the Living Dead* (1968) evokes the painful history of American race relations and overseas wars by featuring a black protagonist leading a group of white survivors against hordes of zombies in rural Pennsylvania; the film blends in footage of lynchings and references to Vietnam to insinuate cultural criticism about past and present alike.[45] Romero's *Dawn of the Dead*, made ten years later, is set entirely in a suburban mall, where survivors hold out against shoppers who have been transformed into idiotic, flesh-eating monsters. These films, like contemporary works of fiction featuring alien life, pose questions about what constitutes humanity and human nature: however one may define these terms, they are always reflected in problematic form in the creatures that heroes encounter.[46] Zombie films commentate the "plebianization"[47] of both the exploited and those who supposedly benefit from prevailing economic relations.

No study of vampires, at this juncture at least, can be complete. Vampires appear regularly in all imaginable media (including animation and video games), and they are likely to continue to multiply for some time yet. Nor can a single work inventory and discuss in detail all the undead that have played starring and secondary roles in cultural productions since the monster's entry into written culture about three hundred years ago. To remain within manageable dimensions, *Metamorphoses of the Vampire* has omitted discussion of works — especially recent ones — too numerous to count.[48]

However, I hope to have extracted, from a mass of data that remains quite extensive, a core set of qualities that illuminates cases not discussed here. Vampires, more fully than their human counterparts, embody incompleteness; their empty core is tenuously held in place by the pressure of the boundaries they transgress. Lacking an identity of their own, vampires contaminate and confuse what surrounds them. The matrix of representation for this disruption is a previously integral body, be it individual or social. The process of vampiric dissolution is caustic and dynamic. Vampires steal and redistribute energy — be it blood, money, sentiment, or "nerve" (chapter 5) — which, under conditions of calm, circulates in fixed pathways. That is why there are so many seemingly contradictory forms that the monster has assumed. Each metamorphosis of the vampire points toward a constant of change: a function of transformation that holds the place of an authentic, proper substance.

Through the comparative analysis of texts that have received extensive commentary, as well as works that have not, *Metamorphoses of the Vampire* has sought not only to dispel misconceptions, but also to demonstrate — whatever qualifications future research may bring — that concrete historical processes and events motivate the sometimes seductive, sometimes terrifying transformations that characterize the many breeds of vampire. Although the vampire is by no means the only monster associated with blood and an unnaturally prolonged life, and although the vampire resembles certain other folkloric creatures, it is a "child" of modern times. This monstrous infant — the term is not as inappropriate as one might think, for decades passed between the vampire's entry into recorded history and the first time it developed a personality and the power of speech (chapter 2) — continues to grow larger and display new potentialities in a way that mirrors its human host. As regimes, relations of production, and social orders change, so, too, does the vampire.

To retain an anthropomorphic vocabulary, there are many members of the vampire family. Individual works present vampires that differ greatly from one another. Gautier's Clarimonde is not Murnau's Nosferatu, and one version of Dracula is not identical to the next. However, all vampires — whether the users of ill-gotten gains in Enlightenment satire or the high-school creeps of *Buffy* — move in the shadows thrown by the world their prey inhabits. Thus, we should not be surprised to see, in an era of globalization, monsters in the cultural productions of the Third World that call to mind the undead of Europe and North America.

Just as the vampire embodied hateful tyranny for polemicists in the eighteenth century, it has now come to represent the power dynamics of a postcolonial geopolitical order. The reggae musician Peter Tosh, in his recorded diaries (the so-called "Red X" tapes), speaks of vampires from North America draining the financial and physical resources of Jamaica.[49] In a similar vein, the South African reggae performer Lucky Dube has a song called "Dracula" in which he compares the vampire and the "New state president/Telling people/What he's gonna do for them," when, in fact, "His heart is as cold as ice," and he intends to suck them of life.[50]

Julio Cortázar drew up a list of vampires even more sweeping than Voltaire's "speculators, tax officials, and businessmen who suck the blood of the people in broad daylight" (chapter 2). The *vampiros multinacionales* that Cortázar enumerates are parasitic international agents who control and manipulate governments, markets, and military forces:

> Se llaman de mil, de diez mil, de cien mil maneras . . . pero se llaman sobre todo ITT, sobre todo Nixon y Ford, sobre todo Henry Kissinger o CIA . . . , se llaman sobre todo Pinochet o Banzer o López Rega, sobre todo General o Coronel o Tecnócrata o Fleury o Stroessner, se llaman de una manera tan especial que cada nombre significa miles de nombres, como la palabra hormiga significa siempre una multitud de hormigas aunque el diccionario la defina en singular.

> [They have a thousand, ten thousand, one hundred thousand names . . . but they are certainly called ITT, certainly Nixon or Ford, certainly Henry Kissinger or the CIA . . . ; they are certainly called Pinochet or Banzer or López Rega, certainly "general" or "colonel" or "technocrat" or Fleury or Stroessner; they possess their names in a special way, so that each one signifies thousands of other names, just as the word "ant" always signifies a multitude of ants, even if the dictionary defines it in the singular.][51]

Since Cortázar inventoried these monsters in the 1970s, the names may have changed, but the number of "multinational vampires" feeding off victim peoples has only increased.

Metamorphoses of the Vampire has taken issue with many scholars' propensity to find vampires everywhere and at all times in history. However, in view of the myth's broad diffusion and the many ramifications of vampirism we have traced, this tendency is understandable. In the context of Cortázar's indictment of economic imperialism as a vampiric activity, as well as the related fields of metaphor mapped out in the preceding pages, a recent study by American anthropologist Luise White warrants mention.

The title of White's examination of Central and East African responses to colonization is *Speaking with Vampires*. White employs the term because, since the late nineteenth century, Africans in territories as diverse as Northern Rhodesia, the Belgian Congo, Uganda, and Kenya have claimed that colonial officers — game rangers, mine managers, and firemen — have captured members of their communities and extracted their blood. White insists on the term "vampire" — informants do not use the word, although the translations of their stories made by mystified colonial authorities do[52] — because it best sums up the qualities of a class of foreign beings able to transgress boundaries, violate intimate space, and steal private and precious substances from the communities where they operate. Discussing a paradigmatic case from Mombasa (Kenya), she observes:

> The power and uncertainty of these stories — no one knew exactly what Europeans did with African blood, but people were convinced that they took it — makes them an especially rich historical source. . . . They report the aggressive carelessness of colonial extractions and ascribe potent and intimate meanings to them.[53]

The very confusion of the reports made by colonial officials provides "a glimpse of the world as seen by people who [see] boundaries and bodies . . . penetrated" — "a world of vulnerable and unreasonable relationships."[54] "Vampire" is an apt term inasmuch as it captures coercive power dynamics that can otherwise be described only by means of an elaborate theoretical vocabulary.

Of course, the African lexicon for supernatural predation is different from the vocabulary we have encountered until now. Are these creatures "really" vampires? Any answer must beg the question. As we have seen throughout the preceding chapters, no absolutely authoritative definition of the word "vampire" exists. The name has been applied to a vast body of beings that are outwardly dissimilar, from Balkan villagers to lordly cosmopolitans. It is conceivable that under other circumstances, an African word might have been disseminated in a manner similar to *vampire;* the cases of foreign domination and upset traditions that White analyzes are not unlike the situation in Serbia some three hundred years ago. However, if this has not occurred, it is in no small part due to the representational syncretism that characterizes the vampire. That is, the name, which mobilizes the "traces"[55] of past significations, fits readily into new contexts, more or less ad libitum, across languages and cultures. This quality — even if it was obtained fortuitously — is not shared by terminology that has remained far more restricted in its circulation. Signs may be inherently arbitrary, as Ferdinand de Saussure famously postulated,[56] but history and politics create relations in which contingency becomes necessity and words lose their neutrality (even if it remains unclear whose interests they serve).

* * *

At any rate, American vampires of the late twentieth century provide the dialectical counterpart of Cortázar's imperialist monsters and the supernatural predators of colonial Africa. A number of academic *Buffy* partisans have claimed that the television show infuses the cultural mainstream with left-wing politics. In the words of critic Jeffrey L. Pasley, "there is a persistent association of capitalist values . . . with literal inhumanity."[57] One episode depicts a vampire "as an über-consumer, living in luxury and sending her scaly minions out to shop"; another shows how the boss vampire known simply as "the Master" contrives to establish "a blood factory where live humans will be transformed into a tasty, nutritious beverage."[58] Thus, the argument goes, Buffy and her friends (who display exemplary solidarity and teamwork in their fight against the shadowy oppressors) combat the monsters of capitalism. Related readings argue that the young heroine represents the feminist ideal of an empowered woman.[59]

Perhaps some viewers have in fact been spurred to become more critical of contemporary society by *Buffy*. However, there is nothing particularly radical about a young woman who wants, more than anything else, to lead a normal teenage existence. Buffy's character is constructed around her assertions of normality. When a boy tells her that she is "not like other girls," Buffy responds, "Yes I am." Other lines spoken by the teenage vampire killer include, "I'm the Chosen One, and I choose to be shopping."

Finding a peer group and withstanding the torments of high school are Buffy's top priorities. As the heroine points out on numerous occasions, she did not choose to be a Slayer any more than she and other teenagers asked to be born. For her, killing vampires is like homework or household chores. Buffy has little insight into the nature or origins of the evil it is her mission to destroy, and she and her friends are neither members of the proletariat nor representatives of the intelligentsia that has, historically, presumed to lead the revolutionary masses. "Excuse me for not knowing about El Salvador," says Buffy when she gets a bad grade on a history exam, "Like I'm ever going to Spain anyway."

As Pasley observes, Buffy and her team "are essentially superheroes."[60] The model superhero, Superman, was created during the New Deal. Superman, Batman, Spiderman, and the rest of their kind operate at the margins of legality, but they assist civil authorities when ordinary means of enforcing the law prove inadequate. Superheroes do not wish to institute new principles of jurisprudence (to say nothing of a more equitable political economy). They are no revolutionaries. Likewise, Buffy and her vampire-fighting friends are outsiders who defend the standing social order; for them, the establishment is right in principle, if not always in fact.

Thematically, *Buffy* remains firmly ensconced in the truisms of a vague liberalism: rooting out injustice, advocating diversity (the heroine's best friend Willow is a Wiccan), "changing the world by changing one's outlook," and so on. The character Angel demonstrates that a vampire can mature and even do good.

This feature of the series amounts to a political blind spot it shares with other shows and films that follow a program of inclusiveness and compassion, for it substitutes fuzzy moral metaphysics ("everyone has a dark side") for the admittedly not-television-friendly business of exploring how vampirism originates in material, and not supernatural, situations.

Buffy's town, though it harbors a "Hellmouth," seems to house no one who does not belong to a utopian middle class. While there are certainly too many vampires in Sunnydale, California, the threat the monsters presumably pose to immigrant farm workers in less affluent townships nearby (to say nothing of victims of vampiric predation in the Third World) is logically much greater. But since these people are largely undocumented, no "Slayer" assists them, and no "Watcher" even notices when they meet a horrible end.

Similarly, Supergirl Buffy may "kick ass" when fighting demons, but if one wants equal rights for women, there are also struggles to be won in the decidedly unglamorous arena of legislation, where the pedantry and bureaucratic formalism of a Dracula (chapter 4) scares off many a young person who wants to save the world and still have perfect hair. There is — as yet, at least — no Rosa Luxemburg the Vampire Slayer.

In its diffusion since the eighteenth century, the vampire myth, like floodwaters covering the earth, has extended over an unequal surface. In valleys and low-lying habitations, the murk gathers thick; elsewhere, it is easier to see to the bottom of things. *Metamorphoses of the Vampire* has sounded the shallows and depths of vampirism. Through this sometimes clear, sometimes cloudy medium, we have seen that vampires can enshroud and penetrate the most varied terrains and human constructions. Submerged Victorian structures house a crustaceous breed of the monster embodying the sexualized threats that thrive in the recesses of the big city. In Serbian villages — that is, at another level of cultural elevation and social density — the vampire is less a submarine entity than an amphibian lurking at the shores of European civilization. If the vampire often appears to be a monster that has crawled out from the dark past or dwells in the hidden angles of the psyche, we should not be deceived: the vampire, like the life it mimics and destroys, is apt to mutate, for the Deluge that brought about vampirism is not divine but man-made. Vampires belong more to the age of Darwin than to an age of Faith.

This convoluted imagery — may the reader pardon the stylistic liberties undertaken by the author at the end of the book — is intended to point elliptically toward the extraordinary power of the vampire to generate new forms. Meetings of religion and science, as well as the intersection of other, competing schemes of understanding the world, always occur in a political dimension — that is, at sites where varying interests compete, conflict, and fuse in unlikely combinations. This study has sought to illuminate the forces that have contributed to the long life of the undead and to show the contours of the territories that vampires inhabit. The liminal location of vampirism in the late twentieth and early twenty-first centuries (whether an adolescent "room of one's own" or outer space) is structurally identical to the positions the vampire occupied in earlier incarnations: contested border lands between East and West in 1730s Serbia; the shifting boundaries between enlightenment and superstition later in the eighteenth century; the lines of demarcation between the ascendant middle classes and the ancien régime in the early- to mid-1800s; the divide between colonizing and colonized cultures at the turn of the twentieth century; and the biological separation of races in the decades before and after 1900.

In addition, *Metamorphoses of the Vampire* has inventoried and analyzed the many forms, mutations, projections, and regressions of the exemplary modern monster. A single name has designated a host of creatures characterized by changing appearances that are outwardly dissimilar. However, examples of the monster uniformly display a hybrid character. More than any other mythic entity, the vampire has the necessary quickness to reincarnate itself in order to meet — and master — new social and historical realities. For this reason, no other creature possesses the vitality of the living dead, who multiply in number with each revolution of the globe.

Notes

[1] Fred Saberhagen, *The Dracula Tape* (Riverdale: Baen, 1999), 2–3.

[2] Saberhagen, 264.

[3] These are, incidentally, also the director's own. See Maurice Yacowar, *The Films of Paul Morrissey* (Cambridge: Cambridge UP, 1993), esp. 55–70.

[4] The same fate befell Ruthven, in the previous century, when the light-opera team of Gilbert and Sullivan produced the vampire farce *Ruddigore* (1887). Avril Horner and Sue Zlosnik have written about the history and conventions of what they call "comic Gothic," which remains understudied ("Comic Gothic," *A Companion to the Gothic*, ed. David Punter [Oxford: Wiley-Blackwell, 2001], 242–53).

[5] Laurence Rickels, *The Vampire Lectures* (Minneapolis: U of Minnesota P, 1999), 217–18.

[6] David J. Skal, in *The Monster Show: A Cultural History of Horror* (New York: W. W. Norton, 1993), examines the effect of war and economic changes on American appetites for horror films.

[7] Edgar Morin, *The Cinema, or the Imaginary Man*, trans. Richard Howard (Minneapolis: U of Minnesota P, 2005).

[8] See Peter Sloterdijk, *Critique of Cynical Reason*, trans. Michael Eldred (Minneapolis: U of Minnesota P, 1988); the book culminates in a discussion of Weimar Germany's divided and self-conflicted perspective on itself and the world — which, Sloterdijk argues, is exemplary of contemporary culture, as well.

[9] Eve Golden, *Vamp: The Rise and Fall of Theda Bara* (New York: Vestal Press, 1997).

[10] Rhona J. Berenstein, *Attack of the Leading Ladies: Gender, Sexuality, and Spectatorship in Classic Horror Cinema* (New York: Columbia UP, 1996), 60–87.

[11] Max Horkheimer and Theodor Adorno, *Dialectic of Enlightenment*, trans. John Cumming (London: Continuum, 1976), 120–67.

[12] Theodor Adorno, "On the Fetish Character in Music and the Regression of Listening," *The Culture Industry: Selected Essays on Mass Culture*, ed. J. M. Bernstein (New York: Routledge, 2004), 29–60.

[13] Wayne Kinsey, *Hammer Films: The Elstree Studio Years* (Sheffield: Tomahawk Press, 2007).

[14] Nina Auerbach, *Our Vampires, Ourselves* (Chicago: U of Chicago P, 1995), 47.

[15] Laura Mulvey, "Visual Pleasure and Narrative Cinema," *Screen* 16.3 Autumn 1975, 6–18. Hence Auerbach's observation that, in the Hammer films, "the staking of female vampires is . . . the licensed torture of a woman who knows women don't need men" (129); "sexual liberation," inasmuch as it does not serve male interests, is punished in a horrifyingly reactionary manner.

[16] Auerbach, 53, The quote is from Andrea Weiss, *Vampires and Violets: Lesbians in Film* (Middlesex: Penguin, 1993), 87.

[17] Stefan Hock, *Die Vampyrsagen und ihre Verwertung in der deutschen Literatur* (Berlin: Alexander Duncker, 1900), 108–15, takes stock of the situation until the beginning of the twentieth century; subsequently, the proportion shifts considerably, but male vampires still predominate.

[18] Bram Dijkstra, *Idols of Perversity: Fantasies of Feminine Evil in Fin-de-Siècle Culture* (Oxford: Oxford UP, 1988), 351.

[19] See Dijkstra, especially chapter 1 ("Raptures of Submission: The Shopkeeper's Soul Keeper and the Cult of the Household Nun," 3–24) and chapter 4 ("The Weightless Woman, the Nymph with the Broken Back, and the Mythology of Therapeutic Rape," 83–118).

[20] For a discussion of the author and auteur's forays into vampire country, see Alain Goulet, "Vampirisme et vampirisation dans l'oeuvre de Robbe-Grillet," in *Les Vampires*, ed. Antoine Faivre (Paris: Albin Michel, 1993), 192–212.

[21] On female empowerment in contemporary vampire fictions, see Gina Wisker, "Love Bites: Contemporary Women's Vampire Fictions," in Punter, 167–79.

[22] See in this respect the pathbreaking study by Eve Kosofsky Sedgwick, *Between Men: English Literature and Male Homosocial Desire* (New York: Columbia UP, 1985).

[23] See Anne Rice, *Called Out of Darkness: A Spiritual Confession* (New York: Knopf, 2008), for the author's explanation of how she rediscovered religion.

[24] For examples, see Deena Weinstein, *Heavy Metal: A Cultural Sociology* (New York: Lexington Books, 1991); Robert Walser, *Running with the Devil: Power, Gender, and Madness in Heavy Metal Music* (Middletown: Wesleyan UP, 1993); Lauren M. E. Goodlad, Michael Bibby, eds., *Goth: Undead Subculture* (Durham: Duke UP, 2007). Richard Davenport-Hines, in *Gothic: Four Hundred Years of Excess, Horror, Evil, and Ruin* (New York: North Point Press, 1998), 62–93, stresses "the strength of backward-looking thoughts" in manifestations of the Gothic, which imply a conservative mentality even in confrontational youth cultures.

[25] Stephenie Meyer, *The Twilight Saga: Slipcased* (New York: Little, Brown Young Readers, 2008). The books have given birth to an equally successful cinema franchise. Significantly, the author's religious background and beliefs are Mormon: once again, vampires emerge from marginal positions within Christianity.

[26] Rob Latham, *Consuming Youth: Vampires, Cyborgs, and the Culture of Consumption* (Chicago: U of Chicago P, 2002), 1.

[27] Gilles Deleuze and Félix Guattari, *Anti-Oedipus: Capitalism and Schizophrenia*, trans. Robert Hurley, Helen R. Lane, and Mark Seem (New York: Viking, 1977).

[28] The novels of Richard Calder, especially *Dead Girls, Dead Boys, Dead Things* (New York: St. Martin's Press, 1998) exemplify this fusion of forward-looking and archaizing fantasies of the undead.

[29] Auguste Villiers de l'Isle-Adam, *Tomorrow's Eve*, trans. Robert Martin Adams (Champaign: U of Illinois P, 2000), 113.

[30] Andreas Huyssen, *After the Great Divide: Modernism, Mass Culture, Postmodernism* (Bloomington: Indiana UP, 1986), 65–81.

[31] For a discussion of this topic, see Michel Houellebecq, *H.P. Lovecraft: Against the World, Against Life*, trans. Dorna Khazeni (London: Orion, 2008).

[32] Howard Phillips Lovecraft, *At the Mountains of Madness and Other Novels*, ed. August Derleth (Sauk City, WI: Arkham House, 1964), 257.

[33] Lovecraft, 251–52.

[34] That said, the story does hint at ethnic and religious conflict between the French and English settlers of colonial America as a possible source of the intrusion from outer space, which was perhaps obtained by occult means (Lovecraft, 248–49).

[25] The other side of Lovecraft's conjectural fiction about life from extraterrestrial sources was his obsession with the roles played by race and heredity; miscegenation and degeneration are a constant theme in his works. His correspondence, edited by S. T. Joshi and David E. Schultz (*Lord of a Visible World: An Autobiography in Letters* [Athens: Ohio UP, 2000], offers considerable insight into the connections between threats from "above" and those from "below" or "within."

[36] Joan Copjec, "Vampires, Breastfeeding, and Anxiety," in *Gothic: Critical Concepts in Literary and Cultural Studies*, eds. Fred Botting and Dale Townshend (New York: Routledge, 2004), 12–29.

[37] Accordingly, a subgenre of science fiction features vampires from other planets and "galaxies far, far away." Cinematic examples include *giallo* pioneer Mario Bava's *Planet of the Vampires* (1965) and *Texas Chainsaw Massacre* director Tobe Hooper's *Lifeforce* (1985).

[38] In this regard, the cinematic Frankenstein (that is, properly speaking, Dr. Victor Frankenstein's creature) made popular in James Whale's 1931 film has many traits of the zombie, as well as a comparably undistinguished social status (see chapter 3).

[39] In Southey's Orientalist romance *Thalaba the Destroyer* (1797), there is a brief appearance of a "vampire corpse" (Book Eight) when the hero's dead beloved,

Oneiza, rises from the grave and must be destroyed. See James B. Twitchell, *The Living Dead: A Study of the Vampire in Romantic Literature* (Durham: Duke UP, 1985), 35–36.

[40] Markman Ellis, *The History of Gothic Fiction* (Edinburgh: Edinburgh UP, 2000), 212.

[41] Ellis, 213–20.

[42] Ellis, 233. The subject matter is drawn from *The Magic Island* (1929), by American occultist and adventurer William Seabrook (1884–1945); "following [its] publication," Ellis writes, "the zombie can properly be said to take on a life of its own in Western culture" (229).

[43] Ellis, 223. The film, which stars Bela Lugosi as the villain, capitalized on the actor's portrayal of Count Dracula the previous year.

[44] The sole exception (perhaps) is Canadian provocateur Bruce LaBruce's *Otto; or, Up with Dead People* (2008), which honors and parodies zombie film conventions by featuring an undead dandy wandering through the wasteland of Berlin nightlife.

[45] Ben Hervey, *Night of the Living Dead* (London: BFI Film Classics, 2008), passim.

[46] See the introduction.

[47] See in this regard Fredric Jameson, "Interview with Stuart Hall," *Jameson on Jameson: Conversations on Cultural Marxism*, ed. Ian Buchanan (Durham: Duke UP, 2007), 113–22.

[48] The latter half of Auerbach's excellent study, which has been cited on numerous occasions in the preceding pages, offers a key point of reference and contains nuanced, feminist readings of books and films from the 1970s on. A worthwhile, if occasionally overly general collection of essays can be found in Joan Gordon and Veronica Hollinger, *Blood Read: The Vampire as Metaphor in Contemporary Culture* (Philadelphia: U of Pennsylvania P, 1996). Petra Flocke, in *Vampirinnen: Ich schaue in den Spiegel und sehe nichts. Die kulturellen Repräsentationsformen der Vampirin* (Tübingen: Konkursbuch, 1999) offers original, if somewhat speculative, readings of the symbolism of female vampires; the study is noteworthy for its exploration of the negation of feminine identity and sexuality in the vampire myth. Austrian Nobel laureate Elfriede Jelinek's works abound in the undead; for a discussion, see, e.g., Sigrid Berka, "'Das bissigste Stück der Saison': The Textual and Sexual Politics of Vampirism in Elfriede Jelinek's *Krankheit oder Moderne Frauen*," *German Quarterly*, Vol. 68, No. 4 (Autumn, 1995), 372–88.

[49] See the 1992 documentary, *Stepping Razor: Red X*, directed by Nicholas Campbell.

[50] Lucky Dube, *Prisoner* (Shanachie, 1991).

[51] Julio Cortázar, *Vampiros multinacionales* (Mexico City: Excélsior, 1975), 40–41.

[52] Luise White, *Speaking with Vampires: Rumor and History in Colonial Africa* (Berkeley: U of California P, 2000), 12.

[53] White, 5.

[54] White, 5.

[55] Cf. Jacques Derrida, *Of Grammatology*, trans. Gayatri Chakravorty Spivak (Baltimore: The Johns Hopkins UP, 1998), passim.

[56] Ferdinand de Saussure, *Course in General Linguistics*, trans. Roy Harris (Chicago: Open Court, 1998), 67–69.

[57] Jeffry L. Pasley, "Old Familiar Vampires: The Politics of the Buffyverse," in James B. South, ed., *Buffy the Vampire Slayer and Philosophy: Fear and Trembling in Sunnydale* (Chicago: Open Court, 2003), 258.

[58] Pasley, 258.

[59] See, for example, Anne Millard Daughtey, "Just a Girl: Buffy as Icon," in *Reading the Slayer: An Unofficial Critical Companion to* Buffy *and* Angel, ed. Roy Kaverney (New York: Tauris Parke, 2002), 148–65, and, in the same volume, Zoe Jane Playden, "What You Are, What's to Come: Feminisms, Citizenship, and the Divine," 120–47.

[60] Pasley, 265.

Works Cited

Primary Sources

Baudelaire, Charles. *Oeuvres completes.* Paris: Laffont, 1980.

Brontë, Charlotte. *Jane Eyre. The Brontës: Three Great Novels.* London: JG Press, 1995.

Burton, Richard F. *Vikram and the Vampire, or, Tales of Hindu Devilry.* Ed. Isabel Burton. London: Tylston and Edwards, 1893.

Byron. *Poetical Works.* Ed. Frederick Page. Oxford: Oxford UP, 1970.

Calder, Richard. *Dead Girls, Dead Boys, Dead Things.* New York: St. Martin's Press, 1998.

Calmet, Augustin. *Dissertation sur les vampires.* Grenoble: Jérôme Millon, 1998.

Clery, E. J., and Robert Miles, eds. *Gothic Documents: A Sourcebook, 1700–1820.* Manchester: Manchester UP, 2000.

Collins, Wilkie. *Armadale.* Oxford: Oxford UP, 1990.

Cortázar, Julio. *Vampiros multinacionales.* Mexico City: Excélsior, 1975.

Deane, Hamilton and John L. Balderston. *Dracula: The Ultimate, Illustrated Edition of the World-Famous Vampire Play.* Ed. David J. Skal. New York: St. Martin's Press, 1993.

Ducasse, Isidore/Comte de Lautréamont. *Maldoror and the Complete Works of the Comte de Lautréamont.* Trans. Alexis Lykiard. Cambridge: Exact Change, 1998.

———. *Oeuvres complètes.* Ed. Hubert Juin. Paris: Gallimard, 1973.

Dumas, Alexandre. *Les Mille et Un Fantômes,* précédé de *La Femme au collier de velours.* Ed. Anne-Marie Callet-Bianco. Paris: Gallimard, 2006.

Du Maurier, George. *Trilby.* New York: Penguin, 1995.

Féval, Paul. *Le chevalier Ténèbre, suivi de La ville-vampire.* Verviers: Marabout, 1972.

———. *La Vampire.* Castelnau-le-Lez: Éditions Climats, 2004.

———. *Vampire City.* Trans. Brian Stableford. Encino: Black Coat Press, 2003.

Gautier, Théophile. *Fortunio et autres nouvelles.* Paris: Garnier, 1930.

———. *Les Jeunes France: Romans Goguenards.* Paris: Édition des autres, 1979.

———. "La morte amoureuse." *Récits fantastiques.* Paris: Flammarion, 1981.

Goethe, Johann Wolfgang. *Faust, erster und zweiter Teil.* Munich: Deutscher Taschenbuch Verlag, 1997.

Görres, Joseph von. *Die christliche Mystik*, 5 vols. Graz: Akademische Druck-u. Verlagsanstalt, 1960.

Hamberger, Klaus. *Mortuus non mordet: Kommentierte Dokumentation zum Vampirismus 1689–1791*. Vienna: Turia & Kant, 1992.

Harbour, Dorothy. *Energy Vampires: A Practical Guide for Psychic Self-Protection*. Rochester: Destiny Books, 2002.

Heine, Heinrich. *Die Romantische Schule und andere Schriften über Deutschland*. Cologne: Könemann, 1995.

Herzen, Alexander. *Selected Philosophical Works*. Moscow: Foreign Languages Publishing House, 1956.

Hoffmann, E. T. A. *Sämtliche Werke in Sechs Bänden*. Frankfurt am Main: Deutscher Klassiker Verlag, 1985.

Hort, Barbara E. *Unholy Hungers: Encountering the Psychic Vampire in Ourselves and Others*. Boston: Shambhala, 1996.

Jacques, Norbert. *Dr. Mabuse, der Spieler*. Eds. Michael Farin and Günter Scholdt. Hamburg: Rogner & Bernhard, 1994.

Joyce, James. *Ulysses*. New York: Vintage, 1986.

Kessler, Joan, ed. *Demons of the Night: Tales of the Fantastic, Madness, and the Supernatural from Nineteenth-Century France*. Chicago: U of Chicago P, 1995.

Kipling, Rudyard. *The Vampire and Other Verses*. New York: Little Leather Library, 1924.

Klingemann, Ernst August Friedrich (Bonaventura). *Die Nachtwachen des Bonaventura*. Ed. and trans. Gerald Gillespie. Austin: U of Texas P, 1971.

Lawrence, David Herbert. *Studies in Classic American Literature*. New York: Penguin, 1971.

Le Fanu, Sheridan. *The Best Horror Stories*. London: Sphere Books, 1970.

Lovecraft, Howard Phillips. *At the Mountains of Madness and Other Novels*. Ed. August Derleth. Sauk City, WI: Arkham House, 1964.

———. *Lord of a Visible World: An Autobiography in Letters*. Ed. S. T. Joshi and David E. Schultz. Athens: Ohio UP, 2000.

Meyer, Stephenie. *The Twilight Saga: Slipcased*. New York: Little, Brown Young Readers, 2008.

Norton, Rictor, ed. *Gothic Readings: The First Wave, 1764–1840*. London: Continuum, 2005.

Novalis, *Gedichte/Die Lehrlinge zu Sais*. Stuttgart: Reclam, 1984.

Polidori, John. *Polidori's Vampire*. Doylestown: Wildside Press, 2002.

Potocki, Jan. *Manuscript Found in Saragossa*. Trans. Ian Maclean. London: Penguin, 1995.

Przybyszewski, Stanislaw. *Kritische und essayistische Schriften*. Ed. Michael M. Schardt. Paderborn: Igel, 1992.

Ranfft, Michael. *Traktat von dem Kauen und Schmatzen der Toten in Gräbern*. Ed. Nicolaus Equiamicus. Diedorf: Ubooks, 2006.

Raphael, Marty. *Spiritual Vampires: The Use and Misuse of Spiritual Power*. Santa Fe: Message, 1996.

Rice, Anne. *Called Out of Darkness: A Spiritual Confession.* New York: Knopf, 2008.

———. *Complete Vampire Chronicles.* New York: Ballantine, 1993.

Rousseau, Jean-Jacques. *Julie or the New Heloise.* Trans. Philip Stewart and Jean Vaché. Hanover: University Press of New England, 1997.

———. *Julie ou la Nouvelle Héloïse.* Ed. R. Pomeau. Paris: Garnier, 1960.

Saberhagen, Fred. *The Dracula Tape.* Riverdale: Baen, 1999.

Sacher-Masoch, Leopold von. *Mondnacht: Erzählungen aus Galizien.* Ed. Karl Emmerich. Berlin: Rütten & Loening, 1991.

Sade, Donatien Alphonse François de. *Les 120 journées de Sodome.* Paris: 10/18, 1993.

———. *Histoire de Juliette, ou les Prospérités du vice, Oeuvres complètes* VIII. Eds. Annie Le Brun and Jean-Jacques Pauvert. Paris: Pauvert, 1987.

———. *Juliette.* Trans. Austryn Wainhouse. New York: Grove Press, 1968.

Schreber, Daniel Paul. *Denkwürdigkeiten eines Nervenkranken.* Wiesbaden: Focus, 1973.

———. *Memoirs of My Nervous Illness.* Trans. Ida Macalpine and Richard A. Hunter. Cambridge: Harvard UP, 1988.

Seabrook, William. *The Magic Island.* New York: Paragon House, 1969.

Shelley, Mary. *Frankenstein or the Modern Prometheus.* London: Penguin, 1985.

Southey, Robert. *Thalaba the Destroyer.* London: Routledge, Warne, and Routledge, 1860.

Stoker, Bram. *Dracula.* Ed. Glennis Byron. Ontario: Broadview, 1998.

———. *Famous Impostors.* London: Sidgwick & London, 1910.

Strieber, Whitley. *The Hunger.* New York: Harper Collins, 1981.

Varma, Devendra P., ed. *Varney the Vampire, or, The Feast of Blood.* North Stratford, NH: Ayer, 1998. 3 vols.

Verne, Jules. *Le château des Carpathes.* Paris: Livre de Poche, 1994.

Villiers de l'Isle-Adam, Auguste. *L'Ève future.* Paris: Gallimard, 1999.

———. *Tomorrow's Eve.* Trans. Robert Martin Adams. Champaign: U of Illinois P, 2000.

Discussions of Vampires and the Supernatural

Abrams, M. H. *Natural Supernaturalism: Tradition and Revolution in Romantic Literature.* New York: W. W. Norton, 1973.

Anderson, George K. *The Legend of the Wandering Jew.* Hanover: Brown UP, 1991.

Auerbach, Nina. *Our Vampires, Ourselves.* Chicago: U of Chicago P, 1995.

———. *Woman and the Demon: The Life of a Victorian Myth.* Cambridge: Harvard UP, 1984.

Baldick, Chris. *In Frankenstein's Shadow: Myth, Monstrosity, and Nineteenth-Century Writing.* Oxford: Oxford UP, 1987.

Barber, Paul. *Vampires, Burial, and Death.* New Haven: Yale UP, 1988.

Bentley, Christopher F. "The Monster in the Bedroom." *Literature and Psychology* 22 (1972). 27–34.

Berenstein, Rhona J. *Attack of the Leading Ladies: Gender, Sexuality, and Spectatorship in Classic Horror Cinema.* New York: Columbia UP, 1996.

Berka, Sigrid. "Das bissigste Stück der Saison": The Textual and Sexual Politics of Vampirism in Elfriede Jelineks's *Krankheit oder Moderne Frauen.*" *The German Quarterly*, Vol. 68, No. 4 (Autumn, 1995). 372–88.

Borrmann, Norbert. *Vampirismus oder die Sehnsucht nach Unsterblichkeit.* Munich: Diederichs, 1999.

Botting, Fred and Dale Townshend, eds. *Gothic: Critical Concepts in Literary and Cultural Studies.* New York: Routledge, 2004.

Bouvier Michel and Jean-Louis Leutrat. *Nosferatu.* Paris: Cahiers du Cinéma/ Gallimard, 1981.

Budd, Mike, ed. *The Cabinet of Dr. Caligari: Texts, Contexts, Histories.* New Brunswick: Rutgers UP, 1990.

Buse, Peter and Andrew Stott. *Ghosts: Deconstruction, Psychoanalysis, History.* New York: Macmillan, 1999.

Byron, Glennis and David Punter, eds. *Spectral Readings: Towards a Gothic Geography.* New York: Palgrave, 1999.

Cain, Jr., Jimmie E. *Bram Stoker and Russophobia.* London: McFarland, 2006.

Case, Alison. "Tasting the Original Apple: Gender and the Struggle for Narrative Authority in *Dracula.*" *Narrative* I.3 (1993). 223–43.

Claes, Oliver. *Fremde, Vampire. Sexualität, Tod und Kunst bei Elfriede Jelinek und Adolf Muschg.* Bielefeld: Aisthesis: 1994.

Cohen, Jeffrey Jerome, ed. *Monster Theory: Reading Culture.* Minneapolis: U of Minnesota P, 1997.

Craft, Christopher. "'Kiss Me with Those Red Lips': Gender and Inversion in Bram Stoker's *Dracula.*" *Representations* 8 (1984). 107–33.

Dadoun, Roger. "Fetishism in the Horror Film." *Fantasy and the Cinema.* Ed. James Donald. London: British Film Institute, 1989.

Davenport-Hines, Richard. *Gothic: Four Hundred Years of Excess, Horror, Evil, and Ruin.* New York: North Point Press, 1998.

Day, Gary. "The State of *Dracula:* Bureaucracy and the Vampire." *Rereading Victorian Fiction.* Eds. Alice Jenkins and Juliet John. New York: St. Martin's Press, 2000. 81–95.

Dijkstra, Bram. *Idols of Perversity: Fantasies of Feminine Evil in Fin-de-Siècle Culture.* Oxford: Oxford UP, 1988.

Dimic, Milan V. "Vampiromania in the Eighteenth Century: The Other Side of Enlightenment." *Man and Nature/L'Homme et la Nature: Proceedings of the Canadian Society for Eighteenth-Century Studies* 3. Ed. R. J. Merrett. Edmonton: The Society, 1984. 1–22.

Dundes, Alan, ed. *The Vampire: A Casebook.* Madison: U of Wisconsin P, 1998.

Eisner, Lotte. *The Haunted Screen: Expressionism in the German Cinema.* Trans. Roger Greaves. Berkeley: U of California P, 1973.

Ellis, Markman. *The History of Gothic Fiction*. Edinburgh: Edinburgh UP, 2000.

Elsaesser, Thomas. *Weimar Cinema and After: German's Historical Imaginary*. New York: Routledge, 2000.

Enright, D. J. *The Oxford Book of the Supernatural*. Oxford: Oxford UP, 1994.

Jones, Ernest. *On the Nightmare*. New York: Grove, 1959.

Faivre, Antoine, ed. *Les vampires*. Paris: Albin Michel, 1993.

Fleig, Horst. *Literarischer Vampirismus: Klingemanns 'Nachtwachen von Bonaventura.'* Tübingen: Niemeyer, 1985.

Flocke, Petra. *Vampirinnen: Ich schaue in den Spiegel und sehe nichts. Die kulturellen Repräsentationsformen der Vampirin*. Tübingen: Konkursbuch, 1999.

Frayling, Christopher. *Vampyres*. London: Faber and Faber, 1991.

Freud, Sigmund. *Three Case Histories*. Ed. Philip Rieff. New York: Collier, 1963.

———. "The 'Uncanny.'" *Sigmund Freud: Collected Papers* (Vol. 4). Trans. Joan Riviere. New York: Basic Books, 1959. 368–407.

Griffin, Gail. "'Your Girls That You All Love Are Mine': *Dracula* and the Victorian Male Sexual Imagination." *International Journal of Women's Studies* 3 (1980). 454–65.

Gelder, Ken. *Reading the Vampire*. London: Routledge, 1994.

Glover, David. *Vampires, Mummies, and Liberals: Bram Stoker and the Politics of Popular Fiction*. Durham: Duke UP, 1996.

Gordon, Joan and Veronica Hollinger. *Blood Read: The Vampire as Metaphor in Contemporary Culture*. Philadelphia: U of Pennsylvania P, 1997.

Gunning, Tom. *The Films of Fritz Lang: Allegories of Vision and Modernity*. London: British Film Institute, 2000.

Halberstam, Judith. *Skin Shows: Gothic Horror and the Technology of Monsters*. Durham: Duke UP, 1995.

Harmening, Dieter. *Der Anfang von Dracula: Zur Geschichte von Geschichten*. Würzburg: Königshausen + Neumann, 1983.

Hervey, Ben. *Night of the Living Dead*. London: BFI Film Classics, 2008.

Hock, Stefan. *Die Vampyrsagen und ihre Verwertung in der deutschen Literatur*. Berlin: Alexander Duncker, 1900.

Houellebecq, Michel. *H. P. Lovecraft: Against the World, Against Life*. Trans. Dorna Khazeni. London: Orion, 2008.

Howes, Marjorie "The Mediation of the Feminine: Bisexuality, Homoerotic Desire, and Self-Expression in Bram Stoker's *Dracula*." *Texas Studies in Language and Literature* 30.1 (1988). 104–19.

Jeandillou, Jean-François. *Supercheries littéraires: La vie et l'oeuvre des auteurs supposés*. Geneva: Droz, 2001.

Jowett, Lorna. *Sex and the Slayer: A Gender Studies Primer for the Buffy Fan*. Middletown, CT: Wesleyan, 2005.

Kalat, David. *The Strange Case of Dr. Mabuse: A Study of the Twelve Films and Five Novels*. Jefferson: McFarland and Company, 2001.

Kaverney, Roy, ed. *Reading the Slayer: An Unofficial Critical Companion to Buffy and* Angel. New York: Tauris Parke, 2002.

Kennedy, J. Gerald, and Liliane Weissberg, eds. *Romancing the Shadow: Poe and Race.* Oxford: Oxford UP, 2001.

Kittler, Friedrich. "Dracula's Legacy." *Stanford Humanities Review* I (1989). 143–73.

Klemens, Elke. *Dracula und 'seine Töchter': Die Vampirin als Symbol im Wandel der Zeit.* Tübingen: Günter Narr, 2004.

Kracauer, Siegfried. *From Caligari to Hitler: A Psychological History of the German Film.* Ed. Leonardo Quaresima. Princeton: Princeton UP, 2004.

Kreuter, Peter Mario. "The Name of the Vampire: Some Reflections on Current Linguistic Theories on the Etymology of the Word *Vampire.*" *Vampires: Myths and Metaphors of Enduring Evil.* Ed. Peter Day. Amsterdam: Rodopi, 2006.

———. *Der Vampirglaube in Südosteuropa: Studien zur Genese, Bedeutung und Funktion.* Berlin: Weidler, 2001.

Latham, Rob. *Consuming Youth: Vampires, Cyborgs, and the Culture of Consumption.* Chicago: U of Chicago P, 2002.

Lederer, Susan E. *Frankenstein: Penetrating the Secrets of Nature.* New Brunswick: Rutgers UP, 2002.

Monleón, José B. *A Specter is Haunting Europe: A Sociohistorical Approach to the Fantastic.* Princeton: Princeton UP, 1990.

Moretti, Franco. *Signs Taken for Wonders: Essays in the Sociology of Literary Forms.* Trans. Susan Fischer, David Forgacs, and David Miller. London: Verso, 1983.

Mücke, Dorothea von. *The Seduction of the Occult and the Rise of the Fantastic Tale.* Stanford: Stanford UP, 2003.

Oinas, Felix J. *Essays on Russian Folklore and Mythology.* Columbus: Slavica, 1985.

Perkowski, Jan L. *Vampires of the Slavs.* Cambridge: Slavica, 1976.

Pick, Daniel. *Svengali's Web: The Alien Enchanter in Modern Culture.* New Haven: Yale UP, 2000.

Posnov, Mikhail Emmanuelovich. *The History of the Christian Church until the Great Schism of 1054.* Trans. Thomas Herman. Bloomington: AuthorHouse, 2004.

Praz, Mario. *The Romantic Agony.* Trans. Angus Davidson. Oxford: Oxford UP, 1933.

Punter, David, ed. *A Companion to the Gothic.* Oxford: Wiley-Blackwell, 2001.

Purkiss, Diane. *The Witch in History: Early Modern and Twentieth-Century Representations.* New York: Routledge, 1996.

Rabaté, Jean-Michel. *The Ghosts of Modernity.* Gainesville: The University Press of Florida, 1996.

Rickels, Laurence A. *Aberrations of Mourning: Writing on German Crypts.* Detroit: Wayne State UP, 1988.

———. *The Vampire Lectures.* Minneapolis: U of Minnesota P, 1999.

Robinson, David. *Das Cabinet des Dr. Caligari.* London: British Film Institute, 1997.

Ronell, Avital. *The Telephone Book: Technology, Schizophrenia, Electric Speech.* Lincoln: U of Nebraska P, 1991.

Roth, Phyllis A. "Suddenly Sexual Women in Bram Stoker's *Dracula.*" *Literature and Psychology* 27.3 (1977). 113–21.

Rudkin, David. *Vampyr.* London: British Film Institute, 2005.

Safranski, Rüdiger. *E. T. A. Hoffmann: Das Leben eines skeptischen Phantasten.* Frankfurt am Main: Fischer, 2005.

Sangsue, Daniel. "Nodier et le commerce des vampires." *Nodier.* Ed. Georges Zaragoza. Dijon: Éditions universitaires de Dijon, 1998.

Schroeder, Aribert. *Vampirismus: Seine Entwicklung vom Thema zum Motiv.* Frankfurt am Main: Akademische Verlagsgesellschaft, 1973.

Schürmann, Thomas. *Nachzehrerglauben in Mitteleuropa.* Marburg: N. G. Elwert, 1990.

Serres, Michel. *The Parasite.* Trans. Lawrence R. Schehr. Minneapolis: U of Minnesota P, 2007.

Silver, Anna Krugovoy. *Victorian Literature and the Anorexic Body.* Cambridge: Cambridge UP, 2002.

Skal, David J. *Hollywood Gothic: The Tangled Web of Dracula from Novel to Stage to Screen.* New York: W. W. Norton, 1990.

———. *The Monster Show: A Cultural History of Horror.* New York: Faber & Faber, 2001.

South, James B, ed. *Buffy the Vampire Slayer and Philosophy: Fear and Trembling in Sunnydale.* Chicago: Open Court, 2003.

Stevenson, John Allen. "A Vampire in the Mirror: The Sexuality of *Dracula.*" *PMLA* 103.2 (1988). 139–49.

Stoichita, Victor I. *Brève histoire de l'ombre.* Geneva: Droz, 2000.

Stuart, Roxana. *Stage Blood: Vampires of the Nineteenth-Century Stage.* Bowling Green: Bowling Green University Popular Press, 1994.

Sturm, Dieter and Klaus Völker. *Von denen Vampiren.* Frankfurt am Main: Suhrkamp, 1994.

Summers, Montague. *The Vampire.* London: Senate, 1995.

Todorov, Tzvetan. *The Fantastic: A Structural Approach to a Literary Genre.* Trans. Richard Howard. Ithaca: Cornell UP, 1975.

Twitchell, James B. *The Living Dead: A Study of the Vampire in Romantic Literature.* Durham: Duke UP, 1985.

Valente, Joseph. *Dracula's Crypt: Bram Stoker, Irishness, and the Question of Blood.* Urbana: U of Illinois P, 2001.

Weiss, Andrea. *Vampires and Violets: Lesbians in Film.* Middlesex: Penguin, 1993.

White, Luise. *Speaking with Vampires: Rumor and History in Colonial Africa.* Berkeley: U of California P, 2000.

Wicke, Jennifer. "Vampiric Typewriting." *ELH* 59 (Summer 1992). 467–93.

Wilcox, Rhonda V. *Why Buffy Matters: The Art of Buffy the Vampire Slayer.* London: I. B. Tauris, 2005.

Williams, Anne. *Art of Darkness: A Poetics of Gothic.* Chicago: U of Chicago P, 1995.

Winthrop-Young, Geoffrey. "Undead Networks: Information Processing and Media Boundary Conflicts in *Dracula.*" *Literature and Science.* Eds. Donald Bruce and Anthony Purdy. Atlanta: Rodopi, 1994. 107–29.

Wolfreys, Julian. *Victorian Hauntings: Spectrality, Gothic, the Uncanny, and Literature.* New York: Palgrave, 2002.

Other

Abramson, Julia. *Learning from Lying: Paradoxes of Literary Mystification.* Newark: U of Delaware P, 2005.

Adorno, Theodor. *The Culture Industry: Selected Essays on Mass Culture.* Ed. J. M. Bernstein. New York: Routledge, 2004.

Anz, Thomas. "Vitalismus und Kriegsdichtung." *Kultur und Krieg: Die Rolle der Intellektuellen, Künstler und Schriftsteller im Ersten Weltkrieg.* Ed. Wolfgang J. Mommsen. Munich: Oldenbourg, 1996.

Bakhtin, Mikhail. *The Dialogic Imagination: Four Essays.* Ed. Michael Holquist. Austin: U of Texas P, 1982.

Bancroft, Angus. *Roma and Gypsy-Travellers in Europe: Race, Space and Exclusion.* Aldershot: Ashgate, 2005.

Barthes, Roland. *Michelet.* Trans. Richard Howard. New York: Farrar, Straus and Giroux, 1987.

Belford, Barbara. *Bram Stoker and the Man Who was Dracula.* New York: Da Capo, 2002.

Bénichou, Paul. *The Consecration of the Writer, 1750–1830.* Trans. Mark K. Jensen. Lincoln: U of Nebraska P, 1999.

Benjamin, Walter. *The Arcades Project.* Trans. Howard Eiland and Kevin McLaughlin. Cambridge: Harvard UP, 1999.

———. *Baudelaire: A Lyric Poet in the Era of High Capitalism.* Trans. Harry Zohn. London: Verso, 1983.

Berman, Marshall. *"All That is Solid Melts into Air": The Experience of Modernity.* New York: Penguin, 1988.

Biale, David. *Blood and Belief: The Circulation of a Symbol between Jews and Christians.* Berkeley: U of California P, 2007.

Brooks, Peter. *The Melodramatic Imagination: Balzac, Henry James, Melodrama, and the Mode of Excess.* New Haven: Yale UP, 1976.

Brüggemann, Heinz. *"Aber schickt keinen Poeten nach London!" Großstadt und literarische Wahrnehmung im 18. Und 19. Jahrhundert.* Hamburg: Rowohlt, 1985.

Buzard, James. "The Grand Tour and After (1660–1840)." *The Cambridge Companion to Travel Writing.* Eds. Peter Hulme and Tim Youngs. Cambridge: Cambridge UP, 37–52.

Bynum, Caroline Walker. *The Resurrection of the Body in Western Christianity, 200–1336.* New York: Columbia UP, 1995.

———. *Wonderful Blood: Theology and Practice in Late Medieval Northern Germany and Beyond.* Philadelphia: U of Pennsylvania P, 2007.

Bynum, W. F. *Science and the Practice of Medicine in the Nineteenth Century.* Cambridge: Cambridge UP, 1994.

Calasso, Roberto. *L'impuro folle.* Milan: Adelphi, 1974.

Canetti, Elias. *Crowds and Power.* Trans. Carol Stewart. New York: Farrar, Straus, and Giroux, 1984.

———. *Kafka's Other Trial: The Letters to Felice.* Trans. Christopher Middleton. New York: Schocken, 1974.

Cannadine, David. *Ornamentalism: How the British Saw Their Empire.* Oxford: Oxford UP, 2002.

Caruth, Cathy. *Unclaimed Experience: Trauma, Narrative, and History.* Baltimore: The Johns Hopkins UP, 1996.

Carver, Terrell. *The Postmodern Marx.* University Park: Pennsylvania State UP, 1998.

Certeau, Michel de. *The Possession at Loudun.* Trans. Michael B. Smith. Chicago: U of Chicago P, 2000.

Chion, Michel. *The Voice in Cinema.* Trans. Claudia Gorbman. New York: Columbia UP, 1999.

Cirkovic, Sima M. *The Serbs.* Oxford: Wiley-Blackwell, 2004.

Clarke, Bruce. *Posthuman Metamorphosis: Narrative and Systems.* New York: Fordham UP, 2008.

Cunningham, Andrew, and Ole Peter Grell. *The Four Horsemen of the Apocalypse: Religion, War, Famine, and Death in Reformation Europe.* Cambridge: Cambridge UP, 2001.

Curley, Thomas M. *Samuel Johnson, the Ossian Fraud, and the Celtic Revival in Great Britain and Ireland.* Cambridge: Cambridge UP, 2009.

Darnton, Robert. *Mesmerism and the End of Enlightenment in France.* Cambridge: Harvard UP, 1968.

Deleuze, Gilles. *Masochism: Coldness and Cruelty.* Trans. Jean McNeil. Cambridge: Zone Books, 1991.

Deleuze, Gilles, and Félix Guattari. *Anti-Oedipus: Capitalism and Schizophrenia.* Trans. Robert Hurley, Helen R. Lane, and Mark Seem. New York: Viking, 1977.

———. *Kafka: Toward a Minor Literature.* Trans. Dana Polan. Minneapolis: U of Minnesota P, 1986.

———. *A Thousand Plateaus.* Trans. Brian Massumi. London: Continuum, 2004.

de Man, Paul. *Allegories of Reading: Figural Language in Rousseau, Nietzsche, Rilke, and Proust.* New Haven: Yale UP, 1982.

Derrida, Jacques. *Margins of Philosophy.* Trans. Alan Bass. Chicago: U of Chicago P, 1985.

———. *Of Grammatology.* Trans. Gayatri Chakravorty Spivak. Baltimore: The Johns Hopkins UP, 1998. [Revised edition.]

———. *Specters of Marx: The State of the Debt, the Work of Mourning, and the New International.* Trans. Peggy Kamuf. New York: Routledge, 1994.

Descombes, Vincent. *Modern French Philosophy.* Trans. L. Scott-Fox and J. M. Harding. Cambridge: Cambridge UP 1981.

Duncan, Ian. *Scott's Shadow: The Novel in Romantic Edinburgh.* Princeton: Princeton UP, 2007.

Dundes, Alan, ed. *The Blood Libel Legend: A Casebook in Anti-Semitic Folklore.* Madison: U of Wisconsin P, 1991.

Eksteins, Modris. *Rites of Spring: The Great War and the Birth of the Modern Age.* Boston: Mariner, 2000.

Elias, Norbert. *The Civilizing Process: Sociogenetic and Psychogenetic Investigations,* trans. Edmund Jephcott. Oxford: Blackwell, 2000.

Evans, Robert John Weston. *The Making of the Habsburg Monarchy, 1550–1700: An Interpretation.* Oxford: Oxford UP, 1984.

Fink, Bruce. *A Clinical Introduction to Lacanian Psychoanalysis: Theory and Technique.* Cambridge: Harvard UP, 1999.

Finke, Michael C., and Carl Niekerk, eds. *One Hundred Years of Masochism: Literary Texts, Social and Cultural Contexts.* Amsterdam: Rodopi, 2000.

Foucault, Michel. *Discipline and Punish: The Birth of the Prison.* Trans. Alan Sheridan. New York: Vintage, 1995.

———. *The History of Sexuality.* Trans. Robert Hurley. New York: Pantheon, 1978.

———. *Madness and Civilization.* Trans. Richard Howard. New York: Vintage, 1965.

———. *The Order of Things.* Trans. Alan Sheridan. New York: Vintage, 1970.

Florescu, Radu R. and Raymond T. McNally. *Dracula: Prince of Many Faces.* Boston: Little, Brown and Company, 1989.

Fussell, Paul. *The Great War and Modern Memory.* New York: Oxford UP, 1975.

Gay, Peter. *Weimar Culture: The Outsider as Insider.* New York: W. W. Norton, 2001.

Gilbert, Sandra M. and Susan Gubar. *The Madwoman in the Attic: The Woman Writer and the Nineteenth-Century Literary Imagination.* New Haven: Yale UP, 2000.

Gilman, Sander L. *Freud, Race, and Gender.* Princeton: Princeton UP, 1993.

———. *The Jew's Body.* New York: Routledge, 1991.

Gilman, Sander L., and J. E. Chamberlin, eds. *Degeneration: The Dark Side of Progress.* New York: Columbia UP, 1985.

Gilman, Sander L., Helen King, Roy Porter, G. S. Rousseau, and Elaine Showalter. *Hysteria Beyond Freud.* Berkeley: U of California P, 1993.

Ginzburg, Carlo. *Clues, Myths, and the Historical Method.* Trans. John and Anne C. Tedeschi. Baltimore: Johns Hopkins UP, 1989.

———. *Ecstasies: Deciphering the Witches' Sabbath.* Trans. Raymond Rosenthal. Chicago: U of Chicago P, 2004.

———. *The Night Battles: Witchcraft and Agrarian Cults in the Sixteenth and Seventeenth Centuries.* Trans. John and Anne C. Tedeschi. Baltimore: The Johns Hopkins UP, 1992.

Girard, René. *The Scapegoat*. Trans. Yvonne Freccero. Baltimore: Johns Hopkins UP, 1986.

———. *Things Hidden Since the Foundation of the World*. Trans. Stephen Benn and Michael Metteer. Stanford: Stanford UP, 1987.

———. *Violence and the Sacred*. Trans. Patrick Gregory. Baltimore: Johns Hopkins UP, 1979.

Golden, Eve. *Vamp: The Rise and Fall of Theda Bara*. New York: Vestal Press, 1997.

Goodlad, Lauren M. E. and Michael Bibby. *Goth: Undead Subculture*. Durham: Duke UP, 2007.

Greenblatt, Stephen. *Renaissance Self-Fashioning: From More to Shakespeare*. Chicago: U of Chicago P, 1984.

Haraway, Donna J. *How Like a Leaf: An Interview with Thyrza Nichols Goodeve*. New York: Routledge, 2000.

———. *Modest Witness@Second Millennium. FemaleMan Meets OncoMouse: Feminism and Technoscience*. New York: Routledge, 1997.

Hardt, Michael, and Antonio Negri. *Multitude: War and Democracy in the Age of Empire*. New York: Penguin, 2004.

Hawkins, Mike. *Social Darwinism in European and American Thought, 1860–1945: Nature as Model and Nature as Threat*. Cambridge: Cambridge UP, 1997.

Hayles, N. Katherine. *How We Became Posthuman: Virtual Bodies in Cybernetics, Literature, and Informatics*. Chicago: U of Chicago P, 1999.

Hobsbawm, Eric. *The Age of Revolution: 1789–1848*. New York: Vintage, 1996.

Holland, Eugene. *Baudelaire and Schizoanalysis: The Sociopoetics of Modernism*. Cambridge: Cambridge UP, 1993.

Hsia, R. Po-chia. *The Myth of Ritual Murder: Jews and Magic in Reformation Germany*. New Haven: Yale UP, 1988.

Hunter, Richard. *The Shadow of Callimachus: Studies in the Reception of Hellenistic Poetry at Rome*. Cambridge: Cambridge UP, 2006.

Huyssen, Andreas. *After the Great Divide: Modernism, Mass Culture, Postmodernism*. Bloomington: Indiana UP, 1986.

Ingrao, Charles W. *The Habsburg Monarchy, 1618–1815*. Cambridge: Cambridge UP, 2002.

Jacobs, Carol. *In the Language of Walter Benjamin*. Baltimore: Johns Hopkins UP, 2000.

Jameson, Fredric. *Jameson on Jameson: Conversations on Cultural Marxism*. Ed. Ian Buchanan. Durham: Duke UP, 2007.

———. *The Political Unconscious: Narrative as a Socially Symbolic Act*. Ithaca: Cornell UP, 1982.

Judah, Tim. *The Serbs: History, Myth, and the Destruction of Yugoslavia*. New Haven: Yale UP, 1997.

Kaes, Anton. *M*. London: British Film Institute, 2000.

Kaplan, Robert D. *Balkan Ghosts: A Journey Through History*. New York: Picador, 2005.

Kelly, Gary. *The English Jacobin Novel 1780–1805*. Oxford: Oxford UP, 1976.

Kinsey, Wayne. *Hammer Films: The Elstree Studio Years*. Sheffield: Tomahawk Press, 2007.

Kitchen, Martin. *Kaspar Hauser: Europe's Child*. New York: Palgrave, 2001.

Kittler, Friedrich. *Discourse Networks, 1800/1900*. Trans. Michael Metteer with Chris Cullens. Stanford: Stanford UP, 1992.

———. *Gramophone, Film, Typewriter*. Trans. Geoffrey Winthrop-Young and Michael Wutz. Stanford: Stanford UP, 1999.

Klaniczay, Gábor. *The Uses of Supernatural Power: The Transformation of Popular Religion in Medieval and Early-Modern Europe*. Trans. Susan Singerman. Oxford: Polity Press, 1990.

Knight, Alanna. *Burke and Hare: Crime Archive*. London: National Archives, 2007.

Kojève, Alexandre. *Introduction to the Reading of Hegel: Lectures on the Phenomenology of Spirit*. Trans. James H. Nichols. Ithaca: Cornell UP, 1980.

Koyré, Alexandre. *Mystiques, spirituels, alchimistes du XVIe siècle allemand*. Paris: Armand Colin, 1955.

Krauss, Friedrich S. *Slavische Volkforschungen: Abhandlungen über Glauben, Gewohnheitrechte, Sitten, Bräuche und die Guslarenlieder der Südslaven*. Leipzig: Wilhelm Heims, 1908.

Kugel, Wilfried. *Der Unverantwortliche: Das Leben des Hanns Heinz Ewers*. Düsseldorf: Grupello, 1993.

Kurtz, Rudolf. *Expressionismus und Film*. Berlin: Verlag der Lichtbildbühne, 1926.

Lacan, Jacques. *Écrits. A Selection*. Trans. Alan Sheridan. New York: W. W. Norton, 1977.

———. *The Seminar, Book III: The Psychoses*. Trans. Russell Grigg. New York: W. W. Norton, 1993.

Lennig, Arthur. *The Immortal Count: The Life and Films of Bela Lugosi*. Lexington: University Press of Kentucky, 2003.

Lenk, Elisabeth, and Katharina Kaever. *Peter Kürten, genannt der Vampir von Düsseldorf*. Frankfurt am Main: Eichborn, 1997.

Lepenies, Wolf. *The Seduction of Culture in German History*. Princeton: Princeton UP, 2006.

Leuschner, Joachim. *Deutschland im späten Mittelalter*. Göttingen: Vandenhoeck & Ruprecht, 2000.

Lothane, Zvi. *In Defense of Schreber: Soul Murder and Psychiatry*. Hillsdale: The Analytic Press, 1992.

Lovell, Mary S. *A Rage to Live: A Biography of Richard and Isabel Burton*. New York: W. W. Norton, 1998.

Lukács, Georg. *The Theory of the Novel*. Cambridge: MIT Press, 1971.

MacCarthy, Fiona. *Byron: Life and Legend*. New York: Farrar, Straus and Giroux, 2004.

Macdonald, David Lorne. *Poor Polidori*. Toronto: U of Toronto P, 1991.

Marcus, Jacob R., ed. *The Jew in the Medieval World: A Source Book, 315–1791.* New York: Atheneum, 1969.

Marshall, David. *The Surprising Effects of Sympathy: Marivaux, Diderot, Rousseau, and Mary Shelley.* Chicago: U of Chicago P, 1988.

Mccalman, Iain. *The Last Alchemist: Count Cagliostro, Master of Magic in the Age of Reason.* New York: Harper, 2004.

McMahon, Darrin M., *Enemies of the Enlightenment: The French Counter-Enlightenment and the Making of Modernity.* Oxford: Oxford UP, 2001.

Menninghaus, Winfried. *Unendliche Verdopplung: Die frühromantische Grundlegung der Kunsttheorie im Begriff absoluter Selbstreflexion.* Frankfurt am Main: Suhrkamp, 1987.

Mitchell, Juliet. *Mad Men and Medusas: Reclaiming Hysteria.* New York: Basic Books, 2001.

Morin, Edgar. *The Cinema, or the Imaginary Man.* Trans. Richard Howard. Minneapolis: U of Minnesota P, 2005.

Mosse, George L. *The Crisis of German Ideology: Intellectual Origins of the Third Reich.* New York: Howard Fertig, 1999.

Mulvey, Laura. "Visual Pleasure and Narrative Cinema." *Screen* 16.3 Autumn 1975. 6–18.

Muray, Philippe. *Le XIXe siècle à travers les âges.* Paris: Gallimard, 1999.

Nelson, Carolyn Christensen, ed. *A New Woman Reader: Fiction, Articles, and Drama of the 1890s.* Ontario: Broadview, 2000.

Niederland, William. *The Schreber Case: Psychoanalytic Profile of a Paranoid Personality.* Hillsdale: The Analytic Press, 1984.

Norton, Robert E. *The Beautiful Soul: Aesthetic Morality in the Eighteenth Century.* Ithaca: Cornell UP, 1995.

Oehler, Dolf. *Ein Höllensturz der Alten Welt.* Frankfurt am Main: Suhrkamp, 1988.

———. *Pariser Bilder I (1830–1848): Antibourgeoise Ästhetik bei Baudelaire, Daumier und Heine.* Frankfurt am Main: Suhrkamp, 1979.

Pagel, Walter. *Joan Baptista Van Helmont: Reformer of Science and Medicine.* Cambridge: Cambridge UP, 2002.

Paglia, Camille. *Sexual Personae: Art and Decadence from Nefertiti to Emily Dickinson.* New York: Vintage, 1991.

Percival, Melissa and Graeme Tytler, eds. *Physiognomy in Profile: Lavater's Impact on European Culture.* Newark: U of Delaware P, 2005.

Pick, Daniel. *Faces of Degeneration: A European Disorder, c. 1848–1918.* Cambridge: Cambridge UP, 1993.

Rentschler, Eric. *The Ministry of Illusion: Nazi Cinema and Its Afterlife.* Cambridge: Harvard UP, 1996.

Ricoeur, Paul. *Freud and Philosophy: An Essay on Interpretation.* Trans. Denis Savage. New Haven: Yale UP, 1970.

———. *Du texte à l'action.* Paris: Seuil, 1986.

Roux, Jean-Paul. *Le sang: Mythes, symboles et réalités.* Paris: Fayard, 1988.

Said, Edward. *Culture and Imperialism.* New York: Vintage, 1994.

———. *Joseph Conrad and the Fiction of Autobiography*. Cambridge: Harvard UP, 1966.

———. *Orientalism*. New York: Vintage, 1979.

Santner, Eric. *My Own Private Germany: Daniel Paul Schreber's Secret History of Modernity*. Princeton: Princeton UP, 1996.

Saussure, Ferdinand de. *Course in General Linguistics*, trans. Roy Harris. Chicago: Open Court, 1998.

Schatzman, Morton. *Soul Murder: Persecution in the Family*. New York: Signet, 1974.

Schmitt, Carl. *The Nomos of the Earth in the International Law of the Jus Publicum Europaeum*. Trans. G. L. Ulmen. New York: Telos, 2003.

———. *Political Romanticism*. Trans. Guy Oakes. Cambridge: The MIT Press, 1986.

Schreiber, Elisabeth. *Schreber und der Zeitgeist*. Berlin: R. Matzker, 1987.

Schulte-Sasse, Linda. *Entertaining the Third Reich: Illusions of Wholeness in Nazi Cinema*. Durham: Duke UP, 1996.

Sedgwick, Eve Kosofsky. *Between Men: English Literature and Male Homosocial Desire*. New York: Columbia UP, 1985.

Sherry, Vincent B. *The Great War and the Language of Modernism*. New York: Oxford UP, 2003.

Showalter, Elaine. *Hystories: Hysterical Epidemics and Modern Media*. New York: Columbia UP, 1998.

Siegert, Bernhard. *Relays: Literature as an Epoch of the Postal System*. Trans. Kevin Repp. Stanford: Stanford UP, 1999.

Sloterdijk, Peter. *Critique of Cynical Reason*. Trans. Michael Eldred. Minneapolis: U of Minnesota Press, 1988.

Smith, Helmut Walser. *The Butcher's Tale: Murder and Anti-Semitism in a German Town*. New York: W. W. Norton, 2003.

Starkie, Enid. *Petrus Borel, the Lycanthrope: His Life and Times*. New York: New Directions, 1954.

Stephens, Walter. *Demon Lovers: Witchcraft, Sex, and the Crisis of Belief*. Chicago: U of Chicago P, 2003.

Stingelin, Martin. "Die Seele als Funktion des Körpers: Zur Seelenpolitik der Leipziger Universitätspsychiatrie unter Paul Emil Flechsig." *Diskursanalysen 2: Institution Universität*. Eds. Friedrich A. Kittler, Manfred Schneider, and Samuel Weber. Opladen: Westdeutscher Verlag, 1989.

Stoye, John. *The Siege of Vienna: The Last Great Trial between Cross and Crescent*. London: Collins, 1964.

Subtelny, Orest. *Ukraine: A History*. Toronto: U of Toronto P, 1994.

Tatar, Maria. *Lustmord: Sexual Murder in Weimar Germany*. Princeton: Princeton UP, 1995.

———. *Spellbound: Studies on Mesmerism and Literature*. Princeton: Princeton UP, 1978.

Ullrich, Volker. *Die nervöse Großmacht 1871–1918: Aufstieg und Untergang des deutschen Kaiserreichs*. Frankfurt am Main: Fischer, 1999.

Viereck, Peter. *Metapolitics: The Roots of the Nazi Mind*. New York: Capricorn, 1965.

Virilio, Paul. *War and Cinema: The Logistics of Perception*. Trans. Patrick Camiller. London: Verso, 1989.

Walser, Robert. *Running with the Devil: Power, Gender, and Madness in Heavy Metal Music*. Middletown: Wesleyan UP, 1993.

Watt, Ian. *Myths of Modern Individualism: Faust, Don Quixote, Don Juan, Robinson Crusoe*. Cambridge: Cambridge UP, 1997.

Weinstein, Deena. *Heavy Metal: A Cultural Sociology*. New York: Lexington Books, 1991.

Widdig, Bernd. *Culture and Inflation in Weimar Germany*. Berkeley: U of California P, 2001.

Winters, Alison. *Mesmerized: Powers of Mind in Victorian England*. Chicago: U of Chicago P, 1998.

Yacowar, Maurice. *The Films of Paul Morrissey*. Cambridge: Cambridge UP, 1993.

Zipser, Richard A. *Edward Bulwer-Lytton and Germany*. Bern: Herbert Lang, 1974.

Filmography

Abbott and Costello Meet Frankenstein. Dir. Charles Barton. Universal Studios, 1948.

Alien. Dir. Ridley Scott. Twentieth Century Fox Productions, 1979.

La belle captive (The Beautiful Prisoner). Dir. Alain Robbe-Grillet. Argos Films, 1983.

Blacula. Dir. William Crain. American International Pictures, 1972.

Blood for Dracula (Dracula cerca sangue di vergine . . . e morì di sete!!!). Dir. Paul Morrissey. Compania Cinematografica Champion, 1974.

The Blue Light (Das Blaue Licht). Dir. Leni Riefenstahl. Leni Riefenstahl-Produktion, 1932.

Bram Stoker's Dracula. Dir. Francis Ford Coppola. American Zoetrope, 1992.

Buffy the Vampire Slayer. Exec. prod. Joss Whedon. Twentieth Century Fox Television, 1997–2003.

The Cabinet of Dr. Caligari (Das Cabinet des Dr. Caligari). Dir. Robert Wiene. Decla-Bioscop AG, 1920.

Close Encounters of the Third Kind. Dir. Steven Spielberg. Columbia Pictures Corporation, 1977.

Dark City. Dir. Alex Proyas. New Line Cinema, 1998.

Dark Shadows. Exec. prod. Dan Curtis. American Broadcasting Corporation, 1966–71.

Dawn of the Dead. Dir. George A. Romero. Laurel Group, 1978.

Dr. Mabuse the Gambler (Dr. Mabuse, der Spieler). Dir. Fritz Lang. Decla-Bioscop AG, 1922.

Dracula. Dir. Tod Browning. Universal Pictures, 1931.

Dracula: Dead and Loving It. Dir. Mel Brooks. Castle Rock Entertainment, 1995.

Dracula: Pages from a Virgin's Diary. Dir Guy Maddin. Vonnie von Helmolt Film, 2002.

The Eternal Jew (Der ewige Jude). Dir. Fritz Hippler. Deutsche Filmherstellungs- und Verwertungs-GmbH, 1940.

A Fool There Was. Dir. Frank Powell. William Fox Vaudeville Company, 1915.

Frankenstein. Dir. James Whale. Universal Pictures, 1931.

The Golem (Der Golem, wie er in die Welt kam). Dir. Paul Wegener. Universum Film AG, 1920.

The Hands of Orlac (Orlacs Hände). Dir. Robert Wiene. Berolina Film GmbH, 1924.

Jew Süss (Jud Süss). Dir. Veit Harlan. Terra-Filmkunst, 1940.

Lifeforce. Dir. Tobe Hooper. Golan-Globus Productions, 1985.

The Lost Boys. Dir. Joel Schumacher. Warner Bros. Pictures, 1987.

Love At First Bite. Dir. Stan Dragoti. Melvin Simon Productions, 1979.

M. Dir. Fritz Lang. Nero-Film AG, 1931.

Mad Love. Dir. Karl Freund. Metro-Goldwyn-Mayer, 1935.

Metropolis. Dir. Fritz Lang. Universum Film AG, 1927.

Night of the Living Dead. Dir. George A. Romero. Laurel Group, 1968.

Nosferatu, A Symphony of Horror (Nosferatu, eine Symphonie des Grauens). Dir. Friedrich Wilhelm Murnau. Prana-Film GmbH, 1922.

Otto; or, Up With Dead People. Bruce LaBruce. Jürgen Brüning Filmproduktion, 2008.

Planet of the Vampires (Terrore nello Spazio). Dir. Mario Bava. America-International Pictures, 1965.

Shadow of the Vampire. Dir. E. Elias Merhige. BBC Films, 2000.

Species. Dir. Roger Donaldson. Metro-Goldwyn-Mayer, 1995.

Starship Troopers. Dir. Paul Verhoeven. TriStar Pictures, 1997.

Sunrise: A Song of Two Humans. Dir. Friedrich Wilhelm Murnau. Fox Film Corporation, 1927.

The Testament of Dr. Mabuse (Das Testament des Dr. Mabuse). Dir. Fritz Lang. Nero-Film AG, 1933.

The Vampire Lovers. Dir. Roy Ward Baker. Hammer Film Productions, 1970.

The Vampires (Les vampires). Dir. Louis Feuillade. Gaumont, 1915.

Vampyr. Dir. Carl Theodor Dreyer. Tobis Filmkunst, 1932.

Vampyros Lesbos. Dir. Jess Franco. CCC Telecine, 1971.

White Zombie. Dir. Victor Halperin. United Artists, 1932.

Index